Insurgency, Terrorism, and Counterterrorism in Africa

Insurgency, Terrorism, and Counterterrorism in Africa

Edited by George Klay Kieh
Jr. and Kelechi A. Kalu

LEXINGTON BOOKS
Lanham • Boulder • New York • London

Published by Lexington Books
An imprint of The Rowman & Littlefield Publishing Group, Inc.
4501 Forbes Boulevard, Suite 200, Lanham, Maryland 20706
www.rowman.com

86-90 Paul Street, London EC2A 4NE

British Library Cataloguing in Publication Information Available

Library of Congress Cataloging-in-Publication Data

Names: Kieh, George Klay, 1956- editor. | Kalu, Kelechi Amihe, editor.
   Title: Insurgency, terrorism, and counterterrorism in Africa / edited by
   George Klay Kieh Jr. and Kelechi A. Kalu.
   Description: Lanham : Lexington Books, [2023] | Includes index. | Summary:
   "This book provides an examination of insurgent movements and terrorist
   organizations, as well as state policies that instigate intrastate
   conflicts in African states. It examines the tactics used by
   anti-government forces, states' counterterrorism responses, and the
   human security impacts of insecurity on citizens in Africa"-- Provided
   by publisher.
   Identifiers: LCCN 2022052164 (print) | LCCN 2022052165 (ebook) | ISBN
   9781793649362 (cloth) | ISBN 9781793649379 (epub)
   Subjects: LCSH: Terrorism--Africa. | Terrorism--Africa--Prevention. |
   Terrorism--Prevention--Government policy--Africa. | Terrorism--Religious
   aspects--Islam.
   Classification: LCC HV6433.A35 I47 2023 (print) | LCC HV6433.A35 (ebook)
   | DDC 363.32517096--dc23/eng/20221101
   LC record available at https://lccn.loc.gov/2022052164
   LC ebook record available at https://lccn.loc.gov/2022052165

Contents

List of Figures and Tables

Acknowledgments

We would like to thank Lexington Books for permitting us to use the following material in chapter 9: "Conclusion: Beyond Civil Wars in Africa" in *Civil Wars in Africa*, edited by Kelechi A. Kalu and George Klay Kieh Jr., (Lanham, MD: Lexington Books), pages 313–34. Additionally, the interviews are anonymized with pseudonyms in chapters 3 and 4, and personal correspondence with Ugwumbu Egbuta and Freedom Onuoha in chapter 6 are published with permission.

Preface

The contradictions and crises that are inherent in the postcolonial state in Africa have generated various conflicts. These conflicts have found expression, for example, in insurgencies, and the use of terrorism as instruments for the articulation of grievances by subaltern forces against incumbent regimes. For their part, African regimes (with few exceptions) have used state terrorism as the deus ex machina for mediating state-society relations. In addition, military-centric counterterrorism has become the dominant state response to insurgencies and "terrorism from below" (Martin 2003:34). Undoubtedly, insurgency, terrorism and counterterrorism have profound multidimensional ramifications for human safety, socioeconomic development, and stability, among others, in Africa. Accordingly, effective ways must be found to address the root causes of insurgencies and terrorism (both by state and non-sate actors).

Against this background, the African Studies and Research Forum (ASRF) commissioned a Research Project on "Civil Conflicts in Africa" in collaboration with the Office of International Affairs at the University of California, Riverside. One of the major areas of the research project is on "Insurgency, Terrorism and Counter-terrorism in Africa." This section of the research project focused on the provision of a theoretical crucible for enhancing the understanding of insurgency, terrorism, and counterterrorism, case studies of insurgencies and terrorism "from below" (Al-Shabab, Boko Haram, Al-Qaeda and the Islamic State of Iraq and Syria), and the counterterrorism regimes and strategies of selected African states, the Economic Community of West African States (ECOWAS), and the United States.

We would like to thank the African Studies and Research Forum (ASRF) and the Office of International Affairs at the University of California, Riverside, for sponsoring the research project that has produced this volume. At the African Studies and Research Forum (ASRF), we would like to thank Samuel Zalanga, the Director of Research and Publications and the members of the Research and Publications Committee for their encouragement and support. At the University of California at Riverside's Office of International Affairs, we would like to thank Mely Fitzgerald, Carmen Rivera, and Reyna Alarcon for their help with coordinating the logistics for the research project with scholars from different parts of the world.

Further, we extend our gratitude to the researchers who participated in the research project, including writing the chapters that constitute this volume. We appreciate their patience in waiting for comments on their draft chapters and for their diligence in addressing the issues raised. Clearly, they have made major contributions to the understanding of the frontier security issues of insurgency, terrorism, and counterterrorism.

Last, but not the least, we would like to thank Lexington Books for publishing this volume. Specifically, we are grateful to Sydney Wedbush of the African Studies Program for her patience, encouragement, and support, which contributed to the publication of this volume. In addition, we would like to thank the Production Department for preparing the book for publication.

George Klay Kieh Jr. and Kelechi A. Kalu

PART I

BACKGROUND

Chapter 1

Introduction

The African Landscape, Insurgency, and Terrorism

George Klay Kieh Jr. and Kelechi A. Kalu

There is a general consensus that with few exceptions the postcolonial era in Africa has failed to fulfill the high hopes and expectations of the African peoples, especially the subalterns. During the dawn of the "first wave" of independence in Africa during the 1950s, and the subsequent "second" and "third" waves in the 1960s and 1970s, the prognostication about the postindependence era was highly optimistic. Ramsay (1993: 3) provides an excellent summation of the euphoria that greeted the postindependence era:

> The times were electric. In country after country, the flags of Britain, Belgium and France were replaced by the banners of the new states, whose leaders offered idealistic promises to remake the continent and the world. Hopes were high, and the most ambitious goals[seemed] obtainable. Even non-Africans spoke of the resource-rich continent as being on the verge of a development take-off. Some of the old, racist myths about Africa were [at] last being questioned.

However, the singing of the requiem for the demise of colonialism and its attendant authoritarian governance model and political economy was short-lived. The majority of the citizens of the various newly independent states became cognizant of the fact that the venalities of the colonial state had been replaced by the postcolonial variants. In sum, the dawn of the era of human-centered democracy and development was a mirage. For example, the authoritarian governance model, including its pivot, state-sponsored terrorism, remained entrenched; and the sordid state of material conditions of the subalterns remained unchanged. By the mid-1980s, the human development

3

deficit reached a crescendo as evidenced by soaring rates of poverty, unemployment, and the vagaries of social malaise. The profundity of the multidimensional crises of human material well-being resulted in the period being referred to as "Africa's lost decade" (Ihonvbere 1991). In addition, by the end of the 1980s, there were only two democratic states on the African continent—Botswana and Mauritius (Freedom House 2022). The other states were ruled by both civilian and military autocrats, whose regimes, among others, asphyxiated the free exercise of political rights and civil liberties.

Disillusioned by excesses of authoritarian governance and the deteriorating standard of living, some Africans decided to use extralegal means such as insurgency as instruments of struggle against some of the authoritarian regimes in countries like Sudan, Senegal, and Somalia. In addition, some of the insurgent groups also employed the use of terrorism as vehicle for harassing, intimidating, and visiting injury and death on civilians. In such cases, insurgent groups such as Al Shabab, which is based in Somalia, and Boko Haram in Nigeria have lost mass support for the original purposes of the insurgency. Similarly, the various authoritarian regimes in Africa have used terrorism as an instrument for mediating state-society relations, thereby leading to the injuries and deaths of real and imagined political opponents, as well as ordinary citizens.

The 9/11 terrorist attacks against the American homeland witnessed the ascendancy of counterterrorism on the national security agenda of the United States, and the agendas of its African "partner states." For example, counterterrorism has provided a veneer for legitimizing state-sponsored terrorism on the African continent. Terrorism has become an "elastic term" that the various authoritarian regimes on the African continent are using to delegitimize opposition groups and to cow them into submission through the use of the American-sponsored counterterrorism architectures that have been established in the various African states (Fisher and Anderson 2013).

Against this backdrop, this chapter has several interrelated purposes. One is to provide the conceptual framework comprising insurgency, terrorism, and counterterrorism that will provide the ideational guidance for the book. Another is to interrogate the travails of insurgency, terrorism, and counterterrorism in Africa. In addition, the chapter will map out the major objectives of the book. Further, the book's theoretical and methodological compasses will be examined. Finally, the various chapters that constitute the book will be summarized.

CONCEPTUALIZING INSURGENCY, TERRORISM, AND COUNTERTERRORISM

Like many concepts, insurgency, terrorism, and counterterrorism have varied meanings. Hence, the purpose is to provide the definitions that will serve as the conceptual guides for the book. In this vein, drawing from Terrorism Research (n.d: 1), an insurgency is a political movement that has a "specific aim." It challenges an incumbent government pursuant to a grievance or grievances. It may have support from a segment or segments of a population. It does not require the use of terror. Betts (2002: 460) uses the term "tripartite" to describe the locus of the conflict dynamics in insurgency: There are three primary actors involved: the government, the insurgents, and the people. Both the government and the insurgents compete for the support of the people.

Similarly, for Obi and Wallace (2021: 1) the concept of terrorism is a "problematic term." One of the major reasons for the conceptual complexity of the term is the tendency to tailor its meaning or definition to the ideological orientation and/or political agenda of the user (Obi and Wallace 2021). In the effort to transcend the ideological, political, and other underpinnings of the term, some of the extant definitions were examined. Consequently, terrorism in this volume is defined as a "method [involving the] deliberate use of violence or the threat of its use against innocent people, with the aim of intimidating [or actually harming them]" (Primoratz 1990: 221; Weinberg et al. 2010: 785–94).

In terms of counterterrorism, we employ Sandler's (2015: 12–13) conceptual framework: "Counterterrorism [is a set of] actions to ameliorate the threat and consequences of terrorism. These actions can be taken by governments, military alliances, international organizations (e.g. INTERPOL), private corporations or private citizens. Counterterrorism comes in two basic varieties: defensive and proactive." In addition, private citizens and private organizations can take counterterrorism measures against state-sponsored terrorism. In sum, counterterrorism is applicable to both privately sponsored and state-sponsored terrorism.

THE TUGS AND PULLS OF INSURGENCY, TERRORISM, AND COUNTERTERRORISM IN AFRICA

Insurgency

Insurgency is not a new phenomenon either on the African continent or globally. As Metz and Millen (2004:1) observed, "Insurgency has existed throughout history but ebbed and flowed in strategic significance. At times, insurgency forms 'background noise' to competition or conflict between great powers. At other times, it is strategically significant, undercutting regional stability drawing outsiders into direct conflicts, and spawning humanitarian disasters." For example, globally, there have been insurgencies in Nicaragua (1978–1979, 1981–1990), Afghanistan (1978–1992), El Salvador (1979–1992), Peru (1980–1992) (Paulet et al. 2010). On the African continent, Dunn and Boas (2017) estimate that over thirty African states have experienced insurgencies since the beginning of the "second wave" of independence in the 1960s. The insurgencies include: Senegal (1982–2002), Sudan (1984–2004), Uganda (1986–2000), Algeria (1992–2004), Zaire (now Democratic Republic of Congo) (1996–1997), and Democratic Republic of the Congo (1998–2003).

Christopher Clapham and Kevin Dunn and Morten Boas have provided typologies of insurgencies in Africa. In the case of Clapham (1998), he identified four major types: secessionist (e.g., Nigeria, Eritrea), liberationist (e.g., Angola, Cape Verde, Guinea-Bissau, Mozambique, South Africa), reformist (e.g., Ethiopia, Rwanda, and Uganda) and warlordist (e.g., Chad, Liberia, Sierra Leone). As for Dunn and Boas (2017), their framework consists of the following: the competing and shifting systems of governance (e.g., Al-Qaeda in the Islamic Maghreb's affiliate in northern Mali and Al Shabab in Somalia took advantage of fragmented systems of governance), attempted systems of governance (e.g., the eastern Democratic Republic of Congo), the "big man syndrome" (e.g., networks of governance), global and national linkages (e.g., Liberia and Sierra Leone), ideological (e.g., global jihadist movements such as Al-Qaeda and ISIS), and non-elite groups (youth and women groups in various African states).

In terms of a balance sheet, there have been three major outcomes of insurgencies: successful, unsuccessful, and ongoing. In the case of the successful ones, they include the Hissen Habre-led seizure of power in Chad in 1979; the Museveni-headed National Resistance Army's capture of state power in Uganda in 1986; and the Kabila-led Democratic Alliance's ouster of the Mobutu regime in Zaire in 1997. As for the cases of unsuccessful insurgencies, they include the failed secession of Biafra from Nigeria (1967–1970), and the Foday Sankoh-headed Revolutionary United Front's efforts to seize state power in Sierra Leone (1991–1997). In the case of the ongoing insurgencies, they include Al Shabab in Somalia and Boko Haram in Nigeria.

Terrorism

Background

Historically, the use of terrorism as an instrument has its roots in the colonial era. The first major use of terrorism was by the European colonial powers—Britain, Belgium, France, Germany, Italy, Portugal, and Spain—after the "Berlin Conference" of 1884–1885: The colonial powers used terror as the method for imposing their control over hitherto independent African political entities (Ake 1996). For example, the German imperialists waged a genocidal war against the Herero and Namaqua ethnic groups that led to the murder of thousands of people (Maelber 2020).

Having established their control over Africa, the colonial powers then established authoritarian governance systems over their respective colonies. Generally, the colonial state relied primarily on the use of terror as the vehicle for mediating relations between the European colonizers and the colonized peoples of Africa (Young 1997). In addition, the colonial state established its hegemony over every sphere—cultural, economic, political, religious, and social—based on the use of terror. This led Ake (1996:3) to refer to the colonial state as "totalistic." Similarly, the various models of the colonial state shared a common core based on the excessive use of terror. For example, the Belgian model, which was referred to as "Bula Matari" ("crusher of rocks") was legendary for terrorizing the colonized Africans in the Congo (Young 1997).

Since the postcolonial African state is the replica of the colonial one, the former (the postcolonial state) inherited and maintained the preponderant reliance on terror as terra firma for state-society relations (Ake 1996). Accordingly, the "first generation" of African leaders and the subsequent ones (with few exceptions) have relied on the use of terror as the motor force for cowing and maintaining the African peoples in submission to their autocratic rule, and the resulting human insecurity.

State-sponsored terrorism

As has been discussed, since the dawn of the postindependence era, African states (with few exceptions) have, and continue to perpetrate terroristic acts spanning the broad gamut from intimidation to murder on their citizens (Martin 2006; Strydom and Neube 2016). Several cases are instructive. For example, during the apartheid era in South Africa, the government's death squad known as the Askanis assassinated several members of the African National Congress (ANC), which was waging a liberation struggle both within and outside South Africa (Martin 2006).

In the case of Egypt, the el-Sisi civilianized military regime has continued the country's history of state-sponsored terrorism, especially during the Mubarak regime (1981–2011). As Al-Anani (2020: 1) laments, "since General Abdel-Fattah el-Sisi took office in 2014, Egypt has become a dark and terrifying place for political activists, opposition groups, journalists, civil society and human rights groups." The el-Sisi regime has employed various methods of terror, including torture, extrajudicial killings, and massacres (Al-Anani 2020). In addition, drawing from the various Egyptian regimes, including el-Sisi's, various cases of state-sponsored terrorism are instructive. For example, on August 14, 2013, state military and security forces killed peaceful protesters during the Rabaa massacre. Similarly, between 2013 and 2018, about 1,520 people "forcibly disappeared" (Stop Force Disappearance Campaign cited in Al-Anani 2020: 2). Further, by June 2019, there were about 492 cases of torture (Al-Nadeem Center for Rehabilitation of Victims of Violence and Torture 2019).

As for Ethiopia, the Zenawi and subsequent regimes that succeeded the ousted Mengistu authoritarian regime have retained and expanded the ambit of state-sponsored terrorism. Several cases are noteworthy. For example, between 2003 and 2004, the Ethiopian National Defense Force repeatedly terrorized the people of Gambella (Human Rights Watch 2004, 2005). Similarly, in 2009, there was widespread torture of prisoners across the country (Human Rights Watch 2010). Further, in 2014, using terror as the implementation instrument, the Ethiopian government forcibly displaced about 1.5 million people in the Gambella region (Human Rights Watch 2015). About six years later, state military and security forces conducted targeted killings "against ethnic Oromo civilians, including medical professionals" (Human Rights Watch 2021: 235).

In the case of Nigeria, in 2001, for example, the military massacred over 250 civilians in various localities in Benue State (Human Rights Watch 2002). Similarly, in 2013, military personnel killed several civilians and destroyed over two thousand buildings in Baga, Borno State (Human Rights Watch 2014). And five years later, the police killed about eleven people, as the result of the police shooting at the protests by the Sharia Islamic Movement of Nigeria (Human Rights Watch 2020).

As for Zimbabwe under the reign of President Robert Mugabe, state-sponsored terrorism through the military, police, and security services were quite routine, especially against the real and imagined enemies of the regime. For example, on April 25, 2008, "armed riot police raided the Harare Headquarters of the opposition Movement for Democratic Change (MDC)" (Human Rights Watch 2008:1). Interestingly, even after Mugabe's removal by the country's military in 2017, his successor, President Emmerson Mnangagwa, continues to use terror as the major vehicle for suppressing dissent. For example, prior to and after the 2017 election cycle, the military, police, and security service regularly terrorized opposition political groups and parties, especially during their rallies (Gavin 2018).

Privately sponsored terrorism

Various non-state actors have, and continue to use terrorism as an instrument in their respective conflicts with African states and the United States and other Western powers (by attacking their interests, including their client regimes in Africa). This genre of terrorism is referred to as "terrorism from below" (Martin 2003:34). This section of the chapter will focus on a brief examination of some of the major non-state actors: Al-Shabab, Boko Haram, Al-Qaeda in the Islamic Maghreb (AQIM), and the Islamic State of Iraq and Syria (ISIS).

Al Shabaab

Al Shabaab or Harakat Al Shabaab al-Mujahideen ("the youth" in Arabic) has its roots in al-Ittihad al-Islami (AIAI or "unity of Islam") (Felter et al. 2021: 1). The AIAI was organized as an opposition movement against the authoritarian regime of Mohammed Said Barre (who ruled Somalia from 1969 to 1991), which visited repression and socioeconomic malaise, including poverty, on the Somali people. After the collapse of the Barre regime and the country's descent into internecine warfare among competing warlordist factions, conflict emerged among the "old guards" and the younger members of the AIAI. The conflict revolved around competing trajectories for the AIAI: On the one hand, the "old guards" were desirous of organizing a political party to contest for state power. On the other hand, the younger members desired "the establishment of 'Greater Somalia' under fundamentalist rule" (Felton 2021: 1). Amid the tugs and pulls, the younger members broke away from the AIAI and joined the Islamic Courts Union. In 2006, the emergent Al Shabaab collaborated with the Islamic Courts Union in seizing state power. However, the alliance was dislodged from power in December 2006 by Ethiopia.

By the end of 2006, Al Shabaab shifted to the use of terrorism as its central instrument in the quest for state power in Somalia. In this vein, Al Shabaab sees Somalia, Kenya, Ethiopia, and the United States as its main targets for terrorist attacks. For example, on September 21, 2013, the group launched a brazen terrorist attack on the Westgate Mall in Kenya, resulting in the deaths of several innocent civilians (Agbiboa 2014). In other words, the attack was indiscriminate, because the group's operatives who carried out the attack shot and killed people without regard to their nationalities.

Boko Haram

Jama'atu Ahlis Sunna Lidda "awati Wal-Jihad—'people committed to the propagation of the Prophet's Teachings and Jihad,'" commonly referred to as Boko Haram ("Western education/culture is forbidden") was organized in 2002 by Mohammed Yusuf in Maiduguri in northeastern Nigeria (Adibe 2014:1). Initially, the organization engaged in peaceful protests against the Nigerian state and the failure of its custodians to address human security. The hope was that the Nigerian state and its regimes would have addressed the legitimate human welfare concerns that the group raised. Unfortunately, the Nigerian state chose to respond to the group's grievances and resulting protests with terror. For example, in 2009, Mohammed Yusuf, the group's founder and leader, was killed in police custody (Forest 2012). When some members of the group protested Yusuf's detention and subsequent killing, the police shot and killed about eight hundred of them (Forest 2021).

The murder of Yusuf by the Nigerian police witnessed a major shift in the group's strategy from protests to the use of terrorism (Forest 2012). Three major terrorist attacks by Boko Haram are noteworthy. In 2011, Boko Haram carried out a brazen terrorist attack against the United Nations Headquarters in Abuja, the capital city of Nigeria. In 2014, the group kidnapped about three hundred girls from their school in Chibok. Later that year, the group began to launch terrorist attacks in neighboring Cameroon and subsequently the Republic of Niger (Center for International Cooperation 2022).

Al-Qaeda in the Islamic Maghreb (AQIM)

Al-Qaeda in the Islamic Maghreb (AQIM) is a by-product of the ongoing transformation and adaptability of Al-Qaeda's (Central) organizational structures. Given the security environments at the national, subregional, regional, and global levels, Al-Qaeda (Central) decided to decentralize both its organizational and operational structures. Thus, AQIM was organized in 2007 with indigenous (mainly Algerian) leadership (Filiu 2009). In addition, historically, the AQIM's origins can be traced to Algeria's postcolonial history of seemingly unending civil conflicts, including the aftermath of the 1992 election, in which "a broad Islamic movement [was] robbed of an impending victory by a military coup that cancelled the election" (Boeke 2016: 918). In this vein, the AQIM's progenitor was the Salafist Group for Preaching and Combat (GSPC), which broke away from the Islamic Armed Group (GIA) in 1998 (Pham 2011).

Operationally, AQIM has carried out several terrorist attacks in the Sahel and broader Saharan regions. A major one was carried out in November 2015, when AQIM and its partner, AJ-Mourobitoun, attacked the Radisson Blue

Hotel in Bamako, the capital city of Mali. Several persons were killed and wounded in the attack. Since then, acting in collaboration with local insurgent groups in Mali, the AQIM has carried out other terrorist attacks in the country and region (Stewart 2013).

Islamic State of Iraq and Syria (ISIS)

One of the major consequences of the retreat by the Islamic State of Iraq and Syria (ISIS) from the two countries and the broader region, amid the counterterrorism offensives that have been launched by the United States and its allies, has been the establishment of footprints on the African continent. This has been done through the establishment of cells on the African continent, especially in the Sahel region, the Horn of Africa, Central Africa, and more recently the southeastern tip of the continent (Muraga 2021).

Collectively, ISIS' cells in Africa, including Islamic State West African Province (ISWAP), a breakaway faction of Boko Haram, have carried out terrorist attacks against various African states that have resulted in the deaths of scores of people: "deaths from ISIS' attacks nearly doubled "in West Africa from 2017–2020, from 2,700 to 5,500" (US Department of State 2021:2). For example, ISIS-Mozambique was responsible for an estimated 1,500 deaths in 2021 (US Department of State 2021:2).

Counterterrorism

National counterterrorism regimes

Cameroon

Cameroon's counterterrorism regime consists of various institutions, including the courts, the military and security services, and the Anti-Terrorism Law of 2014. In the case of the Anti-Terrorism Law, its key provisions include:

1. Terrorist crimes: The intimidation of the population, provoking a situation of terror, disturbing the normal operation of public services (Library of Congress 2014).
2. Punishment: The punishment for terrorist offenses include capital punishment for certain acts of terrorism, including "provid[ing] or mak[ing] use of arms and war materials" (Library of Congress 2014:1).

The implementation of the country's counterterrorism law has drawn major criticisms for two major reasons. One is that the law suppresses dissent. This is because it has targeted the political opponents of the Biya regime for the purpose of silencing them. Another reason is that the law has been used to censor the media. Overall, the law has been criticized for providing a propitious legal environment for the state to terrorize its citizens. As Ashukem (2021:119) asserts, "Since the enactment of Cameroon's anti-terrorism law in 2014, the government has embarked on systemic violation of fundamental human rights and freedoms."

Egypt

The Egyptian constitution (2007) provides the legal panoply for the country's counterterrorism regime. Article 179 "stipulates the State's responsibility to counter the dangers of terrorism and on that basis, establishes that legal provisions relating to the leading of inquiry and investigation procedures required to encounter these dangers shall not be hindered by constitutional provisions that guarantees the judicial oversight of detention, home search, and surveillance or seizure of communications" (International Foundation of Human Rights 2010:11). Drawing from the constitution, the Anti-Terrorism Laws of 2014 and 2015 were enacted as the centerpieces of the emergent anti-terrorism regime. Under these laws, there are provisions that define terrorism, a terrorist, a terrorist group, terrorist crimes, and the types of weapons. In addition, the laws provide for the penalties for those, who are found guilty of committing acts of terrorism—life sentence and capital punishment are the two major categories.

Thus, the Egyptian military and security forces, which are the enforcers of the anti-terrorism laws, derive their enormous unchecked powers from Article 179 of the country's constitution, as well as the anti-terrorism acts. For example, the military and security forces have carte blanche power to undertake any activity they deem to be part of counterterrorism operations. In this vein, the el-Sisi regime has used this broad and unchecked power to crack down on dissent, including harassing, intimidating, and imprisoning political opponents, as well as the leaders of various civil society organizations (Magdy 2020).

Ethiopia

Ethiopia established its counterterrorism regime in 2009 under Anti-Terrorism Proclamation No. 652. In 2020, the law was amended. Two of the major provisions of the anti-terrorism law are: the definition of a terrorist organization as an organization "intending to advance a political, religious or ideological cause by coercing the government, intimidating the public or section of the public" (Matfess 2017:1) and the Ethiopian Parliament's authority to ban terrorist organizations (France 24 2020). Further, the military and security services under the direction of the prime minister, the courts, and the parliament are the key institutions for implementing the country's anti-terrorism regime.

The anti-terrorism regime has several shortcomings. A major one is that it is vague. Most of the provisions are not clearly articulated, including the definition of a terrorist group. Another weakness is that the law has provided the legal cover for the government to suppress political dissent (Matfess 2017). This is because, among other things, political dissent is being recurrently classified as acts of terrorism.

Nigeria

Like all national counterterrorism regimes, the Nigerian one consists of two major components: laws and institutions. In the case of the laws, the Terrorism Prevention Act of 2011 (which was amended in 2013) is the fulcrum. As for the institutions, they include Office of the National Security Advisor to the President, the military, security services, the Joint Special Task Force, and the courts. Two of the key provisions of the anti-terrorism laws are the definition of terrorism—"an act which is deliberately done with malice after forethought which may seriously harm or damage a country or an international organization" (Ejeh et al. 2019: 190); and terrorism offenses, which include murder and kidnapping.

In terms of an assessment, the counterterrorism regime has several major weaknesses. One is that the Nigerian military and security services are using Boko Haram's terrorist activities as the pretext for committing human rights violations. As Human Rights Watch (2021:1) laments, "The [Nigerian] military continued to detain thousands of people. They arbitrarily arrested and detained those suspected of links to Boko Haram. Detainees were denied access to their family members and lawyers and were not brought before the courts." Another is that the use of air strikes as part of the military operations under the counterterrorism operations has led to the deaths of innocent civilians. For example, in 2017, air strikes by the Nigerian Air Force killed over one hundred people in a displaced persons' camp in Borno State (Ewang 2021).

South Africa

The cornerstone of South Africa's counterterrorism regime is the Protection of Constitutional Democracy Against Terrorism and Related Activities Act, 2005. Some of the key provisions of the act are: the establishment of terrorism as an offense; making it illegal for an individual to belong to a designated terrorist group, the identification of terrorist offenses to include hijacking aircraft or ships and hostage taking, and the punishments for terrorist offenses to include life imprisonment. Two of the major notables of the South African counterterrorism law are its avoidance of the definition of terrorism and the legitimization of certain actions: Under Section 1(4), "any act committed during a struggle waged by peoples, including any action during an armed struggle for national liberation, self-determination, and independence against colonialism, or occupation of aggression or domination by alien of foreign forces" (Protection of Constitutional Democracy Against Terrorism and Related Activities Act 2005:1).

Among the act's major shortcomings are two provisions: the obligation to report, and the burden of proof for some who are accused of aiding the funding of terrorism. In the case of the former, a legal obligation is imposed on those who have information about suspected terrorist information to report them immediately or face liability under the law. The other is that any individual who is accused of aiding and abetting terrorism, including providing funding, has the burden of proof to establish his or her innocence (Hubschle 2015).

The African Union's counterterrorism regime

The African Union's counterterrorism regime predates the 9/11 terrorist attacks on the homeland of the United States. The development of the regime commenced in the 1980s with the Organization for African Unity's (OAU) Convention for the Elimination of Mercenarism in Africa in 1985. This was followed by the development and promulgation of several major corpuses of anti-terrorism rules. One of the major ones is the Algiers Convention on the Prevention and Combating of Terrorism, 1999. The centerpiece of the convention was the characterization of terrorism as an anathema to human rights (Algiers Convention on the Prevention and Combating of Terrorism 1999). The convention's major provision includes the obligations of the state parties to the convention, including the protection of their peoples against all terrorist attacks, as well as the prevention of terrorist training on their territory (Omenma and Onyango 2020). Another is the African Model Anti-Terrorism Law, 2011, which, among other things, stipulates the categories of the offenses of terrorism, and the resulting penalties.

In terms of the evaluation of the AU's anti-terrorism regime, while the rules that are contained in the various conventions and laws contribute to the prevention and combating of terrorism, it has three major weaknesses. A key one is the perennial problem of state sovereignty, which undermines the imperative of continental cooperation. This is because a state's national interests are the major determinants of its compliance with the anti-terrorism rules. Another shortcoming is the lack of enforcement. The AU lacks the capacity to ensure that its member states that are parties to the various anti-terrorism rules comply with them. In addition, all the rules that undergird the regime are exclusively focused on terrorism by non-state actors. In other words, state terrorism is not taken into consideration.

African subregional organizations' counter-terrorism regimes

The Economic Community of African States (ECOWAS) is the only African subregional organization that has a well-developed counterterrorism regime. The anchor of ECOWAS' counterterrorism regime is Article 58 of the Revised 1993 Charter (Revised Charter of the Economic Community of West African States). The derivatives (anti-terrorism rules) are the ECOWAS Convention on Mutual Assistance in Penal Matters, 1992; Protocol Relating to the Mechanism for Conflict Prevention, Management, Resolution, Peacekeeping and Security, 1999; Convention on Extradition, 1994; ECOWAS' Conflict Prevention Framework, 2008; and ECOWAS' Political Declaration on a Common Position Against Terrorism, 2013. There are several major challenges that have hamstrung ECOWAS' capacity to implement the menu of rules that constitutes the foundation of its counter-terrorism regime. Two of the major ones are the lack of political will by the members states—what Akanji (2019:104) refers to as the "lackluster approach of the organization and its member states to implement counter-terrorism decisions and legally binding instruments"—and financial constraints.

In the case of the Southern African Development Community (SADC), it promulgated a Declaration on Terrorism in 2002; it is anchored on the OAU, AU, and UN conventions on terrorism. Similarly, although the East African Community developed a Regional Strategy for Peace and Security in 2006, like SADC, it has not developed a comprehensive counterterrorism regime.

THE OBJECTIVES OF THE BOOK

The book has several major purposes. First, it is intended to interrogate the domestic and external factors that contribute to the use of insurgency and terrorism by non-state actors as vehicles for expressing grievances against a regime or regimes and their external patrons. Second, it will decipher the factors and ways that contribute to non-state actors shifting from the use of insurgency to terrorism. Third, it will examine the under-researched phenomenon of state-sponsored terrorism. This is because the bulk of the scholarly literature and the discussions in both the corridors of policy-making and among the citizenry focuses on terrorism by non-state actors like Al-Qaeda, the Islamic State of Iraq and Syria (ISIS), Al Shabab, and Boko Haram. Fourth, insurgency, terrorism, and counterterrorism will be problematized by probing their nature and dynamics, especially in the African context. Fifth, the theoretical and methodological approaches of the book will be articulated. Finally, the various chapters that constitute the book will be summarized with succinct accounts of their respective foci.

METHODOLOGICAL AND THEORETICAL ISSUES

The book uses the qualitative research tradition as its methodological tapestry. Drawing from this tradition, all the chapters with the exception of the introductory and theoretical ones employ the case study method. The rationale is that the case study method enables the thorough and in-depth examination of selected insurgent and terrorist groups, as well as American counterterrorism policy and strategies in Africa.

In terms of the theoretical orientation, the book uses multi-theoretical approaches. That is, the book's theoretical chapter maps out various approaches for studying insurgency, terrorism and counter-terrorism. This then enabled each contributor to draw from, and add to (if necessary) to theoretical toolbox, and use the framework or frameworks that are appropriate for their respective cases. Both the book's interdisciplinarity and theoretical toolbox contribute to is analytical rigor, and the resulting lessons that can be used to help inform policy-making and praxis.

THE ORGANIZATION OF THE BOOK

In addition to the introductory and concluding sections, this book has seven core chapters. In chapter 1, the introduction to the book, George Klay Kieh Jr. and Kelechi A. Kalu lay the foundational pillars for the book. Specifically, they provide the book's conceptual framework against the backdrop of the conceptual chaos that characterizes the concepts of insurgency and terrorism. Kieh and Kalu then examined the nature and dynamics of insurgency, terrorism, and counterterrorism on the African continent. In the case of insurgency, they interrogate its nature, context, and dynamics, as well as the shift by insurgent groups to terrorism. This is followed by the examination of the multidimensionality of terrorism, including the motor forces that propel it, and state and non-state actors as the principal drivers of the phenomenon. That is, they argue that contrary to the dominant view in the scholarly literature, states or countries also engage in terrorism (state-sponsored terrorism). In addition, they map out the book's theoretical and methodological approaches. Finally, the chapter summarizes the highlights of each of the chapters that constitute the volume.

In chapter 2, "Explaining Insurgency and Terrorism in Africa," Kalu examines why many postindependence states in Africa remain mired in political instability, banditry, terrorism, and insurgencies. He argues that the incomplete projects of state formation and nation-building within a framework that promotes economic development and political inclusion are at the root of terrorism and insurgencies in Africa.

According to Kalu, given the internal and external dimensions of terrorism and insurgency in Africa, official development assistance (ODA) and external security support enhance the well-being of the governing elites. These parasitic elites have no interest in bringing terrorism and insurgencies to an end because the "war on terrorism" against a segment of their people is a source of foreign aid and security support. More significantly, the "war on terrorists" provides a good excuse and alternative explanations for government incompetence exhibited in economic underdevelopment and unwillingness to institute governance structures that promote accountability and political inclusion that empowers the masses. These challenges with economic and political development issues have bedeviled various governments since political independence.

He concludes that, internally, to end insurgency and terrorism in many African countries, the various governments need to deal with economic development issues that provide access to functional education, create employment opportunities for the masses (especially youth), provide physical and economic security, and govern as if people mattered.

In chapter 3, "Al-Shabab's Insurgency in Somalia," Mohammed Ingiriis examines the origin and long-standing nature of the conflict between the government of Somalia and Al Shabaab. An insurgent group, Al Shabaab has been agitating for power-sharing and political inclusion that balances the clan sentiments as a strategy for sustainable peace in Somalia.

Ingiriis's chapter is framed around such questions as: why is the armed conflict in Somalia unresolvable? Why do fragile states fail to negotiate power-sharing agreements to achieve political stability? Why do fragile states fail to engage political opposition in ways that improve governance performance through power-sharing? Why do marginalized communities' resort to violence and make it difficult for fragile states to gain and maintain domestic legitimacy?

Using the ethnographic field research method, Mohammed Ingiriis examines "the interplay between armed conflict and power-sharing in Somalia; explains why the armed conflict in Somalia remains "so protracted from the perspective of power-sharing," and explores how the local political contexts complicate various power-sharing discussions and reconciliation efforts. He argues that the armed conflict in Somalia is sustained by "the absence of genuine political power-sharing, economic power-sharing, and territorial power-sharing." He concludes that it is "the absence of local elements in power-sharing agreements, aggravated by bad governance, community grievances, and external interventions that help to sustain the protracted conflict and insecurity in Somalia."

In chapter 4, "Boko Haram Insurgency in Nigeria," Sylvester Odion Akhaine examined the internal and external nexus of the Boko Haram insurgency in Nigeria and its impacts on neighboring states. With a succinct critical insight and presentation, Odion Akhaine identifies "poverty, power struggle, religion, and corruption," as the internal drivers of the Boko Haram insurgency in Nigeria. He argues that the Boko Haram insurgency in Nigeria is sustained by internal and external factors. The external factors, according to Odion Akhaine, are the West and the Arabs, especially the French, Britain, Saudi Arabia, and Qatar as supporters of various aspects of the Boko Haram anti-government activities in Nigeria and other states in the region. He concludes that the Nigerian government should have the political will to identify the internal sponsors and drivers of Boko Haram and use carrots and sticks to engage them to resolve the grievances that drive anti-government forces' activities in the country. Additionally, he advocates for a strategic engagement with the external forces—the West and Arabs—to find a sustainable resolution to the Boko Haram conflict.

In chapter 5, "Al-Qaeda: Scoping and Countering Jihadist Nebula in West Africa," Al Chukwuma Okoli presents West Africa as the backdrop to examine the activities of Al Qaeda in the region and its global and adaptational strategies. His research focuses on generating theoretical and practical insights for understanding and countering the threat posed by Al Qaeda in the subregion. Knowledge-based action helps counter the threats of Al-Qaeda in West Africa. Analytically, Okoli's research reveals "the sundry adaptational dynamics of jihadist extremism in West Africa in the context of the contemporary dialectics of local and international counterterrorism crusade" that pits Jihadists in an existential struggle against the "apostate world" from which they seek their freedom. And, according to Okoli, part of what analysts and governments need to pay attention to is the dynamic nature of Al-Qaeda and how, like a chameleon, it metamorphoses to adapt into the colors of grievance depending on the location.

It is Al-Qaeda's "strategy of asymmetric mutations and alignments" that has enabled the organization and its network to survive globally, especially in the West Africa region. To counter the transnational Al Qaeda network in West Africa, Okoli advocates for functional collective security architecture and "a wider trans-regional counterterrorism strategy" in the Western Sahel and Lake Chad axis." He concludes that combating transnational terrorism in west Africa requires strengthening state control of its territories and robust "strategic domestic intelligence, counter-radicalization, and sustainable peace-building" efforts.

In chapter 6, "The Rise and Influence of ISIS in Sub-Saharan Africa," Angela Ajodo-Adehanjoko provides a historical account of the emergence and spread of the Islamic State of Iraq and Syria and the extent to which it has spread its ideological tentacles across the Middle East and Africa, despite drone decimation of its core leadership. Ajodo-Adehanjoko argues that the combination of "weak states and institutions, porous borders, poor governance, socio-economic factors, and the prevalence of internal conflict" provide opportunities for the incursion of various Jihadists and other terrorist networks that infiltrate and occupy spaces in African states. And, that the presence of these extremist groups—Boko Haram, al-Qaeda in the Islamic Maghreb (AQIM), and Islamic State in the West Africa Province (ISWAP)—foment instability and humanitarian crisis across states in sub-Saharan Africa because of ineffective strategic responses to violent extremism by African and non-African governments.

Similar to other contributors to this volume, Ajodo-Adehanjoko contends that a combination of "ungoverned spaces, poverty, injustice, local conflicts, existing extremist networks and ideology in many parts of sub-Saharan Africa" intensified existing internal agitations and insecurity, which exposed vulnerable communities to infiltration by "ISIS to regroup and recruit millions of young people in the region" into anti-government activities. Thus, the existence of under-governed or ungoverned spaces, socioeconomic challenges, perceived injustices, a preexisting network of aggrieved extremists like Boko Haram, ideology, and the politicization of ethnic and religious sentiments are factors that have made it possible for the rise and active presence of the Islamic State in sub-Saharan Africa.

Ajodo-Adehanjoko concludes that the ISIS loss of territories in Syria and Iraq is directly connected to the proliferation of terrorist cells, albeit with local flavors, in Africa. To counteract Islamic State's influence requires a combination of tactics like regional cooperation to deny ISIS safe havens and disrupt their financial flows. Further, there would need to be better border security to disrupt the flow of foreign fighters into various states in Africa, effective and strategic communication to counter Islamic State propaganda, and effective efforts by various states to provide better governance and security to its citizens, especially in the neglected or ungoverned spaces.

In chapter 7, "Assessing the Economic Community of West African States (ECOWAS) Counter-Terrorism Strategy: Achievements, Challenges, and Prospects," Clayton Hazvinei Vhumbunu undertakes an evaluation of the extent to which the counterterrorism strategy adopted by the ECOWAS in Yamoussoukro, Cote d'Ivoire in February 2013, has achieved its objectives of regional collaboration to combat terrorism and maintain regional peace, stability, and security. Based on the ECOWAS documented Regional Counter-Terrorism Strategy, Vhumbunu's research "focuses on measuring the extent to which the agreed interventions as outlined in the ECOWAS Counter-Terrorism Strategy have been implemented, and the extent to which ECOWAS interventions in several instances have contained and eliminated

terrorism as threats within the sub-region." Based on the three-legged stool
of the ECOWAS counterterrorism strategy—prevent, pursue, and repair—
Vhumbunu states that the prevention aspect of the ECOWAS strategy aims
to stop terrorism before it happens.

The first leg of the stool requires policies that dictate, address, and eliminate conditions—such as poverty, unemployment, economic and political
marginalization, human rights abuses, corruption, and insecurity — that
create a conducive environment for the emergence of terrorism. The second
leg of the stool—pursue—adopts tactics such as "proactive and operational
capabilities that detect and eliminate the conditions that make terrorism more
likely. These tactics include 'early warning systems, suppressing financial
sources for terrorist groups, strategies to prevent violent extremism and
radicalism, and the promotion of democratic governance practices.' Also, the
strategy calls on member states to ratify and implement regional, continental,
and international protocols and conventions, and legal frameworks against
terrorism, improve border control, surveillance, disrupt terror finance network, and protect critical infrastructure." The last leg of the stool—repair—is
more akin to peacebuilding. It is a call on member states to reconstruct their
communities and governance structures "to protect the victims of terrorism,
uphold their fundamental human rights, reconcile communities, repair the
social contract with citizens, and develop strategies to prevent future occurrence of terrorism."

Vhumbunu concludes that while the ECOWAS has managed to establish an
institutional framework for coordinating their anti-terrorism efforts, it is "the
lack of operational capacity and capabilities" that has rendered ECOWAS
efforts less than commendable. And, in addition to lacking effective coordination, individual member states with fragile economies and security architecture have not been very successful in countering terrorism at the domestic
level. Instead, these states—Mali, Burkina Faso, and others—rely on international partners and donors to shore up their capacities. Thus, an effective
regional counterterrorism strategy requires domestic capacity and capabilities
to complement the institutional and cross-border efforts of the ECOWAS
to enhance the efficacy of regional security against political and religious
extremism across west Africa.

In chapter 8, "United States Counterterrorism Regime in Africa," George
Klay Kieh Jr. argues that Africa was on the back burner of the US national
security interest until the terrorist attack on the US homeland on September
11, 2001. It was Al-Qaeda's brazen attack against the United States that cata-
pulted Africa into the front burner of the US national security interest—principally because of the framing of the fight against Al-Qaeda as the "Global
War on Terror" by the George W. Bush administration. Given the fact that
many states in Africa have a majority and significant Muslim populations,

the US desire is to prevent al Qaeda from using the so-called "failed states" to which many African states were categorized as a base for further terrorist attacks against Western interests and to ensure continuing access to African natural resources that are needed by several industries in the West, especially the United States.

Consequently, and against the backdrop of the global war on terror, Kieh argues that in promoting US national security interests in Africa, the United States unwittingly sowed the seeds that have germinated into autocratic governments and facilitated the emergence and active engagement of anti-government forces in the form of terrorists in the continent. The initiatives such as "The Pan-Sahel Initiative," "The East African counter-Terrorism Initiative," "The Trans-Saharan Counter-terrorism Partnership," "The African Coastal and Border Security," "The U.S. Africa Command (AFRICOM)," "The Gulf of Guinea Maritime Security Initiative," and the drone program under the Obama administration have resulted in the training of some African military and security agents in counterterrorism. The counterterrorist initiatives have also enhanced the acquisition of equipment and logistics for various governments and led to the capturing and killing of some Al-Qaeda leaders. However, Kieh contends that the successful countering and termination of terrorist networks and cells are challenged by the adaptable capacity of jihadists to recruit new leaders and disgruntled youths as loyal foot soldiers into anti-government activities. Thus, the war on terrorism fought on African territories has led to minimal success, and with dire consequences to life and limbs of the masses.

Kieh concludes that "counter-terrorism initiatives are fraught with major problems — military centricity, the primacy of American national security interests at the expense of the security of the participating states, loss of lives of the citizens, the politicization of counterterrorism, and human rights violations by the local security and military units that are involved in counterterrorism operations." The US-led counterterrorism strategy can enhance the fight against terrorism only to the extent that new policy implementations promote human security and democratic governance.

In chapter 9, George Klay Kieh Jr. and Kelechi A. Kalu weave together the lessons learned from the constituent chapters of the book and they include the legacy of the authoritarian colonial state as evidenced in the performance of the postcolonial state in Africa (with few exceptions): The non-reconstituted postcolonial African state has continued to rule by violence. In addition, its custodians have used the agency of their respective offices to engage in the personal accumulation of wealth by plundering and pillaging state resources. As panaceas, they suggest the imperative of reconstituting the state, and stablishing a system of democratic governance and the promotion of human security that includes, inter alia, ethnic pluralism and the associated tolerance.

CONCLUSION

The chapter has attempted to lay the foundation for the volume in several major ways. First, it provided a conceptual framework that embodied the definitions of the three major terms that undergird the book—insurgency, terrorism, and counterterrorism. The rationale was to avoid the conceptual chaos that attends these key concepts, amid the divergent definitions of them. In sum, the study's conceptual framework provides the meanings of these key terms from the perspective of this book.

Second, the chapter problematized the major pillars of the volume by interrogating their historical development, nature, and dynamics. For example, terrorism both from "above and below" were examined (Martin 2003: 34). The reason was to examine the two major dimensions of the terrorism problematic state-sponsored and privately sponsored. Such an approach is useful for formulating and implementing policies that are designed to address the menace of terrorism, especially in Africa. Similarly, the chapter probed the counterterrorism regimes of some African states, the African Union (AU), and regional organizations. The purpose was to gain insights into the ways the AU, regional organizations, and various African states are addressing terrorism from "below" (Martin 2003:34).

Finally, the introduction provided the overarching theoretical and methodological thrust of the book, as well as insights from its constituent chapters. In the case of the theoretical and methodological lens, the introductory section explicated the book's interdisciplinary locus, and the resulting imperative of employing multiple theoretical and methodological approaches. In addition, the introduction provides summary snapshots about the various chapters, including their foci and findings.

REFERENCES

Adibe, Jideofor.2014. "Explaining the Emergence of Boko Haram." *Africa in Focus*. May 6. www.brookings.edu/blog/africa-in-focus/2014/05/06/explaining-the -emergence-of-boko-haram. Accessed July 24, 2022.

Ake, Christopher. 1996. *Development and Democracy in Africa*. Washington, DC: The Brookings Institution Press.

Al-Anani, Khalil. 2020. *State Terror in Egypt: Is it Time for Accountability?* Arab Center. Washington, DC.

Al-Nadeem Center for Rehabilitation of Victims of Violence and Torture. 2019. *Forced Disappearances and Torture in Egypt*. www.alnadeem.org. Accessed March 20, 2022.

Ashukem, Jean Claude. 2021. "To Give a Dog a Bad Name to Kill It: Cameroon's Anti-terrorism Law as a Strategic Framework for Human Rights Violations." *Journal of Contemporary African Studies*. 39(1): 119–34.

Betts, R. K. 2002. "The Soft Underbelly of American Primacy: Tactical Advantages of Terror." *Political Science Quarterly*. 117(1): 19–36.

Boeke, Sergei. 2016. "Al Qaeda in the Islamic Maghreb: Terrorism, Insurgency or Organized Crime?" *Small Wars and Insurgencies*. 27(5): 914–36.

Center for International Cooperation. 2022. *Terrorism*. Stanford, CA: Stanford University.

Clapham, Christopher. 1998. *African Guerillas*. London: James Currey.

Dunn, Kevin, and Morten Boas. 2017. "The Evolving Landscape of African Insurgencies." In *Africa's Insurgents*. Edited by Kevin Dunn and Morten Boas. Boulder, CO: Lynne Rienner Publishers, 1–21.

Ejeh, E. U. et al. 2019. "Nature of Terrorism and Anti-Terrorism Laws in Nigeria." *Nnamdi Azikiwe University Journal of International Law and Jurisprudence*. 10(2): 186–92.

Ewang, Anietie. 2021. "Counter-terrorism and Human Rights: Striking the Rights Balance. Testimony at the Tom Lantos Human Rights Commission." *Human Rights Watch*. October 26.

Felter, Claire et al. 2021. *Al-Shabab: A Backgrounder*. New York: Council on Foreign Relations.

Filiu, Jean-Pierre. 2009. *Al-Qaeda in the Islamic Maghreb: Algerian Challenge or Global Threat?* Carnegie Papers. Washington, DC: Carnegie Endowment for International Peace.

Fisher, Jonathan, and David M. Anderson. 2013. "Authoritarianism and the Securitization of Development in Africa." *International Affairs*. 91(1): 131–51.

Forest, James J. F. 2021. *Confronting the Terrorism of Boko Haram in Nigeria*. Monograph 12–5. Hurlburt Field, FL: Joint Special Operations University.

France 24. 2020. "Ethiopia Adopts New Version of Much Criticized Terrorism Law." March 1, 1.

Gavin, Michelle. 2018. *Political Violence in Zimbabwe*. June 25. www. cfr.org/blog/political-violence-zimbabwe. Accessed June 27, 2022.

Hubschle, Annette. 2005. "South Africa's Anti-terror Law: Among the Least Restrictive?" *African Security Review*. 14(4): 105–18.

Human Rights Watch. 2002. *World Report, 2001*. New York: Human Rights Watch.

Human Rights Watch. 2005. *World Report, 2004*. New York: Human Rights Watch.

Human Rights Watch. 2006. *World Report, 2005*. New York: Human Rights Watch.

Human Rights Watch. 2008. *Zimbabwe: Surge in State Sponsored Violence*. April 25.

Human Rights Watch. 2009. *World Report.*, 2008 New York: Human Rights Watch.

Human Rights Watch. 2010. *World Report, 2009*. New York: Human Rights Watch.

Human Rights Watch. 2011. *World Report, 2010*. New York: Human Rights Watch.

Human Rights Watch. 2014. *World Report, 2013*. New York: Human Rights Watch.

Human Rights Watch. 2015. *World Report, 2014*. New York: Human Rights Watch.

Human Rights Watch. 2020. *World Report, 2019*. New York: Human Rights Watch.

Ihonvbere, Julius. 1991. "Economic Crisis in Sub-Saharan Africa: Issues, Responses and Prospect for Recovery." *Pakistan Horizon.* 44(4): 41–56.

International Foundation of Human Rights. 2010. *Egypt: Counter-terrorism Against the Background of an Endless State of Emergency.* Paris, France: International Foundation of Human Rights.

Library of Congress. 2014. *Cameroon: New Law on Repression of Terrorism Passed.* December 18.

Magdy, Samy. 2020. "Egypt Moves Toward Toughening Up Draconian Anti-Terror Law." AP. February 10, 1–2.

Matfess, Hilary. 2017. "Ethiopia: Counter-terrorism Legislation in Sub-Saharan Africa." *Small Wars Journal.* www.smallwarsjournal.com. Accessed March 26, 2022.

Martin, Gus. 2003. *Understanding Terrorism: Challenges, Prospects, and Issues.* 1st ed. Thousand Oaks, CA: Sage.

Melber, Henning. 2020. "Germany and Namibia: Negotiating Genocide." *Journal of Genocide Research.* 22(4): 502–14.

Metz, Steven, and Raymond Millen. 2004. *Insurgency and Counterinsurgency in the 21st Century: Reconceptualizing Threat and Response.* Monograph Series. Carlisle, PA: Strategic Studies Institute, Army War College Press.

Muraga, Daniel. 2021. "ISIS in Africa." *CQ Researcher.* October 21. www.library.cqpress.com. Accessed April 5, 2022.

Obi, Alex Vines, and Jon Wallace. 2021. *Terrorism in Africa.* London, UK: Chatham House.

Omenma, J. Tochukwu, and Moses Onyango 2020. "African Union Counter-terrorism Frameworks and Implementation Trends Among Members States of the East African Community." *India Quarterly.* 76(1): 103–19.

Pham, John Peter. 2011. "Foreign Influence and Shifting Horizons: The Ongoing Evolution of al Qaeda in the Islamic Mahgreb." *Orbis.* 55(2): 240–56.

Primoratz, Igor. 1997. "The Morality of Terrorism." *Journal of Applied Philosophy.* 14(3): 221–33.

Ramsay, Jeffress. 1993. "Introduction: The Struggle for Development." *In Global Studies: Africa.* Edited by Jeffress Ramsay. Guilford, CT: McGraw-Hill/Dushkin, 1–3.

Sandler, Todd. 2015. "Terrorism and Counterterrorism: An Overview." *Oxford Economic Papers.* 67(1): 1–20.

Stewart, Donna. 2013. *What is Next for Mali? The Roots of Conflict and Challenges to Stability.* Monograph Series. Carlisle, PA: Strategic Studies Institute, Army War College.

Strydom, Hennie, and Swikani Neube. 2016. "State and Sub-State Terrorism in Africa." *Kazan Journal of International Law and International Relations,* 16–25. www.researchgate.net.publications. Accessed September 26, 2021.

Terrorism Research. N.D. *Differences Between Terrorism and Insurgency,* www.terrorism-research,com. Accessed March 2, 2022.

United States Department of State. 2021. *Country Reports on Terrorism, 2020.* Washington DC: US State Department.

Weinberg, Leonard. 2010. "The Challenges of Conceptualizing Terrorism." *Terrorism and Political Violence.* 16(4): 777–94.

Young, Crawford. 1997. *The African Colonial State in Comparative Perspective.* 1st. ed. New Haven, CT: Yale University Press.

Chapter 2

Explaining Insurgency and Terrorism

Kelechi A. Kalu

This chapter explains the persistence of terrorism and insurgencies in many countries in Africa, dating back to the early periods of political independence in the 1960s. Stories and images in newspapers published within and outside the continent, data, and analyses of terrorism-related incidents lead to one conclusion—that Africa is saturated by violent conflicts and low-intensity wars. Waged mostly by anti-government forces, these wars are characterized as terrorism, insurgency, banditry, and civil wars. One dimension of the conflict is persistent violent armed extremism that challenges government authority, and territorial and human security within and across countries. The hub for several of the armed violent extremisms is in politically and economically neglected communities in natural resource–rich countries such as the Democratic Republic of the Congo (DRC), Nigeria, Niger, and Mozambique. These ungoverned and neglected communities are characterized by the absence of government-provided security, low economic development, lack of employment opportunities, and political exclusion. It will take a capable and effective developmental state to mitigate these insecurities, especially in rural and border communities, with enforceable policies that promote human security and the political inclusion of marginalized communities.

As Kalu and Kieh, (2013: 179–81) note, effective states are characterized by a government's capacity for providing security, education, health, a well-maintained road network, energy, and other infrastructures that enhance the lives of citizens across communities. Failure to provide such basic services leaves the communities and the people vulnerable to occupation by drug cartels, religious and ethnic entrepreneurs, and as a base for anti-government activities. Indeed, the "information superhighway is the real ungoverned and perhaps ungovernable space" (Kalu and Kieh 2013: 181) that insurgents, criminal gangs, and terrorists use as locations for buying weapons and selling protection in communities to foreign mining staff of oil and resource extraction companies. These ungoverned spaces within the Sahel and the Niger Delta, and other remote areas offer ease of access to and exit from such locations because of globalization-induced "interdependence of open society, open economy, and open technology infrastructure" (Love 2019: 2) that enables untraceable financial and resource transactions and transfers. The global and domestic dimensions intersect in the low capacity of most African countries, whose weak institutional structures impact their ability for effective negotiations with multinational corporations that extract African natural resources and global economic institutions that help to undermine policy autonomy in African countries in the name of free market doctrines. The result is weak government institutions with low capacity for revenue generation, and an inability to provide effective security and economic development that leaves some communities politically excluded and therefore vulnerable to occupation by insurgents and criminal gangs. Thus, unable to provide effective security and economic governance, many of the African governments facing insurgencies rely on external military and security support for dealing with their internal economic development challenges, hence the persistence of terrorism, insurgencies, and armed extremism in the name of religion or ethnicity.

Thus, this chapter argues that, with the persistent presence of "insurgents and terrorists" in many countries in Africa, governments are not interested in bringing terrorism and insurgencies to an end for two main reasons. First, a persistent "war on" terrorists, insurgents, and criminal gangs serves a useful purpose for the government's access to economic and military aid from Western powers. Second, persistent "war on terrorists" provides a good excuse and alternative explanations for the incompetence, and lack of capacity, of many governments in the region in dealing with economic and political development issues that have bedeviled them since political independence.

And, as a corollary to the above: continuing "the war on terrorism" advances the political interests of various Western governments, especially France, Britain, and the United States, in the fight against global terrorism—a politically strategic position—for the benefit of domestic constituencies' perceptions of their security against external terrorist attacks. It is a marriage of mutually reinforcing conveniences for African leaders and their foreign external security and commercial partners.

CONCEPTUAL UNDERSTANDING OF
INSURGENCY AND TERRORISM IN AFRICA

Insurgencies[1] can challenge government authority to the extent that such a movement has popular support, and can rely on a segment of the community and security forces, and sometimes, external sponsors. An insurgency fails if it cannot mobilize popular support and/or external sponsorship for its cause. That was the case with reductions in external support for insurgencies and guerrilla movements across Africa at the end of the Cold War. The initial challenge for most affected countries in the region was that the military support received by the government to battle guerrilla movements during the Cold War ended, or was significantly reduced; that was also the fate of various rebels and insurgents. The decline in external military supports for governments against armed resistance by insurgents in Angola, Mali, Niger, Nigeria, and Mozambique forced the governments, albeit temporarily, to accede to the demands for political inclusion in the form of elections and transitions from autocracy to democracy in the 1990s. However, the push for political inclusion was short-lived as many of the autocrats transitioned themselves from military uniform into civilian garb, and from appointed autocracy to elected ochlocracy. The result was a claimed electoral mandate that enhanced the legitimacy of governments in many of the countries and helped to intensify the exploitation of natural resources, political exclusions, and marginalization of communities perceived as neglectable. And, with declined external support for insurgencies, various anti-government forces took over and occupied neglected communities in northern Mozambique, the Niger Delta region and northeastern part of Nigeria, southwest Cameroon, and across the Sahel.

With political exclusion and government neglect of some of its territories and peoples, existing grievances provided opportunities for anti-government forces to take over and occupy neglected or ungoverned territories as a hub for anti-government activities and other forms of exploitation. And, vulnerable to occupation by terrorists, insurgents, and criminal gangs, these territories become a base for anti-government forces to use terrorism as tactics, to appropriate the communities' grievances against government policies of neglect and exploitation, and to advance the economic, political, and sociocultural objectives of the insurgents/terrorists. The point here is that the global war on terrorism in Africa advances the Western strategic security battle inside Africa, and its overriding objective is the protection of Western security and military interests at home and abroad. For Africans, the insurgency and terrorist challenges are driven by political exclusion and economic exploitation by both anti-government forces and the government's countermeasures against armed extremists. Armed extremists like Boko

Haram, insurgent groups like Al-Shabab, and other anti-government forces are generally lumped together as terrorists. As explained above, terrorism is a tactic used by insurgents in their anti-government activities. A conceptual understanding and analysis of terrorism in the literature and how it is used in this volume will help clarify the argument that terrorism in Africa is more of an economic issue, arising from political exclusion and neglect, than the ideological and religious basis of terrorist activities and claims elsewhere, such as in the Middle East.

TERRORISM EXPLAINED

As Neumann and Smith (2005: 574) state, "terrorism is the deliberate creation of a sense of fear, usually by the use of threat or the use of symbolic acts of physical violence, to influence the political behavior of a given target group." Conceptually, the analytical challenge is to explain why and when terrorism occurs. To do so requires a consistent and broad understanding of what terrorism is—because the idea of *terror* and therefore terrorism is not a tangible event that can be observed, except by its effects. As such, fear induced by terror can emanate from any unexpected but frightening action by individuals or groups. Consequently, a full understanding of the concept of terrorism should lead us to ponder whether government violent actions that rain fear and terror in communities occupied by non-state and anti-government forces should be labeled and analyzed as terrorism. Given that, for Wight (2009), political communication is a component in any useful definition of terrorism. For example, how should we label and analyze the leaflet that US bombers dropped on Japanese cities in 1945? According to Daugherty (1958),[2] the leaflet warned Japanese citizens that:

> These leaflets are being dropped to notify you that your city has been listed for destruction by our powerful air force. The bombing will begin in 72 hours.
>
> We give the military clique this notification because we know there is nothing they can do to stop our overwhelming power and our iron determination. We want you to see how powerless the military is to protect you.
>
> [The] systematic destruction of city after city will continue as long as you blindly follow your military leaders . . . (Cited in Merari 1993: 216).

And, as Solomon (2021: 6) argues, "If the birth of the French Republic gave us fraternity, liberty, and equality, it is also true that it gave us the guillotine, *fear,* and *terror*" (my italics). In contemporary scholarship, a realist view of the state as the main actor, with the legitimate right to use violence domestically and in the international system—if the calculations lead such a state to believe that its gains will outweigh the costs—is generally accepted as a given. And, even though the origin of terrorism as a tactic for inflicting fear and pain on communities and anti-government forces goes back to Robespierre and his minions who deployed state terror against anti-government forces in France between 1793 and 1794, the contemporary scholarly view—often colored politically and ideologically—remains that violence against the state by non-state actors is illegitimate and qualifies as terrorism. To be sure, the tactics—physical violence, denial of basic rights, and creation of an atmosphere of constant fear and distrust among neighbors—used by anti-government forces have the same effects on communities as when legitimate government rains terror on a segment of its people. It is the labeling of state violence as legitimate and non-state violence as illegitimate and therefore terrorism that differentiates government actions from anti-government forces' use of violence; but the effects of violence on affected communities remain the same—the loss of security and liberty, amid conditions of economic and psychological vulnerabilities.

In an interview that Marche (2022: 58) had with Peter Mansoor on insurgencies and counterinsurgencies in Iraq and the possibility of anti-government forces succeeding in the United States, the retired army colonel argued that government forces' control of the population is key to the success and failure of both insurgencies and counterinsurgencies. According to Mansoor:

> In Baghdad, we did that by segmenting . . . the city with cement barriers, by instituting martial law and censuses. There was a curfew. There were checkpoints all over the place. We went into people's homes in cordon-and-search operations looking for arms and munitions. We had a full-scale intelligence operation to ferret out the terrorist and insurgent leaders. We had an unblinking eye over the city taking 24/7 surveillance. It's very invasive for civil rights. It became essentially impossible for the terrorists and insurgents to move or communicate. (Marche 2022: 58)

And, as Marche states, "Areas of [the] population were broken down by ethnicity and by 12-foot steel-reinforced blast walls. Citizens were interrogated every time they left or entered their neighborhood. Anyone suspicious was arrested" (ibid.). In such an environment, it is not difficult to understand why affected individuals become vulnerable to recruitment by anti-government forces or why they will take it upon themselves to be distrustful of any promises of political freedom devoid of human dignity and economic opportunities. Thus, by the scale of tactically deployed action in controlling a community in the first instance, any effort aimed at changing their hearts and minds against recruitments by insurgents and terror groups is lost.

The coalition efforts as described by retired army colonel Mansoor are consistent with the definition that a US task force had established as a definition of terrorism in 1986. According to Schmid and Jongman (1988: 33), the task force report specifically defines terrorism as "the unlawful use or threat of violence against persons or property to further political or social objectives. It is generally intended to intimidate or coerce a government, individuals or groups to modify their behavior or policies." And, while acknowledging challenges with a unified definition for terrorism, the State Department Office of the Coordinator of Terrorism (State Department 1990: v) states that:

> we consider terrorism to be premeditated, politically motivated violence perpetrated against noncombatant targets by subnational groups or clandestine state agents, usually intended to influence an audience. "International terrorism" is terrorism involving the citizens or territory of more than one country.

To be sure, the US State Department's definition of terrorism is not spectacularly different from the British government's perspective. And, as Schmid and Jongman (1988: 34) state, for the British government, terrorism is "the use of violence for political ends and includes any use of violence . . . [to put] . . . the public or any section of the public in fear." The foregoing perspectives and definitions—even though similar tactics are deployed by state agents in response to insurgencies—are consistent in focusing attention on the political objectives, the tactic of fear, and violence as the main tool of engagement by anti-government forces. However, Naude's (2021: 14) definition of terrorism as

> a form of organized (sic) violence, directed at non-state actors and organizations (sic) who are not the intended final targets of the attack; that is designed to evoke extreme psychological stress, anxiety or revulsion in the civilian population; and that is carried out in service of ideological, religious and political views that may or may not be shared by those outside of the organization (sic) . . .

is a better nuanced and more inclusive definition for understanding terrorism as an action undertaken by non-state actors. Naude's definition also makes it possible for analysts to understand and explain when government agents' *legitimate violence* crosses the line of providing security into inflicting pains, fear, and insecurity in ungoverned territories used as a base by insurgents, as countermeasures against terrorists and insurgent forces.

From a structural realist view, Wight (2009: 102) argues that any definition of terrorism necessarily "involves the deliberate attempt to enact harm on non-state actors through the use of illegitimate violence with the expressed aim of communicating a political message." Thus, and consistent with realism, Wight's view is that state actions within their territorial boundaries are legitimate. As such, actions taken by anti-government forces—irrespective of why such actions were initiated are considered illegitimate and therefore must be opposed by state agents. More specifically, Wight (2009: 102) suggests that any helpful definition of terrorism must include four elements—"a form of violent political communication, illegitimate use of violence, intentional targeting of non-state actors and institutions, and that the intended recipients of the political message are not always the victims."

Analytically, Wight (2009) and Naude (2021) offer two contrasting, yet similar perspectives—understanding and appreciating that the Westphalian state defines what is legitimate and acceptable behavior by individuals and organizations within each state's borders. This means that any violent action that involves political protests, rebellion and insurgencies, terrorism, and other forms of resistance against the state are considered illegitimate use of violence. It also means that, by extension, in response to anti-government forces, any violent action deployed by *state agents* in contemporary global politics can be seen as legitimate. Thus, I explain, in the rest of this chapter, why violent anti-government activities and government responses have rendered several African states "active sites of contestation, resistance and transgression" (Naude 2021: 15).

THE AFRICAN STATES AS SITES OF CONTESTATION AND RESISTANCE

Generally, states with effective government rarely, if ever, face violent armed challenges from a segment of their population. It is often the existence of governments with a low capacity for effective governance, law, and political inclusion that trigger the desire for some groups in society to plot the overthrow of a government they perceive as ineffective and weak. The core objective of such an action is often leadership transition or the formation of a new government controlled by the insurgents. Given the autocratic governance system that was colonialism, the national liberation movements against the British, French, and Portuguese, and the apartheid regime in Africa were insurgent, as are the various coups after political independence during the Cold War.

However, as the Cold War ended and without reforming the colonial states to focus on the political and economic development of their societies, the objectives of insurgent movements in many conflict areas in the Democratic Republic of the Congo, Nigeria, Mozambique, Somalia, and elsewhere have transitioned from national liberation to economic opportunism. To be sure, the nature of unreformed and unrestructured colonial states in Africa continues to underperform in its basic function of providing physical security for persons and properties that have resulted in the persistence of insurgencies and terrorism in the region. The post–Cold War objectives of various governments in sub-Saharan Africa, especially in Nigeria, Chad, Mali, Cameroon, Angola, and the DRC are not that different from those of the so-called terrorists, bandits, and insurgents whose core objectives are the capturing of a piece of territory and setting up shop for collecting rents from foreign and domestic interests' exploitations of the natural resources in the land. For example, it is the absence of effective, accountable, and inclusive governments in the northern and eastern DRC, Niger Delta region of Nigeria, the northern part of Mozambique, and across Somalia that create space for the active competition between shadow governments, insurgents, and bandits who terrorize the people, recruit them into anti-government activities, and subject them to penury while carting away the economic rents from the community's natural resources.

Citing Tilly (1985), Kalu (2022: 2) argues that the Westphalian states emerged out of deliberate violence between competing forces for control of territories, resources, and the people. That "coercive exploitation . . . banditry, piracy, gangland rivalry, policing, and war making" (Tilly 1985: 169) were strategies deployed in capturing, settling, and eventually building state structures and institutions with a social contract that maintained relative peace and stability with the people. Tilly's (1985:169) core argument on the functions of states is summarized thus:

> state's war making function is to eliminate or neutralize external rivals for the same territory; (2) state making results from neutralizing all internal rivals within the claimed territory; (3) neutralize the state's chief supporter's enemies by . . . [protecting] those who paid for their services; and (4) secure resources extraction it needs to hold and maintain state security essential for successful implementation of its functions of war making, state making, and protection.

The importance of the foregoing argument should be part of any research that seeks to explain why terrorism occurs and why the strategic use of "illegitimate violence" is a preferred tactic by anti-government forces, especially in sub-Saharan Africa. With no overarching government and institutions to define what was legitimate before the emergence of the Westphalian states in 1648, state formation was based on "illegitimate violence." Thus, new state institutions and structures of governance had to rely on "standing militaries, police services, judicial systems for conflict resolutions, governance structures such as parliaments or national assemblies, and financial resources extractions through taxation and import duties" (Kalu 2021: 3) to establish norms of legitimacy, especially about questions of violence. Taxation policies were not just about collecting revenues from the people; they were and are strategies for legitimizing the government and ensuring that the people are included in political and economic decisions in their communities, and consequently enable people to hold their government accountable. Indeed, efficient and effective taxation capacity undergirds the sovereignty of a state. It is this norm of legitimacy and the continuing institutional, political, and economic exclusions of some members of a society/country that fuel anti-government forces, insurgencies, and criminal gangs that attract the labeling of their tactics as "illegitimate use of violence" and terrorism across African countries.

The foregoing is important because the function of the state in Africa (similar to its European, colonially created counterpart) has been on resource extraction—not building political-economic structures that create enabling states for citizens to feel included and valued by their communities and states. And, African states have not needed state building to survive, because they seek and receive external support for maintaining authoritarian policies and neglect many parts of their territories.

Understanding various violent armed conflicts across African states, like Chad, Central African Republic, the Congo, Niger, Nigeria, Cameroon, Sudan, and Mozambique as contestations for economic and political inclusion helps to differentiate between the ideologically, religiously, and politically motivated terrorism in the Middle East, the United States, and many European countries. The so-called terrorism in sub-Saharan Africa reflects economic and regional elites' dominance of government posts without much regard to the people's agitations for the practice of liberal democratic theory. Instead, like insurgents and criminal gangs, these religious and ethnic entrepreneurs in various government offices in Chad, Burkina Faso, Mali, Niger, and Nigeria appropriate religious and ethnic sentiments, symbols, and grievances of the people to maintain themselves in power, while various communities remain under Boko Haram and Islamic jihadist siege.

With support from outside the continent in the battle against global terrorists, governments in the above-mentioned states have no incentives for policy autonomy to build and maintain institutions and economic structures for the benefit of the people. The outcome is persistent agitations in places like the Niger Delta in Nigeria, eastern Congo in the DRC, and northern Cabo Delgado province in Mozambique, where state power uses "legitimate violence" in the form of military operations that have mostly sustained the violence and counterviolence by bandits, criminal gangs, and economic terrorists within those regions. Because the state is a prize that elites fight over at the expense of the masses, the result is an increasing number of peri-urban communities and other "ungovernable spaces . . . abandoned to non-state actors in the rural areas and unguarded forest regions of sub-Saharan Africa, e.g., Boko Haram in Nigeria and Al Qaida in Mali, and Al Shabab in Somalia" (Kalu 2021: 5). These spaces, abandoned by state government security institutions, are now governed by anti-government forces, insurgents, criminal gangs, and terrorists who appropriate community grievances in their public rhetoric to recruit young people and turn communities into anti-government fortresses.

STATES MIDWIFE VIOLENT EXTREMISM IN AFRICA

Thus, the actions of state agents—government and its security institutions—midwife the emergence and persistence of anti-government forces in African countries. To the extent that government policies are not inclusive, and are perceived as unjust, and unfair by many citizens who are negatively impacted by such policies, resistance and anti-government forces are likely to find a fertile mind and ground. It is common sense that aggrieved individuals can and will seek ways and means of addressing their grievances. Such grievances against the government often lead to organized peaceful or violent resistance depending on the nature and governance in the country. Theoretically, in *Why Men Rebel*, Gurr (1970) popularized the concept of *relative deprivation*—to capture and analyze sources of popular discontent, understand peoples' justifications or beliefs about the utility of political action, and examine how people are organized to demand change from the state, and the capacity of the government to resolve their demands without resorting to violence.[3] Thus, understanding why and how certain communities become a playground of anti-government forces helps explain the behavior and or policies of political leaders and their consequences within the structure of the state. Also, understanding who is included or excluded in government policies helps explain how government policies impose differential impacts on ethnic, religious, and other minorities, especially when government policies fail in their raison d'être to protect the security and property of all citizens. For example, based on published interviews (Punch Newspapers Nigeria 2022) with Mallam Turkur Mamu, a representative of Sheikh Ahmad Gumi, who is highly respected by various leaders of the Boko Haram organization, the Boko Haram group's grievances stem from their desire to spread their religious ideology but were consequently attacked by government forces, government neglect of their communities, corruption in government, and the absence of socioeconomic development in their communities. Thus, according to Boko Haram, it is the failure of the Nigerian government to reform state structures and institutions to protect all its communities since independence that is directly connected to the emergence of anti-government forces like Boko Haram.[4] The claim by Boko Haram is made possible by low government capacity to discharge its responsibilities and corrupt practices that provide opportunities for terrorist organizations like Boko Haram to occupy, terrorize, and slaughter Nigerians, and coordinate kidnapping activities with impunity. It first started in the northeastern part of Nigeria and without effective government, the response has since 2020 brazenly extended its terrorizing activities from the Sambisa Forest in the boundary between Nigeria and the Cameroons to the southwestern and southeastern regions of Nigeria.

The seeming lack of capacity of the Nigerian government to enable state institutions and security forces to carry out their responsibilities to protect the people and enable economic activities to advance the interest of ordinary people has resulted in constant claims of marginalization by the Nigerians in the eastern part of the country, several communities in the middle belt, Niger Delta, and more recently, citizens from the southwestern part of the country. It is an issue of perceived relative deprivation and a grievance that stems from political exclusion, unjust, and unfair implementation of government economic policies. Ake's (1996: 1–3), and Kalu 2022) argument that the postcolonial state remains untransformed in its total control of government appointments without merit, failure to integrate economic production processes into regional and social economies of scale, excessive consumerism without production, neglect of educational institutions, and therefore, human capital production, nonexistent or poorly constructed and maintained roads, energy, health infrastructures, excessive dependence on commodities export and the importation of manufactured goods, including food, have created spaces of uncertainties, anxiety, and fear across communities.

One of the consequences of the foregoing is the absence of transparent, fair, and accessible mediating structures as conflict resolution platforms between citizens, communities, and in many instances, between government and groups that seek political inclusion. Each of the countries across sub-Saharan Africa that are experiencing anti-government/terrorist activities and insurgencies—Burkina Faso, Chad, Central African Republic, Cameroon, Niger, and Nigeria—are legacies of colonial state coercive institutions of violence that postcolonial leaders quickly co-opted to advance their ochlocracy and deployed against agitators for political inclusion, conveniently labeled terrorists. Indeed, for postcolonial states in many African countries, the question is not whether the emperor is wearing new clothes, the real question is whether the emperor is wearing any clothes at all (Kalu 2021: 9). From Angola, DRC, and Guinea, from Mali to Nigeria, Mozambique, and Zambia, the state is effectively under the control of an organized party, enabled by international economic institutions and foreign mining corporations, from the West and Asia, against the masses. While the creation of the colonial state was an event, the underlying ideology of imperialism and its associated violence remains a process that continues to unfold across postcolonial states in Africa.

For the colonial state, the naked and abrasive use of soldiers to respond to political demands, and the reliance on external support remains visibly present in how the postcolonial state in Africa sought foreign security assistance to complement the military counteroffensive against anti-government forces (see

Mlambo and Masuku 2020: 9); and that strategy continues to prove ineffective in combating extremism because the challenge across Africa is political and economic, not military. Thus, as Ake (1996: 4–5) notes, the postcolonial state "continues to be totalistic in scope," remains an "apparatus of violence" with a very "narrow social base," and relies on the institutions of coercion rather than authority in making and implementing public policy (Kalu 2021:9). As securing political independence did not lead to state restructuring and reform, the attention of the leaders shifted from agitation for independence and national development to competition for naked power; that is, to control the state apparatus and associated economic rents. In this respect, political parties have largely become platforms or clubs hijacking the government for purposes of sharing (among themselves) natural resources rent paid by foreign corporations. And, with the lowering of the colonial flags and raising of the newly independent state flags, the "attention [of the leaders] turned from the colonial regime to one another; and eventually, the competition among these groups came to dominate political life" (Ake 1996: 5) and winners proceeded to barricade themselves in the fortress of state power and security. This means that political parties are no longer platforms for organizing and aggregating the interests of many to secure good governance for all, instead, it is an ochlocracy, a club for the elite sharing of the "national cake."

One of the consequences of the foregoing is that losers in the competition for state power sometimes become sponsors of agitators or, in many instances, adopt insurgency tactics to advance their cause of securing a portion of state resources as in Chad, Niger, Mali, and Nigeria. And with government economic and political policies not winning the hearts and minds of ordinary people, the insurgents can use the grievances of ordinary people as a base to orchestrate anti-government activities. This is illustrated by the foreign policy impact on African governments and insurgents of the terrorist attacks against the United States on September 11, 2001.

At the end of the Cold War in 1991, the US government's foreign policy of providing support to some autocratic governments and rebels fighting anti-communist battles, for example in Angola, the DRC, Mozambique, Nigeria, and elsewhere, was ended or significantly scaled back. But, after the September 11, 2001, terrorist attacks in New York and Washington, DC, the US government reversed course and resumed military and security support to African governments as part of its fight against global terrorism. On the one hand, that action by the US government enabled weak African governments, seeking increased external military support against anti-government forces, to redefine and repurpose internal agitations for political inclusion and economic development as battles against global terrorism.

On the other hand, for various agitators, the "success" and notoriety Al-Qaeda enjoyed after 9/11 provided a rallying cry for recruitment to address grievances against various governments. And one of the direct consequences of the new externally defined and supported "global war on terror" in Africa was that it turned the Sahel into a terrorist and anti-terrorist battleground. And, with the destabilization and destruction of the government of Libya and its leadership, and redefining the internal battle in Africa, the United States, its Western allies, and African ochlocrats unwittingly unleashed religious fanatics against ordinary Africans. To be sure, the United States and its allies, without accountability and transparency in their economic and resources interests in Arica, are complicit in the devastations that anti-government forces have unleashed on communities across the continent, especially in natural resource–rich countries like the Democratic Republic of the Congo. However, many of the solutions remain internally with the people and their government. So, by prescribing remedies for ending violent extremism that they either initiated or intensified in Africa, the Western powers lack moral and just standing to hold African leaders accountable for illiberal political exclusions that fuel violent anti-government activities that manifest as terrorism in the region. The development issues facing African countries are many; however, it is the deliberate absence of effective government presence, political exclusion of some groups, and the lack of a development agenda for enhancing the lives of ordinary citizens that enable anti-government forces to seize on community grievances as a platform for insurgency and terrorism across Africa.

Therefore, any study of terrorism that focuses mainly on how non-state actors' anti-government activities impact states and their citizens elide the complicity of state policies that lead to persistent anti-government forces and terrorism in Africa. Privileging the effect of terrorism on Westphalia states and ignoring the role of the state in the persistence of anti-government forces in Africa undermines genuine agitations and potential policies for pacifying affected communities. Many of the neglected spaces that have become staging grounds for anti-government activity are communities and peoples whose agitations are mostly driven by the government's inattention to political inclusion and economic development needs of the people. Also, focusing mainly on the impact of anti-government actions without similar attention to how the government's counterterrorism actions impact citizens in affected communities, fails to account for how government actions help to increase popular support for anti-government actions in affected communities across the Sahel, the horn of Africa, and parts of southern Africa.

To be sure, terrorism is not new to African countries and peoples. Terrorism against communities in the Congo, Kenya, Senegal, South Africa, and Nigeria was deployed in the enslavement of people and later occupation of their lands and communities. Subsequently, terrorism was used by colonial and postcolonial governments as a tactic to pacify African peoples' and communities' agitations against forceful exploitation of their resources as the Herero and Nama genocide in Namibia and the Mau Mau massacre in Kenya demonstrate. The memories of these past terrorist activities remain in the oral narratives and symbols across many coastal towns and hinterlands in Africa. The memories and symbols are often conveniently evoked by contemporary groups, e.g., Boko Haram and ISWAP, challenging what they consider as continuing Western government presence in the form of anti-terrorist, military, and intelligence support for governments that continue to terrorize their citizens in Burkina Faso, Cameroon, Chad, Central African Republic, Mali, Mozambique, Niger, Nigeria, Somalia, and Sudan.

TERRORISM AND INSURGENT ACTIVITIES IN NIGERIA AND MOZAMBIQUE

Generally, in its "Key Trends in Global Terrorism Index 2022 report," the Institute for Economics & Peace finds that while "global terrorist attacks increased to 5,226 in 2021, deaths declined slightly by 1.2%, [but] sub-Saharan Africa accounted for 48% of global terrorism deaths" in the same period. And, that "The Sahel is home to the world's fastest growing and most deadly terrorist groups." Specifically, in Niger, the Islamic State (IS) replaces the Taliban as the world's deadliest terror group in 2021, with fifteen deaths per attack.[5]

On his visit to Nigeria in May 2022, the United Nations Secretary-General, Antonio Guterres, received an official account of Nigeria's effort to deal with the security challenges posed by Boko Haram and the Islamic State of West Africa Province (ISWAP) in the region. At a meeting of the UN Global Counter-Terrorism Coordination Compact in June 2022, Guterres stated that "terrorist groups like Al-Qaeda, the Islamic State, and their affiliates continue to grow in the Sahel and make inroads into Central and Southern Africa. They exploit power vacuums, longstanding inter-ethnic strife, internal weaknesses, and state fragilities."[6]

According to the UN Secretary-General (*Manila Times* 2022), terrorism intensifies cycles of violence, fuels instability, and undermines peace efforts and development goals in conflict countries like the Democratic Republic of the Congo, Libya, and Somalia. "Such groups also exploit and manipulate grievances in society and mistrust governments in largely peaceful countries, such as Mozambique and Tanzania."[7] However, given insurgent actions and government counterterrorism operations in northern Mozambique, many residents in the conflict-affected Cabo Delgado province are likely to disagree with Secretary-General Guterres's characterization of their country as peaceful.

Many of the communities that suffer from persistent insecurity perpetrated by bandits, terrorists, and insurgents are equally impacted by government counterinsurgencies and anti-terrorist policies that have not yielded resolutions to the conflicts. Most of the conflicts are identity-based conflicts—politicized religious and ethnic differences, resources-driven insurgent activities, and opportunistic criminal gangs that governments often label as terrorists in Burkina Faso, Chad, Mali, Mozambique, Nigeria, Niger, and Somalia. It is the absence or low government presence in affected communities that are invariably linked to the "excluded group's" occupation of communities as a base for active resistance against government forces and infrastructure in countries like Mozambique, Nigeria, the Democratic Republic of the Congo (DRC), and Somalia.

For example, the Ahlu Sunna Wal Jama has been fighting the government of Mozambique in the Cabo Delgado province, the northern part of the country, since the end of its civil war in 1992. However, with insurgent attacks against security forces, buildings, and civilians in August 2017, the contemporary insurgency in Mozambique intensified in earnest. As Matsinhe and Valoi (2019: 3) states:

> The attacks . . . targeted mainly five isolated districts—Mocímboa da Praia, Macomia, Nangade, Palma and Quissanga [located on the border between Mozambique and Tanzania and the Indian Ocean]. These districts, except Nangade, are coastal areas overlooking the Mozambican Channel, and Macomia has a large plateau area that stretches into the interior. Although Mocímboa da Praia is the birthplace of this violent group, it was in Macomia that the group launched most of its attacks. It is noteworthy that in these districts, most of the population are Mwani and Makwe speakers who practice Islam.

Similarly, the historical context of the Boko Haram insurgency in Nigeria locates the movement at the deathbed of the leader of the Yan Tatsine, Mohammed Marwa, popularly known as Maitatsine. Maitatsine's objections to Western influences date back to the Cameroons in the 1940s—first against the British, and later the government of Nigeria. Maitatsine's activities in Nigeria started with the end of the Nigerian civil war in 1970 as the movement intensified its objections against the Nigerian government, the policies of which were perceived by Maitatsine as "permissible" of Western influences against Islamic beliefs. Thus, its offshoot, Boko Haram, has been fighting various communities in the northern part of the country, especially in the northeastern part of Nigeria, and border communities with Chad, Niger, and Cameroon. The Yan Tatsine birthed the Boko Haram insurgency that has been fighting the Nigerian government, kidnapping schoolchildren, and killing and maiming young and the old and that has perfected the business of kidnapping for ransom with impunity since 2002.

The Ahlu Sunna Wal Jama in Mozambique and Boko Haram in Nigeria insurgencies and "terrorists" are located in the northern part of each country. The leaders and their followers profess the Islamic faith. Occupied communities are characterized by ineffective educational opportunities from an early age to university levels, poor healthcare services, high levels of unemployment, especially among the youth, and corruption-induced breakdown of community morals and ethics that saw politicians as "big men" and everyone else expected to fend for themselves. Furthermore, the neglect of basic security functions of government *provides* opportunities for a small group of local and foreign individuals to recruit and indoctrinate young people into believing their luck in life is better with insurgents and terrorists; and more importantly, the recruits are brainwashed into believing that human life of those perceived as unbelievers is not worth preserving.

The above perfect storm of insecurity and hopelessness, created by government neglect of its basic duties, especially in the rural areas and increasingly in peri-urban communities left ungoverned territories as the theatre of mayhem, fear, and conformity—with consequences for the devaluing of lives by young men and women whose strengths are based on drugs, machetes, clubs, and Kalashnikovs that are constantly at their disposals, to terrorize and destroy peoples' hopes in Mali, Nigeria, Chad, Cameroon, Burkina Faso, Somalia, and elsewhere in Africa.

EFFECTS OF INSURGENT AND TERRORIST ACTIVITIES IN SUB-SAHARA AFRICA

In the case of Nigeria, the Catholic Bishop of the Diocese of Sokoto, Matthew Kukah, a respected public intellectual, in his 2022 Easter Message/Sermon titled, "To mend a broken nation: The Easter metaphor," he laments the absence of effective government and governance in Nigeria and worries about the consequences of the rudderless political leadership on the future of the country. According to Bishop Kukah, "the greatest challenge for Nigeria is not even the 2023 elections. It is the prospect for the reconciliation of our people."[8] Bishop Kukah argued that:

> The challenge of fixing this broken nation is enormous . . . [because] . . . everything [has] . . . broken down, . . . Nigeria . . . has become one big emergency national hospital with full occupancy. Our . . . hearts, homes, churches, mosques, infrastructure . . . and family dreams are broken. Nigeria's educational system . . . children's lives and future[s] are broken. Its politics . . . , economy . . . , energy and security systems and infrastructures are broken; so are the roads and rails—all broken. Only corruption is alive and well.[9]

Bishop Kukah's timely sermon and reflections easily apply to many countries beset by violent extremism, banditry, terrorism, and insurgency in Africa. For example, a snapshot of one week of violent armed conflicts, by the Armed Conflict Location & Event Data Project (ACLED)[10] across Africa, documents a series of continuing challenges facing various countries. Violent conflicts are common in the southwestern region of Cameroon, especially in the border towns with Nigeria where Boko Haram operates freely. South Sudan, Kenya, and Ethiopia are not immune from persistent armed violence by Al Shabaab and other jihadists.

For example, the Al Qaeda–affiliated Jama'at Nusrat al-Islam wal-Muslimin (JNIM) and Islamic State Sahel Province (IS Sahel) attacks in the Center-North of Burkina Faso and Sahel continue unabated. Between June 25 and July 1, 2022, JNIM's violence in the Center-North increased by 155 percent as flagged by ACLED's Subnational Threat Tracker (2022), and in "response, Burkinabe forces conducted ground operations and several airstrikes in the Center-East, Center-North, East, and South-East regions." Also, in Mali, JNIM and IS Sahel jointly attacked the regions of Mopti and Gao. And, JNIM confronted Malian military forces while attacking its rivals—Dozo and Dan Na Ambassagou militias—across Mopti and Segou regions. Farmers, Malian military, and UN peacekeeping (MINUSMA) vehicles in Segou, Tombouctou, and Kidal regions have all suffered attacks by Jama'at Nusrat al-Islam wal-Muslimin. Similarly, IS Sahel attacked farmers and Nigerien government forces in the Tillaberi region while carting away farm livestock. The entire Sahel region is littered with factions of extremist groups flying the flag of the Islamic religion—whether authentic or not. As in Burkina Faso, Mali, and Niger, some of these groups coordinate their attacks while at the same time fighting off rival gangs.

The Islamic State West Africa Province (ISWAP) Lake Chad faction and Boko Haram, also known as Jama'atu Ahlis Sunna Lidda'adati wal-Jihad (JAS), originated from the Yan Tatsine group and remains active in the northeast region of Nigeria, especially in Borno, Katsina, Yobe, and Adamawa states in Nigeria. ISWAP Lake Chad faction clashed with Boko Haram (JAS) in Bama Local Government Area (LGA), killing dozens of mostly innocent citizens. Violence across the northwest, and north-central regions, and increasingly in the southeast and southwest, remain a challenge for Nigerian security forces. Indeed, ISWAP and Boko Haram have been linked to the killing of dozens of people inside churches in the southwest[11] and detonating explosive devices that have crippled train rides between Kaduna and Abuja.[12] Kidnapping for ransom remains a regular occurrence across the country. And, in a brazen operation, Boko Haram operatives stormed and freed their colleagues from the Kuje prison complex in Abuja and in the process, freed over eight hundred other prisoners. Indeed, as Udegbunam (2022) reports, Boko Haram storming and freeing their "soldiers" is not new because between 2020 and 2021, it attacked various prisons in the country which resulted in the escape of five thousand of its members. Boko Haram's brazen attacks include storming military facilities and other security posts—killing military officers and civilians with impunity. A conservative estimate indicates that the Boko Haram insurgency in Nigeria has killed at least 100,000 Nigerians (ibid.).

In Somalia, Al Shabaab has become a government in the shadows—collecting taxes from residents in the regions of Somalia that it controls. The capacity to collect taxes is a sustainable strategy for ensuring state sovereignty and maintaining the legitimacy of government and ensuring a productive relationship between the citizens and their leaders. Residents in regions Al Shabaab control willingly comply with Al Shabaab's tax assessments, and taxpayers are afforded the opportunity by Al Shabaab agents to negotiate a low rate if there is evidence that the value of the assessed property is less than previously valued.[13] In this case, it is not strange that Al Shabaab is a quintessential insurgent that "targets government security forces, African Union Transition Mission in Somalia (ATMIS), and politicians . . . [and] attacked the home of a former Hirshabelle deputy minister and ambushed special forces near Mahadaay town" (ACLED data 2022) with the intent to unsettle and eventually unseat the government.

As the site of greedy global competition for natural resources, especially since the assassination of Patrice Lumumba in 1961, the case of the Democratic Republic of Congo does not need much elaboration. Armed conflicts and criminal gangs supported by different external entities remain persistent with a focus on controlling territories that are mined for their riches. For example, Al Jazeera reports that "fighting and exchanges of territorial control between military forces (FARDC) and March 23 Movement (M23) in Rutshuru, North Kivu, resulted in scores of fatalities, kidnapping, and sexual violence against civilians" between June 25 and July 1, 2022. And while conflicts persist in the Watalinga area of Beni and in South Kivu with no end in sight, these armed conflicts, mostly with external support, have essentially rendered the DRC a no-man's-land where the government only exercises effective and legitimate control of a small portion of the vast territory. And, while external support has been instrumental in sustaining several insurgents and terrorist gangs, these attacks persist because insurgents and extremist groups have taken over and occupied spaces and communities the government neglected.

However, ultimately, the challenges and solutions to problems of political exclusion, the government's failure to provide expected services for most of its citizens, and issues of poor leadership are internal in many African countries. It is the lack of development agenda and unwillingness to engage in economic and public policies that create employment, fund educational facilities, healthcare services, reliable energy, and expand opportunities for the youth that provide opportunities that extremists and terrorists exploit across sub-Saharan Africa.

Unfortunately, most of the traceable external support that African countries continue to receive has not resulted in enhanced well-being for ordinary people or led to sustainable political and economic stability in Burkina Faso, Cameroon, Chad, Niger, Nigeria, Mali, DRC, Mozambique, and other countries in Africa that are challenged by violent extremists. For example, as Figure 2.1 (based on data in Table 2.1) shows, on average, multilateral official development assistance (ODA) for Mozambique between 1990 and 1999 went from $470 million annually to $857 million between 2000 and 2009. That is an increase of approximately 82 percent from the last ten years of the Cold War to the first ten years of the post–Cold War period. For the same periods, 1990–1999 and 2000–2009, the average ODA to Cameroon increased from $225 million to $425 million, an increase of 89 percent. The annual value (averages of ODA) for the Democratic Republic of the Congo (DRC) increased from $138 million between 1990 and 1999 to $831 million between 2000 and 2009. Comparing the 1990–1999 to 2000–2009 values, that means, on average, DRC received a 502 percent ODA increase annually.

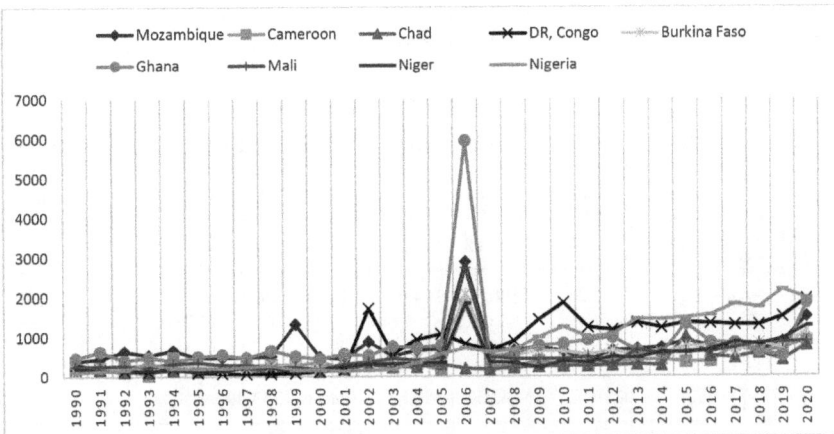

Figure 2.1. Multilateral Official Development Assistance: Total Disbursements for Selected Countries, 1990–2020 (Unit: in Million US Dollars, Current)
Source: Compiled by the Author from OECD Statistics Database

Similarly, the average ODA for Chad increased from $166 million annually between 1990 and 1999 to $217 million annually between 2000 and 2009, or a 31 percentincrease. On average, for Burkina Faso, annual ODA in 1990–1999 was $240 million and $592 million annually between 2000 and2009; an increase of approximately 147 percent. The percentage increases for the same periods for Ghana was 130 percent, Mali, 128 percent, Niger, 174 percent, and on average, annual ODA to Nigeria was $197 million in 1990–1999 and $446 million annually between 2000 and 2009; an increase of 126 percent.[14] Table 2.1 displays the actual annual multilateral ODA for these countries.

Table 2.1-1. Multilateral Official Development Assistance (Total Disbursements), 1990–2020 (Unit: in Million US Dollars, Current)

Recipients Year	Mozam-Bique	Cameroon	Chad	DR Congo	Burkina Faso	Ghana	Mali	Niger	Nigeria
1990	384.98	181.31	193.62	301.12	133.04	458.78	258.16	204.2	113.8
1991	443.28	227.34	183.9	206.15	220.06	628.07	256.03	156.78	130.75
1992	633.62	198.55	128.41	155.99	237.16	406.48	273.13	139.06	167.28
1993	531.29	34.18	113.1	120.07	320.51	476	225.88	143.74	316.36
1994	655.17	471.85	157.67	203.99	252.8	384.29	321.53	165.94	202.81
1995	465.13	131.07	145.38	99.39	296.61	493.23	355.06	112.35	193.16
1996	471.38	183.32	234.41	78.15	198.6	542.52	286.09	139.14	205.69
1997	480.05	255.57	187.95	66.15	222.82	460.45	290.5	224.51	225.79
1998	507.34	289.82	138.01	68.17	256.27	648.56	221.4	227.1	260.16
1999	1317.48	271.65	179.67	82.77	252.88	503.29	232.76	110.6	158.32
2000	484.11	358.49	126.18	118.22	198.81	436.81	165.84	167.79	153.46
2001	431.47	197.31	190.56	164.04	313.76	560.08	310.28	247.27	131.57
2002	869.48	340.67	276.77	1710.05	370.16	519.68	355	303.48	149.82
2003	498.11	219.53	242.57	559.66	388.56	753.49	449.94	311.46	168.93
2004	653.15	297.14	229.26	925.01	423.93	714.45	392.4	321.48	337.48
2005	675.81	162.1	293.98	1063.35	460.86	779.81	459.12	346.56	564.97
2006	2885.03	1800.1	193.37	816.32	2073.49	5947.5	2731.44	1841.39	705.29
2007	715.01	250.05	167.28	644.44	535.84	467.06	475.27	351.7	606.63
2008	642.54	240.94	213.55	887.55	512.47	571.75	432.32	330.33	658.49
2009	732.85	379.74	241.56	1425	641.55	765.58	425.49	219.36	987.24

Table 2.1-2.

2010	614.56	280.61	246.88	1853.51	614.36	814.47	425.33	372.72	1237.56
2011	387.67	296.84	248.34	1234.77	529.49	903.95	482.02	344.25	986.41
2012	635.98	360.55	270.55	1162.91	643.09	977.46	280.09	484.91	1054.72
2013	679.2	396.33	282.29	1345.98	531.77	624.4	663.86	455.25	1437.08
2014	712.08	413.75	270.33	1222.59	567.24	549.84	554.63	597.45	1434.91
2015	891.67	349.82	1006.68	1352	738.8	1318.85	616.49	587.83	1476.03
2016	749.59	363.46	492.77	1328.8	758.18	848.61	613.83	651.54	1538.62
2017	706.27	751.46	462.76	1299.23	601.44	827.66	706.3	860.19	1816.31
2018	626.78	573.19	579.25	1298.47	838.84	609.66	835.64	795.93	1740.8
2019	866.14	701.79	405.92	1503.66	696.78	503.43	843.91	940.3	2177.29
2020	1500.8	890.87	771.14	1939.11	1148.39	1849.54	876.59	1263.97	1958.58

Source: Compiled by the Author from OECDS Statistics Database

In addition to the above data in Figure 2.1, the bilateral ODA that the United Kingdom (Figure 2.2) and France (Figure 2.3) gave to Anglophone and Francophone countries was maintained at pre–Cold War levels, slightly increased, or significantly decreased. And, in cases where France and the UK decreased ODA to their former colonies, the United States increased its ODA (Figure 2.4) to those, and other African countries.

As calculated from Figure 2.2, the average ODA that the UK extended to Ghana between 1990 and 1999 and 2000 and 2009 decreased from $168 million to $154 million annually. That is a 126 percent decrease in ODA from the UK to Ghana in that period. Furthermore, the average ODA that the UK gave to Nigeria increased from $17 million per year from 1990 to 1999 to $617 million annually from 2000 to 2009, which is more than a 3500 percent increase over the period.

Figure 2.3 shows that the annual ODA from France to Burkina Faso averaged $142 million between 1990 and 1999 and $118 million annually between 2000 and 2009. That represents a yearly reduction in France's ODA to Burkina Faso of approximately 17 percent. And, similar to Burkina Faso, France's ODA to Cameroon for the same period decreased from $418 million to $305 million annually, which is a 27 percent reduction.

For the United States, the most dominant economic and political power in the global system between 1990 and 2009, its economic wealth was essential for extending its diplomatic reach, especially in the areas of US security interests. Figure 4 provides data on the average ODA that the United States extended to various African countries during the critical period of 1999–2009.

For the 1999–2009 period, the U.S. briefly went from supporting global engagement during the Cold War to disengagement following the end of the Cold War; and again, to bold global re-engagement in the aftermath of the terrorist attacks against the U.S. homeland in 2001.

For example, except for reductions in ODA from the United Staets to Cameron between 1990 and1999 ($39 million) to $21 million in 2000–2009, a decline of 46 percent; and $37 million in 1990 to $32 million in 2000–2009 to Niger; a decline of approximately 14%, the average ODA that the United States extended to several African countries saw significant increases. To wit, between 1990–1999 and 2000–2009, Mozambique received $115 million to $187 million per year; an increase of approximately 63 percent; and the average ODA to Chad increased from $19 million in 1990–1999 to $60 million during the 2000–2009 period; an increase of 216 percent. On average, in the 1990–1999 period, the United States extended $26 million in ODA to the Democratic Republic of the Congo. For the 2000–2009 period, that amount was increased by 1554 percent, or $430 million. For Burkina Faso, the average ODA that the United States extended for the 1990–1999 period was $23 million, compared to the $33 million ODA Burkina Faso was given by the United States in the 2000–2009 period, a 43 percent increase. Similarly, for

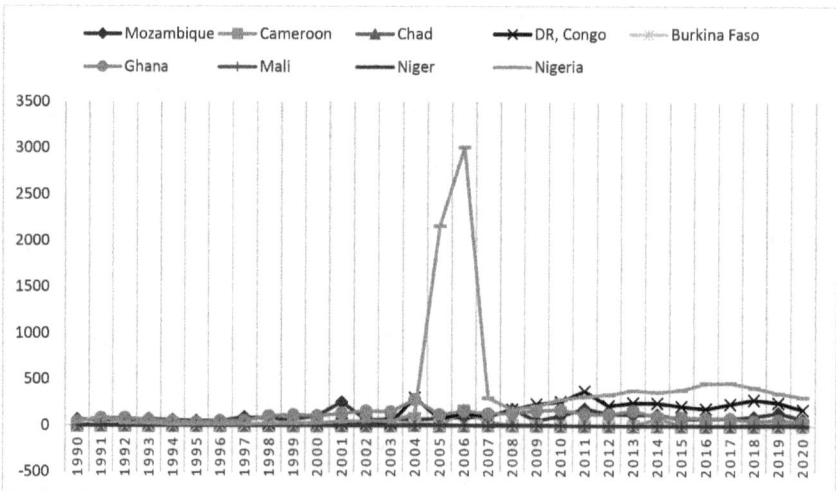

Figure 2.2. United Kingdom's Official Development Assistance (Total Disbursements), 1990–2020 (Unit: in Million US Dollars, Current)

Source: Compiled by the Author from OECD Statistics Database

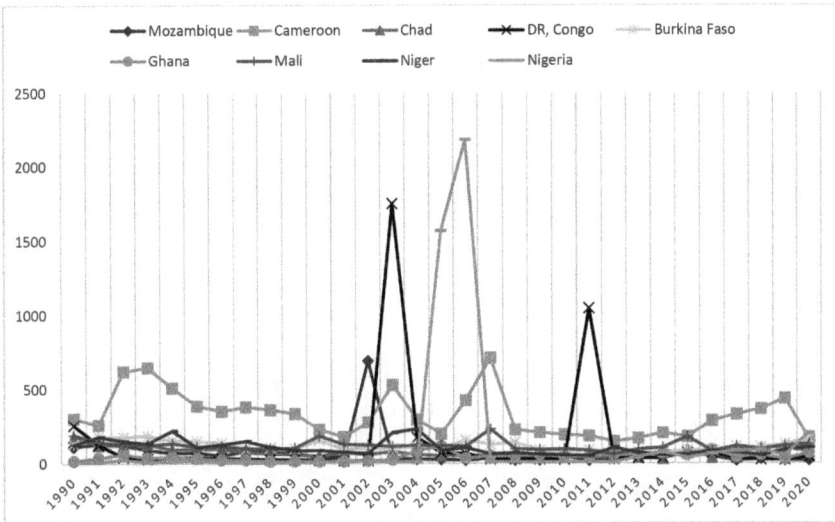

Figure 2.3. France's   Official Development Assistance(Total Disbursements), 1990–2020(Unit: in Million US Dollars, Current)

the 1990–1999 period, Mali received an average of $49 million per year from the United States. That amount was significantly increased to $74 million per year or a 51 percent increase during the 2000–2009 period.

Source: Compiled by the Author from OECD Statistics Database

As with its existing foreign policy practice toward Anglophone countries (Kalu 2014: 62–82), US bilateral ODA to Ghana and Nigeria follows the same pattern as the UK's security approaches to its former colonies in Africa. Thus, while the United States gave an average ODA of $83 million yearly to Ghana during the 1990–1999 period, the amount for the 2000–2009 period was $102 million annually, representing an increase of 23 percent. For Nigeria, the United States provides official development assistance to the tune of $24 million per year from the 1990–1999 period. That amount increased to an average of $276 million per year in the 2000–2009 period, which amounts to a 1050 percent increase.

IN LIEU OF CONCLUSION: *QUO VADIS*, AFRICA?

As previously argued, challenges stemming from insurgency, banditry, violent extremism, and terrorism in Africa are rooted in internal economic problems, political exclusion, and government neglect of segments of its population. Yet, while external economic and security support to fight extremism

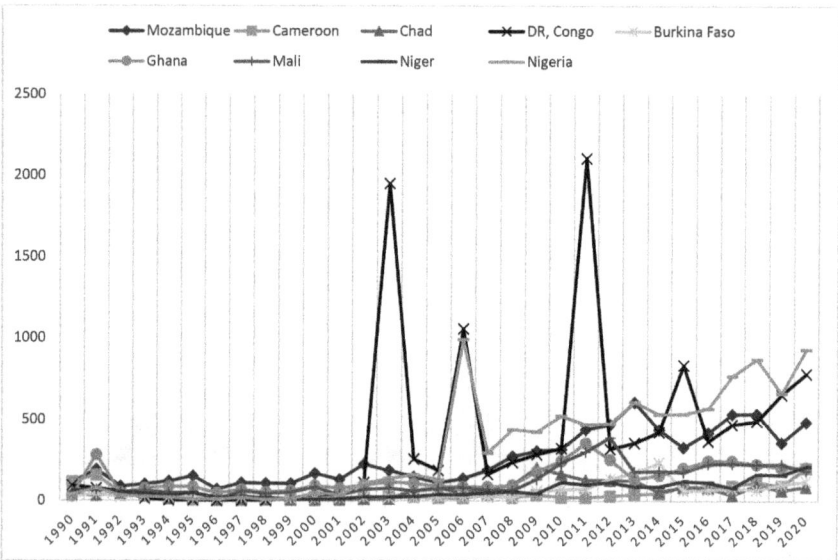

Figure 2.4. United States' Official Development Assistance (Total Disbursements), 1990–2020 (Unit: in Million US Dollars, Current)
Source: Compiled by the Author from the OECD Statistics Database

in Africa may be helpful, and in some instances exacerbate insecurity, the solutions to armed violence and anti-government forces across Africa are internal to each country.

Thus, based on the ODA data, the important question is: to what extent has the external financial and security support to African countries enhanced the lives of the masses, stabilized the political system, and/or enabled the leaders to design and implement public policies that address expressed grievances by members of its society? To what extent have these governments designed policies that expand political inclusion and access, and expand educational and employment opportunities for the young people who are more easily recruited into extremist organizations because they lack purpose and hope for the future? As politics—defined as the distribution of scarce economic resources based on values—drives effective governance, economic development, security, and perceptions of fair and just public policies, the challenges African countries and their leaders must confront in dealing with violent extremism are internal to each society and these have spillover effects because of porous borders in the Sahel, the West, and Central Africa regions. Thus, without outright destruction of the geography of the continent, which will be sad, no amount of foreign support will be sufficient to arrest the devastating presence of Al-Qaeda in the Maghreb, the Islamic State Sahel, Al Shabaab, Boko

Haram, or the Islamic State of the West Africa Province. This is because the internal problems are driven by politics that fails to provide equitable access to educational, economic, and employment opportunities and a governance structure characterized by political inclusion.

Thus, as the US Africa Command concluded, there is a need for changing strategies for dealing with insecurity in Africa, because insurgents, jihadists, and bandits continue to grow in strength, especially in West Africa. This is often with the support of Russian mercenaries, in the case of Mali and with devastating impact on civilian deaths across the continent.[15] What is clear is that military strategies and operations to counter insurgents and terrorist organizations, as the French are finding out in Mali[16] and across sub-Saharan Africa, are wrongheaded applications of tactics that sustain instability, insurgencies, kidnapping for ransom, and environmental destruction of communities in many African countries. For example, despite the "large amount" in ODA that the United States and other donors have given African countries, other databases, like the Global Peace Index (GPI)[17] data can be used to conclusively show that the impacts of external support for African countries do not have positive impact on the people—principally because of internal politics of bitterness and exclusionary consumption.

The GPI is helpful for understanding the internal dynamics in African countries that lead to peace or instability. They are made up of twenty-three and twenty-four quantitative and qualitative indicators, respectively, each weighted on a scale of 1–5. The lower the score the more peaceful or less violent the country[18]. Some of the core variables used in measuring the peacefulness or lack of violence of a country—"acceptance of the Rights of others, equitable distribution of resources, free flow of information, good relations with neighbors, high levels of human capital, low levels of corruption, sound business environment, and well-functioning government"[19]—are all related to persistent extremism, banditry, terrorism, and insurgency that pose internal security challenges in African countries.

For example, Table 2.2 data indicates that selected African countries remain less peaceful and mired in violent conflicts driven by political exclusions and lack of economic and educational opportunities. Most citizens in these countries remain employed in agriculture with fewer and fewer opportunities for employment in industry and the service sector. It is the agricultural base of many of the neglected communities that leaves the residents vulnerable to occupation, hostage-taking, and killings by insurgents, terrorists, and opportunistic criminal gangs. For example, over 60 percent of workers in Mali, Mozambique, Niger, DRC, and Chad are employed in backbreaking jobs in the agricultural sector. Most of the mechanized farms in these countries are either foreign-owned or partly owned by the same elites that are part of the government. The ordinary farmers suffer from crop losses and with the encroaching effects of climate change are often left without a social support network. In addition, most of these countries are resource extraction economies—again owned by foreign firms that pay economic rent to corrupt elites who invest their gains overseas instead of spurring economic development in their home countries.

Also, youth unemployment is rampant in these countries. As Table 2.2 shows, for each of the countries listed, youth employment is higher than general employment data. Indeed, the official youth unemployment and the general unemployment data should be taken with a grain of salt.[22] And educational attainment, as measured by the mean years of schooling for males, youth unemployment, employment opportunities in the service and agricultural sectors may be related. Countries with higher mean year of schooling for males, tend to have a higher percentage of their population employed in the service sector and a smaller percentage working in agriculture. Thus, increasing educational attainment may increase the percentage of the labor force working in industry and the service sector but only if the jobs are available. To be sure, increased educational attainment without the availability of good jobs is a recipe for a less peaceful country. Likewise, less education, especially for young men, may decrease opportunities for useful and dignified employment and produce discontent as in resource extraction economies, where the young men are left to work in the mines with little return for their hard work. In communities where oil drilling is the base of the economy, such as Nigeria and Chad, or mineral resources extraction, such as the DRC, Mozambique, Mali, Niger, and Ghana, the foreign-owned firms, supported by international financial and economic institutions in Chad, Ghana, and the DRC focus mostly on extractions, not sustainable investments and expansion of economic opportunities in the various countries. Thus, quite often, existing but non-conflictual grievances are manipulated by insurgents, terrorists, and criminal organizations to galvanize the youth in these countries/regions to become part of anti-government forces. The likes of Boko Haram, Al-Qaeda in the Maghreb, the Islamic State Sahel, Al Shabaab, and the Islamic State of the West Africa Province represent the last bastion of hope to which poorly educated, unemployed, and "expectations of becoming someone important" are most vulnerable to become part of willingly or unwittingly.

A different, but related, way of understanding the impact of violent extremism driven by internal economic and political challenges across these countries is the data on internally displaced persons (IDPs). Except for Ghana with a low, but an increasing number of IDPs, each country in Table 2.2 with over 100,000 internally displaced persons is also experiencing violent extremism and insurgency—largely driven by agitations for political inclusion and access to economic opportunities. As anyone who has been on the ground

Table 2.2: Socioeconomic Indicators for Selected African Countries, 2019–2022[20, 21]

Country	Mean Schol2019	Agric 2019	Industry2019	Services2019	Y-UNE 2021	UE-2021	GPI 2022	PPI 2022
Ghana	8.10	30	21.00	49.00	9.6	4.70	1.759	2.986
Burk. Faso	2.30	26	25.00	49.00	7.7	4.80	2.786	3.436
Mozambique	4.50	70	9.00	21.00	8.1	4.00	2.316	3.695
Niger	2.80	73	7.00	21.00	1.0	0.80	2.655	3.766
Nigeria	7.70	35	12.00	53.00	19.6	9.80	2.725	3.836
Mali	3.00	62	8.00	30.00	17.3	7.70	2.911	3.844
Cameroon	8.00	43	14.00	42.00	6.6	3.90	2.709	4.005
DRC	8.40	64	10.00	26.00	10.1	5.40	3.166	4.306
Chad	3.80	75	2.00	23.00	2.4	1.90	2.591	4.374

in these countries near the conflict zones will attest to, the official figures in Table 2.2 do not reflect an accurate picture of the number of IDPs. For example, noticeable traffics jam in Abuja, the Federal Capital of Nigeria, reflect temporary IDPs—governors and their entourage across the northeast and some northwestern states that relocate their "offices" to Abuja every evening to escape the menace of Boko Haram in their states. There are also the regular IDPs who have formed a ring around Abuja in their millions. Many of the IDPs around Abuja include those from Chad, Niger, and Mali who blend easily with the Hausa-Fulani population. The same is the case in Accra, Ghana, where IDPs are increasing within the capital, most visible around the Nima area. It is here that many individuals—both Ghanaians and non-Ghanaians—especially from Burkina Faso, Niger, and Mali are relocating as a result of increasing tension in the northern region and border towns that seems to have largely been under the radar of government officials. Lastly, both the global peace index and positive peace index reflect the contested and contentious nature of internal politics characterized by elite corruption, political exclusion, and the lack of a sustainable economic development agenda. Additional features include the lack of access to education and employment opportunities for the masses, autocracy, and politicized ethnicity and religion. These factors enable anti-government forces to galvanize the masses and neglected communities into religious and ethnic extremism with violent outcomes for the most vulnerable in communities neglected by the government.

Thus, it is the neglect of internal nation-building that has enabled bandits, extremists, violence entrepreneurs, and jihadists to occupy spaces long vacated or ignored by various governments in Burkina Faso, Cameroon, Chad, the DRC, Ghana, Mali, Mozambique, Niger, and Nigeria. Some of the drivers of instability and violent extremism—lack of economic and educational opportunities, youth unemployment, insecurity-induced internally displaced persons, and political exclusion—are the same factors that make African countries less peaceful. Reversing these trends requires intentional government engagement with their citizens, designing socioeconomic policies that expand economic and employment opportunities and grant access to functional educational facilities for the masses. Government will need to govern as if the people mattered, which means political inclusion and physical security within a constitutional framework that holds everyone accountable for their actions as citizens and residents in these countries. Like people everywhere, Africans seek a home that provides them a sense of belonging, security, and a place to honor their ancestors and build a future for their families. A home provides ontological security,[23] social customs, norms, and behaviors on what is acceptable and what attracts public opprobrium. It is a place that inspires pride and fosters community acceptance. Conversely, the absence of home drives the young into the arms of violent extremists. Therefore, unless the various governments work to provide and maintain a homeland for all, the long winter of dead bodies and cracked skulls across the farmlands, government and religious offices and houses, and infrastructure will continue across the Sahel, West Africa, and other regions in the continent in the foreseeable future.

NOTES

1. See "Insurgency" in *Britannica Online Encyclopedia* at https://www.britannica.com/print/article/1527994 accessed May 29, 2022.

2. See Ariel Merari, "Terrorism as a Strategy of Insurgency," *Terrorism and Political Violence*, 1993, 4(4): 213–51. For the original text, see W. E. Daugherty, 'Bomb Warnings to Friendly and Enemy Civilian Targets' in William E. Daugherty and Morris Janowitz, *A Psychological Warfare Casebook* (Baltimore: Johns Hopkins UP, 1958), 359–62.

3. See Gurr, Ted Robert, *Why Men Rebel* (Princeton, NJ: Princeton University Press). Also, Kalu 2022. "Theories and Explanations of Civil Conflicts and Wars in Africa."

4. See Godwin Isenyo's interview with Mallam Turku Mamu, a negotiator between a sect of the Boko Haram group and various communities, "Abductors of Abuja-Kaduna train passengers said they read news of how politicians, others steal billions without punishment," at https://punchng.com/abductors-of-abuja-kaduna-train

-passengers-said-they-read-news-of-how-politicians-others-steal-billions-without -punishment-negotiator-mamu/ accessed July 10, 2022.

5. Institute for Economics & Peace, accessed July 11, 2022 here: https:// www.economicsandpeace.org/wp-content/uploads/2022/03/2022_Global_Terrorism _Index_PR.pdf.

6. *Manila Times*, "Terrorism deaths up in Africa, down elsewhere," 2022. https: //www.manilatimes.net/2022/06/10/news/world/terrorism-deaths-up-in-africa-down -elsewhere/1846775?utm_source=iterable&utm_medium=email&utm_campaign =4448901_ Accessed June 11, 2022.

7. Ibid.

8. See, Bishop Matthew Hassan Kukah. 2022. "To Mend a Broken Nation: The Easter Metaphor." An Easter Message delivered by the Bishop of the Diocese of Sokoto on April 17th, 2022, paragraph 7, 2.

9. Ibid., paragraph 15, p. 4.

10. In addition to personal interviews and observations during a recent travel to the West Africa region, the brief summary of various Islamic Jihadists attacks in various countries are based on data from ACLED. "Regional Overview of Africa" https:// acleddata.com/2022/07/07/regional-overview-africa-25-june-1-july-2022/ accessed July 13, 2022.

11. The terrorist attack at Owo church on June 5,2022 was just one of several such attacks across churches in Nigeria and other churches in the sub-Sahara Africa region. For example, see "We thought there was war when terrorists attacked Owo church, rained bullets on us—survivors" https://punchng.com/we-thought-there-was -war-when-terrorists-attacked-owo-church-rained-bullets-on-us-survivors/ accessed July 24, 2022.

12. On March 26, 2022, Boko Haram deployed over two hundred motorcyclist riders to attack the Kaduna International Airport; and on March 28, 2022, they attacked a Kaduna-Abuja bound train. While the federal government and various other government and leaders have expressed the need for action against insecurity perpetrated by insurgents, while the government remains unable to provide effective response, the kidnapped Nigerians remain in captivity pending ransom payments. For example, see "Kaduna-Abuja train attack: Buhari, National Assembly, governors demand tough actions, survivors recount ordeal," https://punchng.com/kaduna-abuja -train-attack-buhari-nassembly-governors-demand-tough-actions-survivors-recount -ordeal/ accessed July 24, 2022.

13. See Mohammed Ingiriis's "Beyond Terrorism: The Case of the Armed Conflict Between the Somali Government and Al-Shabaab," in this volume. Also, my observa- tion here is partly based a privileged conversation with a former Somali government official (without attribution) in May 2022.

14. The annual average ODA to these countries were calculated from the raw data generated from the OECD Statistics Database.

15. John Vandiver, "Security Threats in Africa Call for a New Approach, Outgoing AFRICOM Leader Says," *Stars and Stripes*, July 26, 2022. https://www.stripes.com /theaters/africa/2022-07-26/africom-terrorism-townsend-6772590.html?utm_source =iterable&utm_medium=email&utm_campaign=4747238_ accessed July 26, 2022.

As General Stephen Townsend, the US Africa Command, notes, "Violence in Burkina Faso, Mali and western Niger surged by 140% since 2020, with militant Islamist groups in the Sahel accounting for 60% of violence against civilians in all of Africa" the United States needs to change its approach for security support to countries in the Sahel and West Africa.

16. John Irish, "Ahead of Mali withdrawal, French Prepares Future Sahel Strategy" https://www.reuters.com/world/ahead-mali-withdraw-france-prepares-future-sahel -strategy-2022-07-13/?utm_source=iterable&utm_medium=email&utm_campaign =4662161_ accessed July 15, 2022. As Irish notes, as "Coups in Mali, Chad and Burkina Faso have weakened France's alliances . . . [with] its former colonies, [this have] emboldened jihadists who control large swathes of desert and scrubland, and opened the door to greater Russian influence. . . . [Thus], Concerns have grown that the exit of 2,400 French troops from Mali - the epicenter of violence in the Sahel region and strongholds of both al Qaeda and Islamic State affiliates - is worsening violence, destabilizing neighbors and spurring migration" [to Europe].

17. The Institute for Economics and Peace accessed here: https://www .economicsandpeace.org/ July 16, 2022. The Global Peace Index (GPI) "presents the most comprehensive data-driven analysis to-date on trends in peace, its economic value, and how to develop peaceful societies. The GPI covers 99.7% of the world's population, using 23 qualitative and quantitative indicators from highly respected sources, and measures the state of peace across three domains: [1] the level of Societal Safety and Security, [2] the extent of Ongoing Domestic and International Conflict, and [3], the degree of Militarization."

18. See the Global Peace Index Score here: GPI-2022-web.pdf, accessed on July 16, 2022. And the Positive Peace Index score here: PPR-2022-web.pdf (economicsandpeace.org), accessed on July 16, 2022.

19. Ibid.

20. Source: The World Bank, the UNDP, and the Institute for Economics and Peace. Mean School - 2019—Mean number of years of schooling for men aged 25 and over, Human Development Report 2020 (356 – 359) hdr2020pdf.pdf (undp.org);

Agric 2019 = Percentage of the population employed in agriculture, Employment in agriculture (% of total employment) (modeled ILO estimate) | Data (worldbank. org);

Industry 2019 = percentage of population employed in industry, Employment in industry (% of total employment) (modeled ILO estimate) | Data (worldbank.org);

Services 2019 = percentage of population employed in Service sector, Employment in services (% of total employment) (modeled ILO estimate) | Data (worldbank.org);

Y-UNE-2021 = percentage of youth unemployed by country, Unemployment, youth total (% of total labor force ages 15-24) (modeled ILO estimate) | Data (worldbank.org);

UE-2021 = percentage of population unemployed, Unemployment, total (% of total labor force) (modeled ILO estimate) | Data (worldbank.org);

EdIndex-19 = Education Index (the most recent available data) published by the United Nations Development Program (UNDP) as part of its annual Human Development Report 2020, https://hdr.undp.org/system/files/documents//hdr2020pdf.pdf.

ED-index is a weighted average of adult years of schooling and expected years of schooling for students under the age of twenty-five. As you UNDP notes, "In every country many people have little prospect for a better future. They are without hope, purpose or dignity, watching from society's sidelines as they see others pulling ahead to ever greater prosperity. Worldwide many have escaped extreme poverty. But even more have neither the opportunities nor the resources to control their lives. Far too often a person's place in society is still determined by ethnicity, gender, or his or her parents' wealth."

21. Positive Peace Index (PPI) is from the Institute for Economics and Peace accessed here: https://www.economicsandpeace.org/ July 16, 2022; and Global Peace Index Score accessed here: https://www.visionofhumanity.org/maps/#/, July 16, 2022

22. During my visits to various countries in West Africa, between April and May 2022, different individuals in Ghana, Nigeria, Cameroon, Chad, and Burkina Faso did indicate that the unemployment data, especially for the youth, are mostly reported to enhance each country's economic outlook. This was especially so in the case of Ghana, where unofficial youth unemployment was said to be between 27 percent and 35 percent, especially in the northern region.

23. See B. Naude. 2021. Op. cit., 18.

REFERENCES

ACLED. 2022. "Regional Overview of Africa" https://acleddata.com/2022/07/07/regional-overview-africa-25-june-1-july-2022/ accessed July 13, 2022.

Ake, Claude. 1996. *Democracy and Development in Africa.* Washington D.C.: The Brookings Institution Press.

ALJAZEERA. 2022. "UN Envoy Warns of Spiraling DRC Conflict." June 30. at https://www.aljazeera.com/news/2022/6/30/un-envoy-warns-of-spiralling-drc-conflict accessed July 13, 2022.

Daugherty, W. E. 1958. "Bomb Warnings to Friendly and Enemy Civilian Targets." In *A Psychological Warfare Casebook.* Edited by William E. Daugherty and Morris Janowitz. Baltimore: Johns Hopkins University Press, 359–62.

Gurr, Ted Robert. 1970. *Why Men Rebel.* Princeton, NJ: Princeton University Press.

Institute for Economics & Peace. 2022. https://www.economicsandpeace.org/wp-content/uploads/2022/03/2022_Global_Terrorism_Index_PR.pdf Accessed July 11, 2022.

Isenyo, Godwin. 2022. "Abductors of Abuja-Kaduna Train Passengers Said They Read News of How Politicians, Others Steal Billions Without Punishment," at https://punchng.com/abductors-of-abuja-kaduna-train-passengers-said-they-read-news-of-how-politicians-others-steal-billions-without-punishment-negotiator-mamu/ accessed July 10, 2022.

Kalu, Kelechi A. 2022. "Theories and Explanations of Civil Conflicts and Wars in Africa." In *Civil Wars in Africa.* Edited by Kelechi Kalu and George Kieh, Jr. Lanham, MD: Lexington Books, 23–55.

Kalu, Kelechi A. 2021. "Re-Building Peace after Conflicts in Africa: Theoretical Issues." In *Peacebuilding in Africa: The Post-Conflict State and Its Multidimensional Crises*. Edited by Kelechi Kalu and George Kieh, Jr., Lanham, MD: Lexington Books, 1–23.

Kalu, Kelechi A. 2014. "U.S.-Africa Security Relations in the Twenty-First Century: Trends and Implications." In *United States-Africa Security Relations*. Edited by Kelechi Kalu and George Klay Kieh, Jr. New York: Routledge, 62–82.

Kalu, Kelechi, and George Kieh. 2013. "West Africa and the U.S. War on Terrorism: The Lessons." In *West Africa and the U.S. War on Terror*. Edited by George Kieh and Kelechi Kalu. New York: Routledge, 178–87.

Kukah, Hassan Matthew. 2022. "To Mend a Broken Nation: The Easter Metaphor." A Text of Easter Message by Bishop Matthew Hassan Kukah, Diocese of Sokoto, Nigeria, April 17, 2022.

Love, Maryann Cusimano. 2019. *Global Issues Beyond Sovereignty*. 5th Edition, Lanham, MD: Rowman & Littlefield.

The *Manila Times*. 2022. "Terrorism Deaths Up in Africa, Down Elsewhere." https://www.manilatimes.net/2022/06/10/news/world/terrorism-deaths-up-in-africa-down-elsewhere/1846775?utm_source=iterable&utm_medium=email&utm_campaign=4448901_ accessed June 11, 2022.

Marche, Stephen. 2022. "Shots Fired: A Significant Portion of Americans Seek the Destruction of Political Authority. What If They Succeed?" *Foreign Policy*: 52–59.

Matsinhe, David M., and Estacio Valoi. 2019. "The Genesis of Insurgency in Northern Mozambique." *A Southern Africa Report*. No. 27. Available here: https://media.africaportal.org/documents/The_Genesis_of_insurgency_in_N_Moz.pdf aaccessed on April 26, 2022.

Merari, Ariel. 1993. "Terrorism as a Strategy of Insurgency." *Terrorism and Political Violence*. 4(4): 213–51.

Mlambo, Victor H., and Mfundo Mandla Masuku. 2021. "Terror at the Front Gate: Insurgency in Mozambique and its Implications for the SADC and South Africa." *Journal of Public Affairs*. 2021; e2700 https://doi.org/10.1002/pa.2700.

Naude, Bianca. 2021. "Beyond Disciplinary Dogma: An Ontological Security Approach to Terrorism and Its Study." In *Directions in International Terrorism: Theories, Trends and Trajectories*. Edited by Hussein Solomon. Singapore: Palgrave Macmillan, 11–31.

Neumann, Peter, and M. L. R. Smith. 2005. "Strategic Terrorism: The Framework and Its Fallacies." *Journal of Strategic Studies*. 28(4): 571–95.

Schmid, Alex P. and Albert J. Jongman. 1988. *Political Terrorism*. Amsterdam: North-Holland Publishing Company.

Solomon, Hussein. 2021. "Introduction." In *Directions in International Terrorism: Theories, Trends and Trajectories*. Edited by Hussein Solomon. Singapore: Palgrave Macmillan, 1–9.

State Department. 1990. *Patterns of Global Terrorism: 1989*. Washington, DC: US Department of State.

Tilly, Charles. 1985. "War Making and State Making as Organized Crime." In *Bringing the State Back In.* Edited by Peter B. Evans, Dietrich Rueschemeyer, and Theda Skocpol. New York: Cambridge University Press, 169–87.

Udegbunam, Oge. 2022. "61,000 Boko Haram Suspects Detained in Northeast Nigeria." *Premium Times* accessed here: https://www.premiumtimesng.com/news/headlines/542329-61000-boko-haram-suspects-detained-in-northeast-nigeria-official.html?utm_source=iterable&utm_medium=email&utm_campaign=4662161_ July 14, 2022.

Vandiver, John. 2022. "Security Threats in Africa Call for a New Approach, Outgoing AFRICOM Leader Say." *Stars and Stripes.* https://www.stripes.com/theaters/africa/2022-07-26/africom-terrorism-townsend-6772590.html?utm_source=iterable&utm_medium=email&utm_campaign=4747238_ accessed July 26, 2022.

Wight, Colin. 2009. "Theorizing Terrorism: The State, Structure and History." *International Relations.* 23(1): 99–106.

PART II

CASE STUDIES

Chapter 3

Al Shabab's Insurgency in Somalia

Mohamed Haji Ingiriis

The political conflict in Somalia remains one of the most violent in sub-Saharan Africa. Every war in the country has proved to be a war out of another war (Besteman and Cassanelli 2000). Lederach (1997: 92) has aptly argued that a deeper understanding of the broader evolution of political problem should be fostered if it is to resolve a conflict. To understand the political contestation behind the continuation of conflict, one has to turn back the clock. Political scientists, such as Hyden (2006), have highlighted that the current armed conflicts in Africa are fundamentally distinct from the previous ones that engulfed much of the continent during the 1990s.[1]

While the war for the state seizure was succeeded in many parts of the continent, the second objective of establishing a stable state system has posed a great challenge. Whereas these uncivil wars were about seizing state power and grabbing economic resources, after the millennium—despite high expectations for a sense of sustainable peace—they were converted into "new wars" (Kaldor 1999). The changing faces of the war followed what Rice (1998) called "a war of the third kind" or what Williams, cited in an Uppsala University study, referred to "one-sided violence" (Williams 2014). The "wars of the third kind" (Hardin 1995; Holsti 1996; Rice 1988) are "hard to end war[s]" (Fearon 2004: 275), especially when "combatants deliberately target civilians rather than armed opponents in prosecuting goals; and atrocities are freely committed as part of strategies aimed at publicizing political statements" (Bangura 1997: 117). As Snow (1996: 1–2) also contends, "these wars often appear to be little more than rampages by groups within states against one another with little or no apparent ennobling purposes or outcome; they are indeed uncivil wars."

The long years of the conflict in Somalia have vividly indicated that the absence of a power-sharing mechanism has frustrated the long-sought solution for the armed conflict. As a result, the search for a solution to the Somali conflict generally fails, mainly because of searching for the solution in the wrong time at a wrong place. In Somalia, like in Sierra Leone, there has been political marginalization, economic and social exclusion that led to "mindless violence" (Richards 1996). As Kasaija (2010: 275) acknowledged, "Somalis have been divided between those who have alleged that their clan or sub-clan is under-represented in government, and those [who] believe that the previous governments maintained clan and regional balance." To be sure, the clan system is a reality in the Somali setting that one can hardly escape (Hansen,2013: 139). Clan bargaining was, after all, "an indispensable means of promoting the change from colonial rule to independence, facilitating societal compromise and co-operation within an ongoing authoritarian regime (that is, hegemonic exchange)" (Rothchild, 1995: 54).

The current conflict in contemporary Somalia has a prolonged propensity with multiple forms and faces, not to mention the multilayered and multidimensional internal and external features contributing to its continuation. One can no longer talk about conflict in contemporary Somalia other than conflicts as they have been fought along interstate, intrastate, clan, regional, and religious lines, internally and externally. Many hands have been involved in the kaleidoscopic fragmentation from inside and outside Somalia. This was mainly because the long reconciliation conferences that took place outside Somalia left some of the most important players in conflict (Kasaija 2010: 261). As such, the problem of the Somali peace processes is that some important players in Somali politics are always excluded or left out. Over the years, there have been dozens of reconciliation efforts to stabilize Somalia and restore a functioning government that rules the whole country, but all those initiatives have failed from time to time (Ehrhart & Petretto 2014). Why do most (if not all) end in vain? Why is armed conflict in Somalia unresolvable? What are the causes and consequences of the continuation of armed conflicts in conflict-ridden zones? How do fragile states fail to negotiate power-sharing agreements to achieve political stability? What obstructs failed and fragile states from reaching out to the political opposition to improve their performance by sharing power with them? Why is there an absence of an agreeable power-sharing formula for most African conflicts? How and why do these marginalized communities resist and resort to violence? To what extent do grievances felt by marginalised groups prevent fragile states from gaining domestic legitimacy? Which is the shortest route to resolving political conflict based on power and resources? The Somali case offers an excellent case study to attend to these pertinent questions.

METHODOLOGY AND APPROACH

Based on field research, empirically grounded ethnographic observations, and interviews in Mogadishu (between 2015 and 2018), and drawing from the political economy approach (Leeson 2007; Mubarak 1996; Reno 2006), this chapter interrogates the interplay between armed conflict and power-sharing in the conflict in Somalia. In doing so, it examines why the armed conflict in Somalia is so protracted from the perspective of power-sharing and explores the failure of power-sharing within the context of armed conflict in order the understand the nature of the Somali conflict (Plank 2017). The chapter shows how the absence of a power-sharing accord leads to the fact that any political conflict revolves around who takes what, where, and why.

For purposes of a clear analytical framework, the attention is given to the significance of power-sharing at the local level. This is to address the role of power-sharing arrangements in facilitating sustainable peace and coopera-tion for the long term in weak and failed states. Other than compromise and power-sharing, the chapter finds that the Somali case indicates that political crisis cannot be resolved merely through war. After outlining the long trajec-tory of the current armed conflict, the chapter discusses the prolongation of the conflict and the implications for the absence of power-sharing toward peace and security. The next section situates the chapter within the existing scholarship on power-sharing and conflicts in Africa. The purpose of the chapter is to contribute to the academic literature on power-sharing by add-ing new perspectives to the internal dimensions of the conflict and navigate a short route to conflict resolution.

THE POLITICS OF POWER-SHARING
AND ARMED CONFLICTS

The politics of power-sharing is undoubtedly oxymoronic. The concept of power-sharing refers to the achievement of an all-inclusive government rep-resenting a broad range of concerned communities, but it "may also include provisions regarding the distribution of bureaucratic posts and new rules for the make-up of the security forces and their subsequent management" (Cheeseman and Tendi 2010: 204). The concept of power-sharing is a pre-ferred model of a shorter-term (as in the case of Djibouti) or a longer-term solution (as in the case of Lebanon) for many war-torn societies, but how it is applied or adopted invariably vary from one society to another. Given that power-sharing agreements have been increasingly recommended for fragile states, it is important to consider the specific contexts in which to be adopted

(Binningsbø 2013). Power-sharing accords have led to the end of violence in some countries, but not others. For instance, while adopted successfully to ending political conflicts in Congo and Kenya, other efforts for power-sharing arrangements have failed in Burundi and South Sudan. The power-sharing agreement in South Sudan in the 2005 Comprehensive Peace Agreement (CPA) theoretically encompassed economic, military, political, and territorial dimensions, although it has not been implemented (Wright 2017).

Why have armed conflicts become unresolvable in some countries and while some vanish in other contexts warrants serious research investigation. The absence of genuine power-sharing agreements makes the armed conflict persistent, perpetual, and pervasive (Plank 2017). One of the main reasons why the protracted armed conflicts have not been resolved is the lack of a genuine power-sharing arrangement, which impedes government legitimacy and public support. Thus, assessing the nexus between armed conflict and power-sharing is of critical importance if we are to understand why the Somali conflict is longer than many others on the African continent.

Even though a vast body of empirical research has analysed how power-sharing agreements became successful or unsuccessful, there is a relatively rare examination of why power-sharing is useful for concomitant and chronic armed conflicts in war-torn societies. Often divergent conclusions are reached as to how proper power-sharing solved and did not solve armed conflicts. Recent research studies on power-sharing agreements resulted in ambivalent observations: some have recognized that power-sharing is a vital approach to ending war in conflict-ridden countries (Curtis 2013; McEvoy and O'Leary 2013; Simons et al. 2013; Tull 2010; Vandeginste 2011; Zanker et al. 2015), while others have found no effective restructuring in power-sharing models in less war-torn zones (Cheeseman and Tendi 2010; Daley 2007; Le Van 2010; Mehler 2009; Ottmann and Vüllers 2015; Tull and Mehler 2005). In line and lineage with the former thesis, the main point in this chapter is that the absence of power-sharing increases the conflict and contributes to its continuation. Power-sharing is the shortest route to resolving armed conflicts based on a power struggle, by allowing opposing parties in a conflict equal access to power.

The very fact that power-sharing arrangements can manage armed conflicts or lessen them may help countries torn apart by perpetual armed conflicts, such as Somalia, to have the time to rebuild peace. Even when power-sharing is not done with much progress, "power-sharing is usually justified principally in terms of the number of lives it is likely to save in the short term" (Cheeseman and Tendi 2010: 225). For many years, power-sharing agreements have been instrumental in achieving the overall objective of "war termination" (Vandeginste, 2009: 63). When carefully crafted, power-sharing agreements can confer legitimacy on incumbent regimes to operate areas held by an opposing party and, most importantly, facilitate a long-term process of reconciliation. A genuine power-sharing arrangement could thus pave the way for "the effective institution reform necessary to [defuse] the underlying roots of instability" (Cheeseman and Tendi 2010: 204; see also Mehler 2009).

Armed conflicts tend to end in one of two scenarios: "either through a military victory or through a negotiated settlement" (Elmi 2010: 11; Elmi & Barise 2006: 32; in wider African context, see Olonisakin and Muteru 2014: 9). None of this scenario has been successful in Somalia. Similar to latter war-torn societies, what is absent in Somalia is "a carefully designed and negotiated power equilibrium" (Vandeginste 2011: 29). Spears (2013) formulates the concept of "informal power-sharing" to propose other ways of power-sharing arrangements in an environment resistant for many years to peacebuilding and statebuilding. For a power-sharing agreement to have a "pacifying effect," it should be extended to "the local content" (Simons et al., 2013: 681). By local content is meant to consider local communities at the periphery of the power spectrum. Previous power-sharing arrangements in Somalia have concentrated on the central level rather than the local level (Hersi 2016; Ugas 2017). Fragile or failed states that share power with political opponents achieve a sense of security and legitimation of authority from the local level. For viable peaceful state structures to build, it is indispensable to enable better engagement between state-society relations locally and facilitate "new forms of social contract" (Tull 2010: 644). The 1989 World Bank report entitled "Sub-Saharan Africa: From Crisis to Sustainable Growth" highlighted that local "political legitimacy and consensus are a precondition for sustainable development."

When windows of opportunity for chances of local power-sharing are closed down, clanically divided plural societies—inherent in segmentary lineage system of the Pritchardian social anthropological term—spark and sustain armed conflicts over state power and natural resources, as evidenced in Somalia and South Sudan (on Somalia, see Lewis 1994; on South Sudan, see Evans-Pritchard 1940). Of Africa, Lemarchand (1962: 415) observed that "regional differences in the distribution of economic resources operated to aggravate latent tensions among ethnic groups, so that economic stratification tended to coincide with tribal divisions. In a sense, therefore, tribal antagonisms must be viewed as symptoms of economic grievances." It has become as legitimate a grievance for the demand by many local communities for real and proper power-sharing arrangement. Recent armed conflicts in southern Somalia have been ignited by the absence of conclusive power-sharing formulae as revealed by empirical examples. The major armed conflict—among a multitude of conflicts—in contemporary southern Somalia is the political conundrum between the federal government and Al-Shabaab insurgents. The current conundrum contributing to the acute insecurity prevailing in Somalia are mainly related to power struggle hardened by insurgency violence by Al-Shabaab, which sees the government as an externally driven imposition supported by the neighboring states such as Ethiopia, which has heavily invested in the formation of the federal government. The very proximity to power tends to moderate the extreme political stances of the (un)armed groups opposing successive incumbent regimes. It remains difficult to analyze power dynamics without considering how the ordinary people think and how the state authorities behave.

Using the contestation between the federal government and Al-Shabaab as a case study, the chapter argues that Al-Shabaab should be understood as a "rentier" insurgency movement, the bulk of whom comprising of young men from peripheral communities feeling marginalized in the current flawed federal system in Somalia. In practice, Al-Shabaab voices violently the growing grievances of the vast members of those communities, who have been excluded in the power dispensation of the federal state structure. The absence of power-sharing agreement provides Al-Shabaab with the popular local support it enjoys in the large swaths of territories it rules, mainly inhabited by marginalized communities. By situating Al-Shabaab within the current political contestations of power and resources, the chapter contributes to the studies on how far power-sharing agreements can help fragile and failing states to kerb armed conflict and insurgency. Apart from the misunderstanding of the emergence and existence of Al-Shabaab, the destructive campaigns of the group are constructed on the basis of three fundamental factors: (1) grievance-based reactions, (2) opportunistic personal gains, and (3) ideological idiosyncrasies (Hansen 2013; Ingiriis 2018a). However, it is the contention of this chapter that the latter two factors or facets can hardly exist without grievance-based reactions. This is what makes Al-Shabaab more powerful and strong, even legitimate, so to speak, than the federal government of Somalia in Mogadishu, which is protected militarily by the African Union troops (AMISOM). The federal government continues to confront a daily threat from Al-Shabaab and targeted assassinations of political opponents are the norm. In conversation with US authorities on the phone, the then AMISOM military commander General Osman Noor Soubagleh noted how power-sharing is necessary for resolving the political conflict in Somalia.[2]

In any post-conflict societies, the will to form a workable power-sharing formula for political contenders is the most difficult form and face of political settlements. How power would be shared and with whom to be shared remains and will remain an enigma. Although the external actors often insist on their rigid policies toward engaging anyone who sits in Villa Somalia or the Presidential Palace (even when one does not have a real power base), the political players consisting of both local and diaspora groups come and depart easily without contributing to peace positively (Elmi 2010; Elmi and Barise

2006; Hashim 1997).[3] When the power to control and command becomes a synonym for governance, it is violently questioned as zero-sum politics—where the people in Villa Somalia would take all the benefits of monopolization of power without considering the opposing parties—is posited as a prerequisite and compulsory for the attempts at finding peace. The insistence of the Mogadishu power holders on monopolizing power and appropriating resources for themselves impedes an end to the ongoing insurgency. The absence of power-sharing with political opponents not only contributes to the patronage politics in Somalia, but hampers the emergence of accountable institutions and sustains the Al-Shabaab attacks. For example, the absence of formal state structures—district-based power-sharing—worked well in Afghanistan (Murtazashvili 2014). The reality in Somalia is that such local-level mechanisms have not been tried before, even though group-based power-sharing arrangements had been pursued in the previous reconciliation conferences in the 1990s.

At the threshold of the everyday Somali politics are personalized power and the politics of the belly, which remain institutionalized and intertwined, especially in war-torn southern Somalia (Hills 2014a, 2014b, 2014c, 2014d). The idea of representation, respectability, and legitimacy is left out in favor of consolidating power, leading to illegitimacy and lack of representation on the part of the federal government. Since it joined the armed conflict after the Ethiopian invasion of southern Somalia (Ingiriis 2018b), Al-Shabaab has rapidly succeeded to consolidate its power from urban to the rural areas. As in many parts of Africa (e.g., Djibouti, Ethiopia and Uganda), the "war on terror" in Somalia has strengthened dictators and war profiteers. In *The Accidental Guerrilla*, Kilcullen (2011) observes that the Western-led war on terror campaign misidentifies insurgents with legitimate grievances with those criminal terrorist networks. The accidental guerrilla groups are fighting small wars in the midst of a big one to resist the externally imposed Western projects. Kilcullen (2011) proposes new policies based on the peacebuilding formula beginning from below to avert a mistake to repeat again. This means that the consequences of the growth and spread of armed conflict in Somalia are no longer confined to the Al-Shabaab insurgency insofar as they draw from internal and external factors perpetuating the conflict by taking sides (at once siding with one group and another).

THE ROOTS OF THE POLITICAL CONFLICT

The delicate interplay between armed conflict and the lack of power-sharing has a long historical trajectory and political continuity. The disintegration of Somalia as a unitary state in January 1991 was precipitated by the refusal of then President Siad Barre to relinquish power peacefully or share it with other armed political players in the country (Ingiriis 2016a). Upon assuming power on October 21, 1969, President Barre wasted no time in swiftly undoing the largely passive civilian bargaining politics of the post-colonial Somali state to over-centralize power in his own hands (Rothchild 1995: 65). However, there was initially a sense of brief power balancing between and among the chief architects of the military regime (News from Somalia undated: 6–8). As he came to power through the barrel of the gun, Siad Barre publicly declared that only "the gun" could tell him the time to leave from power. His intimidating public speeches led to "violent politics and the politics of violence" and fighting for and over power became institutionalized (Besteman 1996). Consolidating power through his clansmen, Siad Barre rebuffed efforts to share power not only with his opponents, but also with his fellow leaders of the military junta. Instead, he (President Barre) insisted on remaining in power until he was forced to flee to his clan territory (Caddow 2001; Gassem 1994).

Throughout his rule, the Somali state remained a combination of a "shadow state"(Reno 1995) and a "vampire state" (Frimpong-Ansah, 1992). While power was hegemonized in the hands of Siad Barre's family, other political actors from major clans had been denied key access to it. Those marginalized political actors, who demanded their share of the state power, were violently oppressed (Africa Watch 1990; Hashim 1997; Samatar 1997; Simons 1995). In response to the state terror unleashed in the 1970s and 1980s, several armed resistance groups came to emerge trying to fend for their clans and overthrow the Siad Barre regime. Eventually one of those groups, the United Somali Congress (USC), without direct active collaboration with the other armed groups, succeeded in toppling the regime and capturing the presidential seat.

Siad Barre's ouster was followed by a power vacuum, as no armed liberation group was strong enough to establish a central authority in the capital, Mogadishu. Ali Mahdi Mohamed and General Mohamed Farah Aideed, the two main USC leaders, competed on the war front for power in 1991/1992, and refused calls for equal power-sharing arrangements to end the armed conflict (Caddow 2001; Compagnon 1991; The Indian Ocean Newsletter 1991). Their rejection resulted in the rise of various factional leaders in the 1990s. For close to a decade of no-peace-no-war years from 1991 through 2000, the conventional wisdom, similar to Sudan, was the temptation to "give war a chance," if it could bring about peace(Luttwak 1999; Prunier 2012).[4] This resulted in a devastating decade in which competing armed factional groups carved up their traditional clan fiefdoms for themselves, creating profitable income-generating public properties, such as airports, seaports, and check-points, to extort money from the public. Most of the armed conflicts were waged in the capital city Mogadishu—in contrast with the countryside—in attempts by all groups to seizing the state spoils. Other major towns, such as Baydhabo and Kismaayo, also witnessed tit-for-tat armed conflicts based on resource and territorial grabbing (Besteman and Cassanelli 2000). The situation was so extreme that some keen observers portended there would be no exit from the Somali conflict (Simons 2004). Reflecting on this political disaster, an American television presenter went even further in 1992 to declare that "the nightmare that is Somalia will never go away."[5]

THE DALIBANIZATION OF THE SOMALI CONFLICT

The so-called "warlord era" affirmed that armed conflict could become a determinant factor in Somali politics. Those who held more firearms and the financial resources gained through the war economy, as well as clan and territorial resources, could only opt for unmatched power. The inclination has not completely changed after a grand reconciliation conference called by President Ismail Omar Geelle was held in Arta, Djibouti (Anonymous, 2000). The subsequent "Arta government," formed after a series of negotiations which left out the warlords, was hailed as a landmark for a new beginning for Somalia to create a peaceful politics. With the creation of a new government in the summer of 2000, many Somalis expressed a high expectation that the time has finally come for political contestants to share power equally to end the years of violence (Anonymous, 2000). The new leadership led by Abdikassim Salaad Hassan, a former Deputy Prime Minister and Interior Minister in the military regime, rarely reached out to the warlords for any viable power-sharing arrangement.[6] Since then, the armed conflict has continued (Tripodi 2005). The coming of Colonel Abdullahi Yusuf Ahmed as the presidential replacement for Abdikassim Salaad in 2004, changed the course by externalizing (or Ethiopianizing) the conflict. Yusuf refused to share power with his political opponents, and sought to defeat them by calling on Ethiopia to intervene on his behalf (Cornwell 2004; Human Rights Watch 2007a).[7]

The beginning of the popular Islamic Courts Union (UIC), which clashed with the warlords supported by the United States, was a continuation of the conflict by politico-religious means (Ingiriis 2018b). The UIC authorities operated under consensus and compromise among themselves, but they preached that peace could only be achieved by counterviolence. Yet, the UIC proved that peace can be reinstated or kept without a state authority in Somalia. Without external donor involvement, the UIC restored peace that was never seen in Somalia for a long time (Rice 2006). Their six-month rule from June until December 2006, in which people living in most of South-Central Somalia enjoyed a peace with a price, was a prominent case in point; but it was not without faults. Unfettered authority was pursued along with harsh court judgements and trials without lawyers. The UIC former leaders could argue that all these measures were suitable to the harsh environment as they were attempting to create peace in a war-torn society long adapted to armed conflicts.[8] However, these measures later backfired and pitted local people against the UIC rule, which failed to last long. By late 2006, the lack of a power-sharing accord between the TFG and the UIC led to another round of conflict, eventually exacerbated by the Ethiopian intervention in Somalia (International Crisis Group 2008: 8). The Ethiopian intervention assisted by US intelligence and air force support came to uproot them.[9] Instead of singling out "moderates" within the UIC and empowering them to overwhelm the "extremists," the United States destroyed all of the UIC's institutions and allowed Ethiopian forces to invade southern Somalia (Ingiriis 2018b). The UIC's disintegration gave rise to a period of violent atmosphere, where southern Somalia witnessed another round of armed conflict, as many external forces fought in a proxy war to prop up local armed groups (Human Rights Watch 2007b). The conflict did not end, even after prominent elements within the UIC were incorporated into top leadership positions in the US- and Ethiopian-backed government formed in Djibouti in January 2009 (Roque 2009; The Indian Ocean Newsletter 2009). This was because the political positions of their local clan constituencies were not counted during the negotiations.

CLANIZING OR TERRITORIALISING STATE POWER

The current armed conflicts in southern Somalia are partially prolonged by a flawed logic of power distribution between and among various competing clans and communities. The formula known as the 4.5 supposedly allocates four equal power positions among the four major clans: the Daarood, the Digil-Mirifle, the Dir, and the Hawiye, and half of that to a cluster of "minority" groups, the so-called "Others."[10] The system of 4.5, basically understood as four equal power-sharing dispensations, is heavily punctuated by the predominance of the Hawiye and Daarood political players; and it is widely accepted that there is no place for the Isaaq, the Rahanweyn, and the Dir clans to assume the presidency or premier positions. Even if these groups do not openly declare what sort of positions of power they prefer, they nonetheless understand what they ought to be obtained from the government through fixed clan allocation. In essence, the 4.5 system is a contested formula of reformed power dispensation that initially began as 2 Hawiye, 2 Daarood, and 1 Digil-Mirifle during the Sodere Conference in 1997, with the declaration of the National Salvation Council (NSC); and again in 2001, with the formation of the Somalia Reconciliation and Restoration Council (SRRC). Although it was remodified as 4.5 in Arte (1 Hawiye, 1 Daarood, 1 Dir, 1 Digil-Mirifle and 0.5 for other clans and communities), the real considerations of political positions are much deeper than that. The formula practically operates as 2.5 cake-cutting exercises between Hawiye and Daarood political actors in the top power positions like the presidency and premiership.

Even when there have been slight alterations and leadership changes in February 2017, the political culture in Mogadishu continues to be based on power dispensation based on the 4.5 clan system. The current government political players like their predecessors are only interested in retaining power rather than sharing it with other competing political opponents. For a long time, the tendency to appoint a loyalist from another clan to a minister, only to demonstrate that the said clan were on board without necessarily reflecting a real representation, has been a marked regurgitation in Somali politics. From the outside, the 4.5 system seems balanced on clan level, but in the inside the competition within subclans is intense and often develops into an armed conflict. The posts of the presidency and the premiership always filled by Hawiye and Daarood political actors are the most competitive power positions. A senior political adviser to the Presidential Palace confided to me that, when a Hawiye president assumes the presidency, the Daarood political actors perceive the outcome as a threat to their future and so is Hawiye when a Daarood president comes to the fore.[11] The political message of Villa Somalia's senior political adviser cannot be taken lightly, as he himself was opting to run for a higher position. Part of his plan was to maximize the Hawiye-Daarood rivalry to argue for a case of non-Hawiye and non-Daarood president. From a historical perspective, the two clan-groups have not been hostile at all times: their political actors bargained to share power in equal measures in the 1960s through "political exchange and shared power" (Rothchild 1995: 56). However, the fact that the Hawiye and the Daarood political actors are mostly uneasy to each other (even on subclan level) underscores that there was no genuine power-sharing accord, even among the dominant clan-groups. The strong reactions to the October 2004, September 2012 and, most recently, February 2017 presidential elections that culminated in the coming of Daarood and Hawiye presidents incited the danger of armed conflict.

During most of the peace conferences held in the neighboring countries in the 1990s and 2000s, the important question was how power would be distributed during the transitional period, but never has been discussed on how power would be equally shared in future (Ingiriis 2005). Quite paradoxically, the 2018/2019 (as was the 2015/2016) conferences in Mogadishu and Kismaayo between the federal government and federal states: Galmudug, Puntland and Southwest regional states, which were expected to produce an agreeable new electoral formula for parliamentary elections, ended up with failure.[12] The dispute was over which formula for elections, but not how power would be shared. Political players representing the federal government and regional states each came up with an electoral system that would allocate their clan constituencies more parliamentarians than they had. The government position was a top-down political approach, but the regional states stood midway between bottom-up and top-down. While the government and some regional states like the Southwest preferred a continuation of the 4.5 formula, other regional states like Puntland insisted on a district distribution in the federal parliament. Both systems were flawed, however. On the one hand, districts created by the ousted military regime to reward some clans and punish others can hardly be expected to create a stable peaceful state system. On the other, the 4.5 formula is an abhorred political system marginalizing the minority communities, but it seems less problematic when it comes to the district formulation. A new formula that first counts the public accurately and then distributes power positions and resources thereafter has not also adopted, even within the regional states.

Credible power-sharing accords with political opponents in fragile societies could even lead to the longevity of authoritarian rules.[13] This is not to suggest the federal government in Mogadishu should follow the same path (even though it has thus far attempted to do so), but to propose new ways of restoring the lost trust and create peace. The New Deal Compact for Somalia signed in Brussels in September 2013 sets out five areas of concentration to deal with the Somali conflict: political inclusion, security, justice, economic foundations, and revenues and services (Press Release 2013). The first and most important area is the political inclusion. Some years have elapsed since the declaration of the New Deal Compact, and nothing tangible was achieved. The London Conference in May 2017 specifically stressed the need for power-sharing arrangement, but did not mention the type of power to be shared and with whom to be shared.[14] Whilst there is no agreeable power-sharing formula on a national level, the fact that the key determinant of peace is power-sharing remains visible. The lack of power-sharing agreements within the regional states also follows the paradigmatic political pattern in Mogadishu.[15] This news story in 2016 about a clan in northeast Somalia fighting against the Puntland state is informative:

> [Abdisamad Mohamed] Galan controls militia forces aligned with the Ali-Saleebaan clan, who are demanding greater political representation in Puntland, which is dominated by the president's Darood/Harti-Majeerteen clan. Galan has threatened Gaas by using his militia forces to protect the relocation of militants loyal to the Islamic State-affiliated Abdulqadir Mumin to Bari region. Since 27 October, Puntland media have reported militia were manning

checkpoints from Bosaso port, which houses the Puntland Defence Forces (PDF), towards Qandala (HIS, 2016).

GRIEVANCES AND DOMESTIC LEGITIMACY

The political and economic grievances concerning power dispensation and resource distribution are more explicit in the capital Mogadishu. The local population realizes that peace can hardly be maintained in Mogadishu without proper power-sharing. One of the most thriving business places in the city is a neighborhood known during the 1990s wars as Bosnia that was-renovated by diaspora returnees. Some people in this neighborhood who are war veterans condemn the government for political exclusion and economic marginalization. As they feel marginalized in the government system, they do not have the venue to express their grievances, let alone attract the ear of the top government authorities. Their grievances are kindled by local political players who clandestinely collaborate with anyone who is opposed to Villa Somalia, while their clan elders exploit the political conflict to project more latent grievances to secure profitable rewards from the regime.[16] A former army colonel in the neighborhood anxiously describes how power positions are distributed within the government, enumerating a list of names who were very close to the president sitting at Villa Somalia.[17] In this long list, the president's political faction is shown to have taken all power positions of Villa Somalia and received most of the government contracts uncontested between 2012 and 2016. The patronage politics has not changed with the current regime that came to power after February 2017.

As grievances against the political system in place are ignored, the road is opened for armed conflict as the only means of weakening the government to extend its authority outside the capital city. The pursuit of politics of winner-takes-all played on zero-sum game leads to the growing insurgency against the government. The reconfiguration of politics upon which political players play to reassert their voice through Al-Shabaab rewrites the rules of the past war field. Those who hold the grievances undermine the government in retaliation for political marginalization by using various methods that combine violent and nonviolent approaches. One extreme one is to provide intelligence data to Al-Shabaab in carrying out deadly suicide attacks against the government-held places, as evidenced by the attacks on the Villa Somalia, Mogadishu airport and seaport, Liido Beach, SYL Hotel, Jasiira Hotel, Central Hotel, Ambassador Hotel, Naasa Hablood 1 Hotel, Naasa Hablood 2 Hotel, Hotel Dayah, the CID Headquarters in Mogadishu, Banaadir Beach, as well as Baydhabo, Gaalka'ayo, and Kismaayo.[18] Some of these suicidal attacks are facilitated by some within the government who feel excluded in real power. For instance, the government political players have attributed the 2015 Jasiira Hotel attack to a particular political player for facilitating the attack and helping Al-Shabaab in launching it. The said person was publicly named, an act that creates a further alienation rather than offering a political solution.[19] Unlike the Somali government, which blamed the hotel attacks on individuals, the Kenyan government realized that, because of grievances against its forces in southern Somalia, a certain Somali clan assisted Al-Shabaab in massacring more than a hundred Kenyan soldiers in the Eel Adde camp in January 2016 (Ombati 2016).

The grievances are not confined to one single clan as it can also be extended to countless other clans and communities. The crucial aspect of the conflict is the contrasting recognition of the problem by the two government authorities. Put it this way, although the implication for the accusation marginalizes a whole clan rather than an individual political actor, it also recognises the bulk of the problem—which is to say, clan-based grievances. Al-Shabaab has gained new ground due to these unsettled grievances.[20] Countless clans have allied themselves with Al-Shabaab in various methods and many ways. Marginalized clans within the Dir, the Digil/Mirifle, the Hawiye, and the Daarood have constantly contributed reinforcement fighters to Al-Shabaab (HIS 2016).[21] One senior government official privately stated that: "clan X and clan Y are Al-Shabaab and I don't want their talk."[22] Such dismissive language prolongs the conflict and does not resolve the bulk of the problem. Even if some Al-Shabaab fighters do not have legitimate grievances and can be linked with radical extremism, they violently reverberate the grievances of marginalized communities. This explains why the bulk of Al-Shabaab foot soldiers come from the so-called minority clans and communities.[23] The news item that *Radio Dalsan*(2016) in Mogadishu has released is revealing: "A member of parliament at federal level has called upon the government of President Hassan Sheikh Mohmaud to include minority groups in power-sharing government. . . . There are several Somali minority groups in the country that do not have representation in the government."

BETWEEN THE WRATH OF AL-SHABAAB
AND THE CLAN-BASED STATES

In recent years, out of the unending conflicts emerged the autonomous regional states based on clan identity (Höhne 2006). The multiplication of these entities changed the rule and framework that the previous political conflict followed. As Mayer (2000: 30) argued, "One of the chief defining circumstances is the breakdown of the state's undivided and centralizing sovereignty into several centers of competing power of impotence, with each center resorting to violence to re-establish a monopoly on the use of force—legitimate force—for itself, either nationally or regionally." The contemporary conflict in Somalia are waged in two ways. On the one hand is a political conflict between the federal government and the regional states. On the other is an armed conflict between the federal government and Al-Shabaab. There has usually been discord between the federal government and the federal mini-states over a myriad of issues that resulted in trivial tit-for-tat tussles. All are related to the question of who should take what and when.[24] Even though the political conflicts have become the means to ensure a political end (War Murtiyeed 2016), they continue not because the Somalis are inclined to solve issues through violence or still should do what they have been doing for so long (cf. Besteman, 1998; Lewis 1998); but because of the government political players who are unwilling to share power with not just emerging entities but also political opponents. The government allocation of power positions through clannism or patron-client clan relationships enable Al-Shabaab to accelerate its insurgent activities.[25]

As long as the political system used is a flawed clan-based system, those who feel marginalized express their grievances through facilitating the activities of the government's enemy, Al-Shabaab. Most of Al-Shabaab's anti-government attacks are viewed as a form of articulation of grievance-based political exclusion. Unlike the case of Al-Shabaab, there are often shifting alliances and allegiances between clans supporting the federal government. The clans who at one time support the government opposes the government once their clansman president or prime minister loses the power. Al-Shabaab capitalizes on the desperation of the marginalized communities to broaden its powerbase and responds to their complaints by targeting not just the government but also the AMISOM. Considered by many as a puppet of the West, the federal government remains too weak to confront Al-Shabaab without leaning heavily on the AMISOM forces who guard the security of the president, the prime minister, the speaker of the parliament, and some other members of the government. Those who feel excluded from the center of power do not see the positive effects of the role of the foreign forces providing support for a government under which they feel marginalized.[26] All these everyday realities help create sustenance for Al-Shabaab, making them saviors who stand as a symbol of national sovereignty. Clapham (2017: 156–157) has noted that "*al-Shabaab* remains better placed than the officially recognised regime to build up its authority from below, by acting as the most visible defender of Somali nationalism and identity against an international attempt to impose political order from above."

The external intervention also exacerbates the situation. The continued Kenyan military intervention and the prolonged Ethiopian military presence in Somalia have given legitimacy to Al-Shabaab, which in turn counted support from Somalis alienated by external interventions.[27] Kenya invaded Somalia and captured some areas in the Jubbaland region of southern Somalia, most notably Kismaayo, drawing the region into an illicit regional economy trade. Al-Shabaab leaders continue to exploit the local grievances of the Somali and other coastal Muslim communities in Kenya, and its discourse employs religious and race issues, the dichotomy of Muslim/Christian and Arab/Black. Al-Shabaab fighters view Kenya as the place in which they would eventually end up retreating when they are to retire fighting in southern Somalia.[28] Using online media, Al-Shabaab has attracted some Somali exiles and their friends to sacrifice as suicide bombers. The movement has become notorious in recruiting soldiers as young as twelve. In southern Somalia, four main reasons—two of which are grievance-based—closely related to the Kenyan case had sparked the rise of Al-Shabaab in the first place. First was the formation in Nairobi of a handpicked interim Somali government invented by Ethiopia. Second was the Ethiopian occupation in 2006/2009. Third with equal importance was the anarchic atmosphere that prevailed Mogadishu and made it one of the most dangerous capital cities in the world (Ferguson 2013). The fourth is the propagation of the pan-Islamic dogmatic orientation, although it is less a factor than a fact, but it helps Al-Shabaab to reach out the diasporic Somali communities.

THE UNCOVERED FACE OF AL-SHABAAB

Many observers assume that Al-Shabaab is solely composed of those notorious militant fighters who hide their faces with their feared trademark mouth cover showing only unblinking eyes. Hardly do these observers consider that some elements also join Al-Shabaab as a result of clan-based grievances against the clan dominance of the government or against rival clans enjoying external support, as was the case in Jubbaland, where the Kenyan forces were blamed for making *gacan-qabasho* (backup) for the Ogaadeen politico-religious group led by Sheikh Ahmed Mohamed Islaam "Ahmed Madoobe," a former deputy leader of Al-Shabaab (Maruf and Joseph 2018: 52), who is now enjoying his political power in Kismaayo.[29] Without an acceptable power-sharing formula, some Jubbaland clans support Al-Shabaab as a result of clan grievances of which the militant movement exploits. One Al-Shabaab defector pointed out how those marginalized clans found psychological healing and military assistance from Al-Shabaab.[30] For instance, Awramaleh, Gaalje'el, Sheekhaal, Mareehaan, and Rahanweyn resist Ahmed Madoobe's Ogaadeen clan dominance with the backing of Kenyan forces.[31] In Puntland, there are vociferous complaints by Ali Saleebaan, Awrtable, Dashiishe, Leelkase, and other clans who feel marginalized within the clan-based regional government. The Galgala armed conflict confrontation between the Dubays/Warsangeli clan in Sanaag region and Puntland authorities is a vivid case in point. This conflict began as a war over the perceived exploitation of local natural resources by Puntland authorities.[32] In reacting to this, the local clan militias organized to defend their territory from Puntland, and they sought and received support from a local militant group that soon joined Al-Shabaab. The clan fighters who felt marginalized in both natural and regional political dispensation formula took to the extreme to ally with Al-Shabaab to avert economic exploitation as Puntland authorities attempted to deploy foreign companies to the Dubais/Warsangeli territories for oil exploration.[33]

Al-Shabaab uses several other subtle ways to exploit the continuation of the armed conflict in southern Somalia, one of which is to excavate new clan-based group alliances. In Kismaayo, it allied with the politico-military Mareehaan faction led by Colonel Barre Aden Shire "Barre Hiiraale" to counter the Kenyan-backed politico-religious Ogaadeen group led by Sheikh Ahmed Madoobe. Although there was no reciprocal relationship between Al-Shabaab and Somali pirates, the movement had attempted to broaden its income channels by negotiating with Harardheere pirates during the peak of piracy in 2008–2011.[34] Al-Shabaab's position on the past piratical attacks was a quite paradoxical: at one point, they described it a crime and on another, they saw the piratical acts as a way of protecting Somali shores from the massive foreign trawlers. Many people who are opposed to the government hold equal opposition toward Al-Shabaab as well.[35] For instance, there is strong opposition to Al-Shabaab's rule from the local population in central Somalia.[36] Many local inhabitants complain about Al-Shabaab's rule, which is based on fear, dictation, and disorder.[37] Yet, Al-Shabaab easily operates in the capital city. Tumultuous and turbulent political crisis as it is, the peripheral party of Mogadishu is controlled by the government during the day and Al-Shabaab at night. Similar to the federal government does, Al-Shabaab taxes Mogadishu residents.[38] The town of Afgooye, not that far from Mogadishu, is now taxed by both Al-Shabaab and the federal government. The consensus among the ordinary people for resolving Al-Shabaab is to "pull out all foreign forces out of the country, dismantle the illegitimate government, remove the barrier for political inclusion and then Al-Shabaab would lose credibility as clans would demand their self-determination and, if Al-Shabaab fighters endanger their independence, they would fight against them."[39] However, this could only be one way of containing the Al-Shabaab insurgency.

CONCLUSION

Critiques on power-sharing accords in war-torn societies have emphasized that sharing power does not necessarily lead to an end to armed conflicts. This chapter has challenged this presupposition by presenting a nuanced empirical study on the prolonged war in Somalia, proposing how the power-sharing agreement is necessary to resolve the current insurgency activities of Al-Shabaab. By adopting a conceptual framework structured around the correlation between the armed conflict and the lack of proper power-sharing agreement, the chapter has assessed the intersection between armed conflict and power and demonstrated that the absence of genuine political power-sharing, economic power-sharing and territorial power-sharing sustains the armed conflict in Somalia (Stratford Global Intelligence 2016). The chapter has shown how the absence of the local element in power-sharing agreements aggravated by bad governance, community grievances, and external intervention contributes to the continuation of the protracted conflict and ensures insecurity. The chapter has argued that power-sharing is essential to assuage protracted conflicts based on power struggle. Recent research has made important examples of the victories and failures of power-sharing arrangements and demonstrated the relative capabilities and constraints (Plank 2017; Wright 2017). In line with the recent studies on militant groups in Africa, among them Al-Shabaab (Dowd 2015: 528), the chapter has argued that exclusionary and alienating engagement with the public by the political actors generates opportunities for militant groups to exploit the legitimate grievances.[40] The exclusion (or sometimes dissatisfaction) of important political actors had contributed to the ongoing armed conflict. From the observations and ethnographic interviews upon which this chapter has drawn, it was interesting to find out that people used many times without naming names "that clan supports Al-Shabaab" and "for clan so and so, their members both in government and in Al-Shabaab work together for the common cause of their clan."

Over the years, numerous international peace conferences have been held in the neighboring countries to find for a solution to the armed conflict in Somalia. Because any regime in Somalia is committed to proving itself as a functional and fundamental authority, the internal rivalry over power makes it a fictional and factional entity. However, it is the lack (or thereof) of failing to resolve the public grievances through genuine power-sharing that also contributes to the continuation of the conflicts. Radicalization, grievance, and ideology are usually intertwined with Al-Shabaab elements in Somalia and elsewhere (Anderson and Jacob 2015). Ideology only becomes powerful in conflict when backed up by accumulating grievances. The symbiosis between armed conflicts and patterns of power-sharing has found no more critical place than in Somalia. Throughout the protracted conflicts in Somalia, there has not been proper Somali translation for "compromise" and "concession." The insistence of the government authorities on personalizing power and making the institutions tools to serve the big man in power through clan power and patronage politics thwarts genuine power-sharing accords. The failure of state legitimacy and public support, which developed from the lack of power-sharing agreement, prevents the federal government from consolidating its authority outside Mogadishu.[41] Ethnographic observations made in the field shows that, without attracting domestic legitimacy through power-sharing accord, it would be uneasy for the government to win over Al-Shabaab. Many people in Mogadishu insist that Al-Shabaab is simply out there because people do not consider the federal government a legitimate authority that has the right to rule.[42] The lack of legitimacy on the part of the Mogadishu government and the acute insecurity in the areas it controls largely favour Al-Shabaab.[43] To achieve a popular legitimacy, the government does not attempt to reach out to local armed actors for a power-sharing arrangement.

This chapter has advanced the most recent study on the importance to navigate a form of negotiation with a peaceful settlement of the conflict between the federal government and Al-Shabaab (Ingiriis 2018a). While the theory of power-sharing at the local level offers a good model conflict resolution in Somalia, it has not yet been operationalized. Somalia is a collapsed but not a conventional country. When a country collapses, peacebuilders and state builders need to try new roads and routes. Somalia is profoundly fragmented, and the dysfunctionality of the state is unprecedented on the African continent. Contemporarily, Somalia has no functioning state and is no longer a state, not even a country, other than a "fake state" competed over by the federal government versus Al-Shabaab and the international community versus Al-Shabaab through unending contestation over power to control Somalia. Since the ouster of the military regime in January 1991, no group or government has been capable of restoring the once unified state, let alone controlling throughout the entirety of Somalia. This is why the conflict and collapse in Somalia are now legendary in Africa. Most important local political players in Somalia are Al-Shabaab and clan-based entities which represent the majority of the Somali population. While power-sharing agreements may not be a panacea for all power- and resource-related armed conflicts (McEvoy and O'Leary 2013), if appropriately adopted it can help contain the insurgency violence and contribute to the peacebuilding in Somalia. Without a genuine power-sharing arrangement in place backed up by domestic legitimacy emerging from reconciliation and peaceful arrangement, any emerging government would hardly operate in areas outside Mogadishu.[44] The East African newspaper in Kenya has recently stressed that a "legitimate government is the only antidote to Al-Shabaab terror in Somalia."[45]

The growing insurgency that the federal government faces—and one it has failed to contain thus far—cannot be resolved by ignoring local grievances. After many years of fighting in the bush, Al-Shabaab has now adapted and adopted living in the hinterland as no other Somalis, let alone non-Somalis. Although Al-Shabaab's war-(re)making is part of the broader state-(re)making adventure elsewhere in the Islamic world where many Muslim communities are trying to reject the Western ideal statehood and choose new one based on literal ancient Islam (Ibrahimi 2017), it is imperative to accommodate political opponents and the moderate nationalist elements within Al-Shabaab and offer power positions in the government (Ingiriis 2018a). Beyond offering amnesty to its defectors, the government does not provide moderate elements within Al-Shabaab with political positions. The notion of dealing with Al-Shabaab fighters with only military force ignores the need to rethink what would permit them to operate under the areas populated by the marginalized communities, even if they are to be defeated on the war front. As Burgess (2013: 306) cautioned, "The process of trying to defeat Al Shabaab, moreover, would upset the balance of power among the Somali clans and lead to a new civil war. A large proportion of Al Shabaab's fighters come from [certain clans], and attacking Al Shabaab would weaken that clan and embolden other clans to take advantage of the power vacuum." The widely-held Somali legend is that in each century, there comes a phenomenon in the Somali territories which spreads like a wildfire. Al-Shabaab appears to be such a twenty-first-century Somali phenomenon. Thus, the local element of power-sharing towards the periphery is worth trying. This should not be taken literally as rationalizing Al-Shabaab attacks, but a new way of resolving the unresolved conflict in Somalia. The received wisdom of Somali conflicts has long been that war would at last end all the wars, something that has not happened and will not happen in the near future.

NOTES

1. Whereas Keen (2005) explored the causes of the Sierra Leonean conflict, Richards (1996) examined its consequences.

2. 'Tel. Press Brief with Marine Corps. General Thomas D. Waldhauser, (AFRICOM); Major General Lamidi Adeosun, (MNJTF); Lieutenant General Osman Noor Soubagleh (AMISOM) Ambassador Francisco Madeira, Special Rep. for the Chairperson of the A.U. Commission,' https://www.state.gov/r/pa/ime/africamediahub/rls/270375.htm (accessed 25 April 2017).

3. One Ethiopian official in Somalia by the name of Colonel Gabregziabher Alemseged Abraha is thought to be the long-standing political player because he has been involved in Somali politics as a way of a "diplomat" or a "mediator" over the last twenty-plus years. *Somalialink*, 'Gabre Ayaa xukuma Madaxda Soomaaliya Farah Macalin,' https://www.youtube.com/watch?v=083xg81d444 (accessed 26 January 2016); *Somalialink*, 'Gabre oo la sheegay inuu u taliyo madaxda Soomaaliya,' undated, http://somalialink.com/2016/01/05/gabre-oo-la-sheegay-inuu-u-taliyo -madaxda-soomaaliya/ (accessed 26 January 2016).

4. For a wider African context, see Larmer, Laudati and Clark (2013: 1–12).

5. 'Yusuf Abdi Ali: The Colonel—the fifth estate,' https://www.youtube.com/watch ?v=PFmnWe6bHfs (accessed 15 March 2015).

6. One exception was concluding successfully negotiation with the local "warlord" Mohamed Qanyare Afrah, who was given a position of power and financial inducement in turn for his support to the Arta government.

7. Menkhaus (2007: 263) maintains that "the impulse to try to marginalize rather than integrate the opposition in a transitional government appears to be irresistible to Somalia's political class. President Yusuf, like TNG President Abdiqassim before him, believed he could impose a victor's peace on his adversaries, by relying on Ethiopian "peacekeepers' to outgun them."

8. Interview, former UIC leaders, Mogadishu, August 2015, June 2016.

9. For a detailed survey on the dynamics that led the UIC to failure, see Menkhaus (2007).

10. As Menkhaus (2007: 363) observed: "In reality[,] the 4.5 formula is nothing of the sort, since clan identity is only one dimension of the much more complex split between the SRRC and Mogadishu Group coalitions. Somali leaders controlling a transitional government have had no difficulty attracting members from all the clans while marginalizing their rivals from those same clans. Foreign donors and mediators have been slow to recognize this weakness of the 4.5 formula." On a different kind of formula also existing in Nigeria as the Big Three (Hausa-Fulani, Yoruba and Igbo), see Ikpeze (2000: 98).

11. Discussions, F. S. A., Mogadishu, August 2015, discussions. Writing in 2007, Menkhaus (2007: 263) argued that "Hawiye clan dominance over the capital is one of a number of critical conflict issues which must be addressed. That clan's leadership has for 15 years acted on the unspoken assumption that its capture of the capital gives it the right to rule over the entire country—one reason why the Mogadishu group is so allergic to federal and confederal models for Somalia." For another observer, echoing similar position, the Hawiye "dominance of Mogadishu has placed it in a position to determine how any government that is established in Somalia functions. Thus, the Hawiye leadership has over the years acted on the unspoken assumption that its occupation of the capital gives it the right to rule over the entire country" (Kasaija, 2010: 276). The widely held perception that the Hawiye dominates the Somali politics is seriously mistaken, because within the Hawiye, there is invisible marginalization among some within the clan-group. On the other hand, Daarood political players stick to federalism but do not resist the restoration of the previous authoritarian military regime.

12. Many Somalis insist that if the government had a genuine power-sharing agreement with the regional states, there would be no need for these conferences. The problem is that the opposing, different political players "cannot agree on how to distribute power among [Somali] elites, clans, and factions." Duffield, "When Do Rebels,' 21. In a widely televised gathering, the Puntland community in Minneapolis admitted that the Somali conflict is generally based on a "contestation over cake." This is how Garowe Online, which supports the Puntland mini-state, puts their grievance-based argument: "Aid resources and its distribution are critical issues in Somalia which can complicity exacerbate conflict if not handled well. Anyone with basic knowledge about the history and dynamics of Somali conflict knows well that violence has often been fuel[l]ed by grievances over inequalities of resources distribution mainly due to abuses in powers concentrated in the hands of corrupt authoritarian regimes and other actors in the post conflict." Garowe Online, "Centralized Somalia, Aid Fuels Conflict," February 16, 2016. Cf. *Horseed Media*, "Agreement between Federal Government of Somalia and the Government of Puntland State of Somalia," April 3, 2016.

13. Magaloni (2008) shows how a proper power-sharing arrangement prolongs the longevity of even authoritarian regimes, making brief remarkable examples of several African and Latin American states.

14. As the press release announced: "We agreed with the key constitutional priorities identified by the Federal Government of Somalia including: power sharing; resource sharing; the type of political system; and federal justice model" (Press Release from the London Conference for Somalia, 2017: 5).

15. Discussions, members of various political parties, Mogadishu, June-July 2016. "Awood Qaysiga Puntland iyo Sacdiyo Salaad," https://www.youtube.com/watch?v=aNQ9y0JzNE4 (accessed February 12, 2016). See also *Allgedo Online*, "Beesha Siwaakhroon oo gaashaanka ku dhufatay xulista wasiirada ee Cabdiweli Cali Gaas," Thursday, January 30, 2014.

16. Interview, Y., Mogadishu, May 6, 2016.

17. Interview, Colonel X., Mogadishu, September 20, 2015.

18. *Voa Somali*, "Muqdisho: Laba Qarax oo ka dhacay Hotel Dayax," January 25, 2017; *Voa Somali*, 'Qaraxyo ka dhacay Agagaarka Garoonka Muqdisho," January 2, 2017; *Radio Risaala*, "DEG DEG: Qarax ka dhacay Nawaaxiga dekeda Muqdisho," December 11, 2016; *Hiiraan Online*, "Somali General, 7 Bodyguards Killed in Car Bomb Attack in Mogadishu," September 18, 2016; *Radio Dalsan*, "Daawo: Qaraxii Ma[a]nta Lagu Weeraray Hotel SYL Ee Magaaladda Mogadishu," August 30, 2016; *Radio Shacab*, "Deg Deg Ah: Qarax xoogan oo ka dhacay Hotel Ambassador ee Magaalada Muqdisho," Wednesday, June 1, 2016; *VOA Somali*, "Qarax Ka Dhacay Hotel Naasa Hablood 1," Bisha Lixaad 25, 2016; *Nuxur*, "Deg Deg: Qarax goor dhawayd ka dhacay Xarunta CID ee magaalada [M]uqdisho iyo Ciidamada Dowlada KMG oo isku gadaamay," Jimco, Febraayo, 17th, 2012; *Banadir News*, "Qaraxii ugu weynaa ebed oo xalay lagu weeraray Hotel SYL ee magaalada Muqdisho," February 27, 2016; *Shabelle News*, "Al Shabaab Attacks Kismayo With Mortar Fire," March 9, 2016; *BBC Somali*, "In ka badan 20 ku dhimatay qaraxyada Baydhabo," Febraayo 29, 2016; *Radio Muqadisho*, 'Ammaanka caasimadda oo lagu wareejiyey Maamulka Gobolka Banaadir," February 28, 2016; *BBC Somali*, "Dagaal ka socda xeebta Liido,"

Jannaayo 21, 2016; *BBC Somali*, "20 ku dhimatay weerarkii xeebta Liido," Jannaayo 22, 2016; *BBC Somali*, "Dad musqul isku xiray markuu weerarkii Liido bilowday," Jannaayo 22,2016; *Xoghoose*, "Madaafiicdii lagu weeraray Madaxtooyada Somaliya oo la ogaaday in laga tuuray Degmada Boondheere," January 11, 2016; *AMSOMTV*, "Hotel Jasiira oo la weeraray (War iyo Sawiro)," July26, 2015; *BBC Somali*, "Weerarka Muqdisho oo la cambaareeyey," Febraayo 20, 2015; and *Horseed Media*, "Madaxtooyada Muqdisho ee Villa Soomaaliya oo la weeraray," July 8, 2014; and *Caasimada*, "Shaki cusub oo ka taagan qaraxyada Muqdisho," (accessed April 12, 2016). Cf. *Shabelle News*, "Security Council Condemns Al-Shabaab Attack on Hotel in Mogadishu," June 2,2016; and *Al Jazeera*, "MPs among the Dead in Al-Shabaab Attack on Mogadishu Hotel," June 2, 2016.

19. *Universal Television*, "NABADA SUGIDA SOOMAALIYA OO KA HADA-SHAY QARAXII LALA BEEGSADAY HOTEL JASIIRA 26 07 2015," https://www .youtube.com/watch?v=bbTMFj0xKFU (accessed 1 February 2016); and *Somaliweyn*, "War Deg Deg:- Cabdi Waal oo Loo Soo Gacan Geliyay Dowlada Federalka Soomaaliya *Dhageyso*," Monday, March 7th 2016. When interviewed at a hotel in Mogadishu, the suspected man was defiant and determined to express grievances other than political in nature. B. M. S., Mogadishu, May 3, 2016, interview. Anderson and McKnight have highlighted how Al Shabaab profited from Muslim grievances toward the Kenyan government. This is also the case in Somalia. Anderson and Jacob, "Kenya at War."

20. Rather than dealing directly with Al-Shabaab, the federal gernment punishes members of Al-Shabaab who belong to "unarmed" clans. Former big fishes of Al-Shabaab who hail from "armed" clans feel safe within the federal government. For instance, Hassan Hanafi (from an unarmed clan) was not an Al-Shabaab member, but a broadcaster for Andaluus Radio, a radio that supports Al-Shabaab. His former boss Daher Mohamoud Geelle (from an armed clan) was appointed as an ambassador to Saudi Arabia. According to one former Al-Shabaab defector, Hanafi had never attended the "*mucaskar*" (training) centers of Al-Shabaab. Interview, former Al-Shabaab defector, Mogadishu, May 4, 2016.

21. For more details, see also Hansen (2013: 52, 56, 63, 95, 121 and 139).

22. Conversations, M. A. D., May 31, 2016, Mogadishu.

23. For the role of minority communities in Al-Shabaab, see Hensen (2013: 52, 56, 63, 95, 121 and 139).

24. Interviews, civil society groups, Mogadishu, May–September 2015 and April–August 2016.

25. *Badweyn*, "XOG:- MD Xasan Sheekh oo magacaabay safiirada Soomaaliya u fariisan doona Maraykanka iyo Turkiga," undated, http://allbadweyn.net/xog-md -xasan-sheekh-oo-magacaabay-safiirada-soomaaliya-u-fariisan-doona-maraykanka -iyo-turkiga-sawirmagacyo/ (accessed January13, 2016). For an empirical analysis on the government politics and policies, see Ingiriis (2016b).

26. Allegations are abundant that these forces not only intervene in Somali issues politically, but also corrupt the Somali people socially. There have been notable cases of Somali women being raped by the African Union troops in Somalia, with some women bearing the children of Ugandan soldiers. Interviews, Afgooye, Somalia,

May 18 and 21, September 10–11, 2015. For comparisons, see Amisom (2016); and *The Somalia Herald* (2014). These complaints reveal how far Somalia still lacks a "constrained, supportive state" capable of protecting its citizens (Leeson 2007: 708).

27. Focus groups, Afgooye residents, Somalia, May 18 and 21, September 10 and 11, 2015. For an overview of the Kenyan intervention, see Anderson and McKnight (2015).

28. Focus groups, Afgooye residents, Somalia, May 18 and 21, September 10 and 11, 2015.

29. Ahmed Madoobe's opponents grudgingly alleged that he still has links with Al-Shabaab. Discussions, Mohamed Abdi Mohamed, Wajir (Wajeer in Somali) airstrip, Kenya, June 26, 2015.

30. Interview, former Al-Shabaab defector, Mogadishu, May 4–5, 2016. Hansen details a variety of factions in which one had to join Al-Shabaab, but misses the grievances (see Hansen 2013). For how the project of Jubbaland remains "security dilemma," see Mwangi (2016) and Moe (2017).

31. In Hirshabelle, most of Al-Shabaab members are other Hawaadle subclans because only Ali Madahweyne or Agoon can assume the Hiiraan regional governorship. At the same time, only Harti Abgaal can assume the Lower Shabelle regional governorship, which heightens the grievances of other clans and communities in the regions.

32. Anon., "Dagaalka Buuraha Galgala: Macdan, Mucaarid, Al-Shabaab iyo Puntland (Maqal iyo Muuqaal), Q. 1aad," *Horseed Media*, December 9, 2012. See also Hansen (2013 121–126); and Hoehne (2014).

33. As one former Al-Shabaab defector simply explained, Al-Shabaab takes advantage of the hostility among the local clans to operate in those areas. Interview, B. B. M., Mogadishu, May 6, 2016.

34. 'Kulan looga hadlayay la dagaalanka burcad badeeda iyo al-qaacidda oo ka dhacay xeebaha Puntland, *Radio Muqdisho*, March 4, 2012, http://radiomuqdisho.net/archives/kulan-looga-hadlayay-la-dagaalanka-burcad-badeeda-iyo-al-qaacidda-oo-ka-dhacay-xeebaha-puntland/ (accessed January 10, 2016). For the intersection between Al Shabaab and piracy, see Murphy (2011).

35. Focus groups, residents, Mogadishu, May–September 2015 and April–August 2016.

36. *Telefishinka Qaranka Soomaaliyeed*, 'Dhibaatooyinka Maleeshiyaatka Shabaab ay ku hayaan Ummadda Soomaaliyeed,' https://www.youtube.com/watch?v=6zvcm9ZWnGU&feature=youtu.be (accessed January 11,2016); and *Horn Cable TV*, 'War 14.02.2012 Banaanbax lagaga soo horjeedo isku biiritaanka Alshabaab iyo Al Qaacida,' https://www.youtube.com/watch?v=k0JtXIeUZew (accessed January 11, 2016).

37. Focus group, residents, Afgooye, September 11, 2015. For Al-Shabaab court rulings, see Skjelderup (2014).

38. Dowladda Hoose ee Muqdisho, Waaxda Canshuuraha, Foomka Diiwaangelinta iyo Canshuurta, Dhulka iyo Guryaha "Castato," Warbixinta Dhulka ama Guriga; and Jamhuuriyadda Soomaaliya, Maamulka Gobolka Banaadir, Degmada Hodan, Lambarka Waraaqda / DH/ 2016, Ujeeddo: Wicid, Guri Lambar 5/37.

39. Focus groups, residents, Afgooye, September 11, 2015.

40. This leads to repercussions "beyond theorizing the emergence of violence, but also in the responses to it: where state actions have further reinforced and entrenched the exclusion and marginalization"(Dowd 2015: 528). The interlinkage between protest and revenge in the past Somali wars has been examined by Bakonyi (2005).

41. It has been emphasized elsewhere a decade ago that, "when a country is driven into a state of war, the best alternative is normally [to strive for] a compromise in order to tackle the wrangle amongst the opposing groups and bring them at the negotiating table. One can vaguely argue that such attempts have been made in the last turbulent years of this bleeding nation's history" (Ingiriis 2005).

42. Focus groups, residents, Mogadishu, May–September 2015 and April–August 2016.

43. Ibid.

44. Most recently, the only female presidential candidate in the 2017 elections had declared before leaving the race that she will talk to Al-Shabaab (All Africa News 2016).

45. The East African, "A Legitimate Government is the Only Antidote to Al-Shabaab Terror in Somalia." Saturday, January 30, 2016. See also Mukinda (2016).

REFERENCES

AMISOM.2016). "Senior Amisom Military Officers Undergo Training on Human Rights and Child Protection." December 15.

Anderson, David M., and McKnight, Jacob. 2015. "Kenya at War: al-Shabaab and Their Enemies in Eastern Africa." *African Affairs* 114 (454): 1–27.

All Africa News. 2016. "I Will Sit Down with Al Shabaab as President, Faduma Dayib." March.14,

Anonymous. 2002. "Government Recognition in Somalia and Regional Political Stability in the Horn of Africa." *Journal of Modern African Studies* 40 (2): 247–72.

Bangura. Yusuf. 1997. "Understanding the Political and Cultural Dynamics of the Sierra Leone War: a Critique of Paul Richard's 'Fighting for the Rain Forest.'" *African Development* 32 (3/4): 117–48.

Besteman, Catherine. 1996. "Violent Politics and the Politics of Violence: The Dissolution of the Somali Nation-State." *American Ethnologist.* 23 (3): 579–596.

Besteman, Catherine. 1998. "Primordialist Blinders: A Reply to I. M. Lewis." *Cultural Anthropology.* 13 (1): 109–120.

Besteman, Catherine. 2003. "The Cold War and Chaos in Somalia." In *The State, Identity and Violence: Political Disintegration in the Post-Cold War*. Edited by R. Brian Ferguson. London: Routledge, 285–99.

Besteman, Catherine, and Lee V. Cassanelli, eds. 2000. *The Struggle for Land in Southern Somalia: The War Behind the War*. London: Haan.

Binningsbø, Helma Malmin. 2013. "Power Sharing, Peace and Democracy: Any Obvious Relationships?" *International Area Studies Review* 16 (1): 89–112.

Burgess, Stephen. 2013. "A Lost Cause Recouped: Peace Enforcement and State-Building in Somalia." *Contemporary Security Policy* 34 (2): 302–23.

Caddow, Axmed Jilao. 2001. *Somalia: Gelbiskii Geerida.* N.P.: N.P.

Cheeseman, Nic, and Blessing-Miles Tendi. 2010. "Power-sharing in Comparative Perspective: The Dynamics of 'Unity Government' in Kenya and Zimbabwe." *The Journal of Modern African Studies* 48 (2): 203–29.

Clapham, Christopher. 2016. *Horn of Africa: State Formation and Decay.* London: Hurst.

Compagnon, Daniel. ''Somalie: l'aube de l'après-Siyaad Barre.'" *Politique Africaine* (41): 129–34.

Cornwell, Richard. 2004. "SOMALIA: Plus ça change . . . ?" *African Security Review* 13 (4): 57–60.

Curtis, Devon. "The International Peacebuilding Paradox: Power-sharing and Post-Conflict Governance in Burundi." *African Affairs* 112(446): 72–91.

Daily Nation. 2016. "Kenyan Troops 'Pull Out From El-Adde.'" Tuesday, January 26.

Daley, Patricia. 2007. "The Burundi Peace Negotiations: An African Experience of Peace-Making." *Review of African Political Economy* 34 (112): 333–52.

Dowd, Caitriona. 2015. "Grievances, Governance and Islamist Violence in Sub-Saharan Africa." *Journal of Modern African Studies* 53 (4): 505–31.

Duffield, Andrew Scott. 2013. "When Do Rebels Become State-Builders?: A Comparative Case Study of Somaliland, Puntland, and South-Central Somalia." *Bildhaan.* (13): 1–29.

Ehrhart, Hans-Georg & Petretto, Kerstin. 2014. "Stabilizing Somalia: Can the EU's Comprehensive Approach Work?" *European Security* 23 (2): 179–94.

Elmi, Afyare Abdi. 2010. *Understanding the Somalia Conflagration: Identity, Political Islam and Peacebuilding.* London: Pluto Press.

Elmi, Afyare Abdi, and Abdullahi Barise. 2006. "The Somali Conflict: Root Causes, Obstacles, and Peace-building Strategies." *African Security Review* 15 (1): 32–54.

Elmi, Omar Salaad. 1992. *The Somali Conflict and the Uncurrent Causes.* Muqdisho: Beeldeeq Printing Press.

Evans-Pritchard, E. E., 1940. *The Nuer: A Description of the Modes of Livelihood and Political Institutions of a Nilotic People.* Oxford: Oxford University Press.

Fearon, James D. 2004. "Why Do Some Civil Wars Last So Much Longer than Others?" *Journal of Peace Research* 41 (3): 275–301.

Frimpong-Ansah, Jonathan H. 1992. The Vampire State in Africa: The Political Economy of Decline. Trenton, N.J., Africa World Press.

Gassem, Mariam Arif. 1994. *Hostages: The People Who Kidnapped Themselves.* Nairobi: Central Graphics Services.

Goede, Meike J. De. 2015. " 'Mundele, It is Because of You': History, Identity and the Meaning of Democracy in the Congo." *The Journal of Modern African Studies.* 53 (4): 583–609.

Hansen, Stig Jarle. 2013. *Al-Shabaab in Somalia: The History and Ideology of a Militant Islamist Group, 2005–2012.* London: C. Hurst.

Hannas, Chris. 2016. "Reports Lists Somalia, North Korea as World's Most Corrupt Countries." *Voice of America*, January 27.

Hardin, Russell. 1995. *One for All: The Logic of Group Conflict*. Princeton: Princeton University Press.

Hashim, Alice Bettis. 1997. *The Fallen State: Dissonance, Dictatorship and Death in Somalia*. Lanham, MD: University Press of America.

Hersi, Abdullahi. 2016. *The Power-Sharing and Management of Clan Conflicts in Somalia*. London: Lambert Academic Publishing.

Hills, Alice. 2014a. "Somalia Works: Police Development as State Building." *African Affairs* 113 (9450): 88–107.

———. 2014b. "Remembrance of Things Past: Somali Roads to Police Development." *Stability: International Journal of Security & Development* 3 (1): 1–14.

———. 2014c. "What is Policeness? On Being Police in Somalia." *British Journal of Criminology* 54 (5): 765–83.

———. 2014d. "Security Sector or Security Arena? The Evidence from Somalia." *International Peacekeeping* 21(2): 165–80.

HIS. 2016. "Anti-government Clan's Support for Islamic State Faction in Puntland Unlikely to Contribute to Increased Somalia-based Piracy." November 9.

Höhne, Markus. 2014. "Resource Conflict and Militant Islamism in the Golis Mountains in Northern Somalia (2006–2013)." *Review of African Political Economy.* 41: 358–73.

———. 2006. "Political Identity, Emerging State Structures and Conflict in Northern Somalia." *Journal of Modern African Studies.* 44 (3): 397–414.

Human Rights Watch. 2007a. Somalia: Shell-Shocked—Civilians under Siege in Mogadishu. New York: Human Rights Watch.

Human Rights Watch. 2007b. Somalia: Mogadishu Clashes Devastating Civilians—Protect Medical Facilities and Aid Workers. New York: Human Rights Watch.

Ibrahimi, S. Yaqub, 2017. "The Taliban's Islamic Emirate of Afghanistan (1996–20021): 'War-Making and State-Making' as an Insurgency Strategy." *Small Wars & Insurgencies* 28(6): 947–72.

Ikpeze, Nnaemeka. 2000. "Post-Biafran Marginalization of the Igbo in Nigeria." In *The Politics of Memory: Truth, Healing & Social Justice*. Edited by Ifi Amadiume and Abdullahi An-Na'im. London: Zed Books, 90–109.

Indian Ocean Newsletter. 2009. "The Inter-Islamist War Has Begun." 10/01/2009, No. 928.

———. 1991. "Somalia: Power Struggle." February 2. No. 928

Ingiriis, Mohamed Haji. 2018a. "Building Peace from the Margins in Somalia: The Case for Political Settlement with Al-Shabaab." *Contemporary Security Policy* 39(4): 512–36

———. 2018b. "From Al-Itihaad to Al-Shabaab: How the Ethiopian Intervention and the 'War on Terror' Exacerbated the Conflict in Somalia." *Third World Quarterly.*39(11): 2033–52.

———. 2016a. *The Suicidal State in Somalia: The Rise and Fall of the Siad Barre Regime, 1969–1991*. Lanham, MD: University Press of America.

———. 2016b. "How Somalia Works: Mimicry and the Making of Mohamed Siad Barre's Regime in Mogadishu." *Africa Today* 63 (1): 57–83.

————. 2015. "Politics as a Profitable Business: Patronage, Patrimony, Predation and Primordial Power in Contemporary Somalia." *Journal of Somali Studies* 2 (1 & 3): 67–97.

————. 2005. "Somalia: Can a Stripping-nation Refurbish its Statehood?" *Somaliweyn*, November 29.

International Crisis Group. 2008. *To Move Beyond the Failed State*. Africa Report, No. 147, Nairobi-Brussels. August 10.

Kaldor, Mary. 1999. *New and Old Wars: Organized Violence in a Global Era*. Cambridge: Polity Press.

Kasaija, Apuuli Phillip. 2010. "The UN-led Djibouti Peace Process for Somalia 2008–2009: Results and Problems." *Journal of Contemporary African Studies*. 28 (3): 261–82.

Keen, David. 2005. *Conflict & Collision in Sierra Leone*. Oxford: James Currey.

Larmer, Miles, Ann Laudati, and John F. Clark. 2013. "Neither War Nor Peace in the Democratic Republic of Congo (DRC): Profiting and Coping Amid Violence and Disorder." *Review of African Political Economy* 40 (135): 1–12.

Lemerchand, René. 1962. "The Limits of Self-Determination: The Case of the Katanga Secession.'" *American Political Science Review* 56 (2): 404–16.

Le Van, A. Carl 2010. "Power Sharing and Inclusive Politics in Africa's Uncertain Democracies." *Governance* 24 (1): 31–53.

Leeson, Peter T. 2007. "Better Off Stateless: Somalia Before and After Government Collapse." *Journal of Comparative Economics* 35 (4): 689–710.

Lederach, John Paul. 1997. *Building Peace: Sustainable Reconciliation in Divided Societies*. Washington, DC: United States Institute of Peace Press.

Lewis, I. M. 1994. *Blood and Bone: The Call of Kinship in Somali Society*. Trenton, NJ: The Red Sea Press.

————. 1998. "Doing Violence to Ethnography: A Response to Catherine Besteman's "Representing Violence and 'Othering' Somalia".' *Cultural Anthropology* 13 (1): 100–8.

Luttwak, Edward. 1999. "Give War a Chance." *Foreign Affairs* 78 (4): 36–44.

Magaloni, Beatriz. 2008. "Credible Power-Sharing and the Longevity of Authoritarian Rule." *Comparative Political Studies* 41(4–5): 715–41.

Malito, Debora Valentina. 2015. "Building Terror While Fighting Enemies: How the Global War on Terror Deepened the Crisis in Somalia." *Third World Quarterly* 36 (10): 1866–96.

Maruf, Harun Dan Joseph. 2018. *Inside Al-Shabaab: The Secret History of Al-Qaeda's Most Powerful Ally*. Bloomington: Indiana University Press.

Mayer, Arno J. 2000. *The Furies: Violence and Terror in the French and Russian Revolution*. Princeton: Princeton University Press.

McEvoy, Joanne, and Brendan O'Leary (eds.). 2013. *Power Sharing in Deeply Divided Places*. Philadelphia: University of Pennsylvania Press.

Mehler, Andres. 2009. "Peace and Power Sharing in Africa: A Not So Obvious Relationship." *African Affairs* 108 (432): 453–73.

Menkhaus, Ken. 2007. "The Crisis in Somalia: Tragedy in Five Acts." *African Affairs* 1 (204): 357–90.

Moe, Louise Wiuff. 2017. "Counterinsurgent Warfare and the Decentering of Sovereignty in Somalia." In *Reconfiguring Intervention: Complexity, Resilience and the 'Local Turn' in Counterinsurgent Warfare*. Edited by Louise Wiuff Moe and Markus-Michael Müller. London: Palgrave Macmillan, 119–40.

Mukinda, Fred. 2016. "Uhuru Kenyatta Urges Somalis to Form Credible Government." *The Daily Nation*. January 22.

Murphy, Martin. 2011. *Somalia: The New Barbary? Piracy and Islam in the Horn of Africa*. London: C. Hurst.

Murtazashvili, Jennifer Brick. 2014. "Informal Federalism: Self-Governance and Power Sharing in Afghanistan." *Publius* 44 (2): 324–43.

Mwangi, Oscar Gakuo. 2016. "Jubaland: Somalia's New Security Dilemma and State-building Efforts." *Africa Review*. 8 (2): 129–32.

News from Somalia. Undated. "SRC and Council of Secretaries Approve 1973 Budget." *News from Somalia*, published by the Embassy of the Somali Democratic Republic in Addis Ababa, 6–8.

Olonisakin, 'Funmi and Alfred Muteru. 2014. Reframing Narratives of Peacebuilding and Statebuilding in Africa. ALC Working Paper, No. 16.

Ombati, Cyrus. 2016. "Kenya: Local clan in El Adde Might Have Betrayed KDF." *The Standard*. January 25.

Ottmann, Martin, and Vüllers, Johannes, 2015. "The Power-Sharing Event Dataset (PSED): A New Dataset on the Promises and Practices of Power-Sharing in Post-Conflict Countries." *Conflict Management and Peace Science* 32 (2): 327–50.

Plank, Friedrich. 2017. "When Peace Leads to Divorce: The Splintering of Rebel Groups in Power-Sharing Agreements." *Civil Wars*. 19 (2): 176–97.

Press Release. 2013. A New Deal for Somalia: A Unique Opportunity to Build a Peaceful Society. http://eeas.europa.eu/archives/new-deal-for-somalia-conference/press-corner.1.html (accessed October 30, 2016).

Press Release from the London Conference for Somalia. 2017. Looking Ahead to the London Somalia Conference 2017. https://www.gov.uk/government/news/looking-ahead-to-the-london-somalia-conference-2017 (accessed May 21, 2017).

Prunier, Gérard. 2012. "In Sudan, Give War a Chance." *New York Times*. May 4.

Radio Dalsan. 2016. "Somali MP Calls for Inclusion of Minorities in Power-Sharing." May 5.

Reno, William. 1995. *Corruption and State Politics in Sierra Leone*. Cambridge, Cambridge University Press.

Rice, Edward E. 1998. *Wars of the Third Kind: Conflict in Underdeveloped Countries*. Berkeley: University of California Press.

Rice, Xan. 2006. "Mogadishu's Miracle: Peace in the World's Most Lawless City—After 16 years of Chaos, the Warlords Have Left and the Capital's Streets are Quiet." *The Guardian*. June 26.

Richards, Paul. 1996. *Fighting for the Rain Forest: War, Youth & Resources in Sierra Leone*. Oxford: James Currey.

Roitsch, Paul E. 2014. "The Next Step in Somalia: Exploiting Victory, Post-Mogadishu." *African Security Review* 23 (1): 3–16.

Roque, Paula Cristina. 2009. "The Battle for Mogadishu: Revealing Somalia's Fluid Loyalties and Identities." *African Security Review* 18 (3): 74–79.

Rothchild, Donald. 1995. "Ethnic Bargaining and State Breakdown in Africa." *Nationalism and Ethnic Politics* 1 (1): 54–72.

Samatar, Ibrahim Megag. 1997. "Light at the End of the Tunnel: Some Reflections on the Struggle of the Somali National Movement." In Mending Rips in the Sky: Options for Somali Communities in the 21st Century Edited by Hussein M. Adam and Richard Ford. Lawrenceville, N.J.: The Red Sea Press, 21–48.

Skjelderup, Michael. 2014. "*Udūd* Punishments in the Forefront: Application of Islamic Criminal Law by Harakat Al-Shabaab Al-Mujahideen." *Journal of Law and Religion* 29 (2): 317–29.

Simons, Anna. 1995. *Networks of Dissolution: Somalia Undone.* Boulder and Oxford, CO: Westview Press.

Simons, Anna. 2004. "No Exit from Somalia." In *Anthropologists in the Public Sphere: Speaking Out on War, Peace, and American Power.* Edited by Roberto J. Gonzalez. Austin: The University of Texas Press, 82–83.

Simons, Claudia, Franzisca Zanker, Andreas Mehler, and Dennis M. Tull, 2013. "Power-Sharing in Africa's War Zones: How Important is the Local Level." *Journal of Modern African Studies* 51 (4): 681–706.

Snow, Donald. 1996. *Uncivil Wars: International Security and the New International World Order.* Boulder: Lynne Rienner.

Somalia Herald. 2014. "AMISOM Should Take Probe on Sex Abuse by its Troops Seriously."

Spears, Ian S. 2013. "Africa's Informal Power-Sharing and the Prospects for Peace." *Civil Wars* 15 (1): 37–53.

Stratford Global Intelligence. 2016. "In Somalia, Stability Is a Distant Promise." February 1.

Stedman, Stephen John. 1997. "Spoiler Problems in Peace Processes." *International Security* 22 (2): 5–53.

Tripodi, Paolo. 2005. "Whatever Happens to Somalia . . . Ignoring it is No Longer an Option." Low Intensity Conflict & Law Enforcement 13 (3): 212–26.

Tull, Dennis M. 2010. "Troubled State-building in the DR Congo: The Challenge from the Margins." *The Journal of Modern African Studies* 48 (4): 643–61.

Tull, Denis M. and Andreas Mehler. 2005. "The Hidden Costs of Power-Sharing: Reproducing Insurgent Violence in Africa." *African Affairs* 104 (416): 375–98.

Ugas, Kamal Hassan. 2017. "Factors Influencing Power-Sharing System in Somali Politics." *Strategic Journal of Business & Change Management* 4 (4): 15–32.

Vandeginste, Stef. 2009. "Power-Sharing, Conflict and Transition in Burundi: Twenty Years of Trial and Error." *Africa Spectrum* 44 (3): 63–86.

Vandeginste, Stef. 2011. "Power-Sharing as a Fragile Safety Valve in Times of Electoral Turmoil: The Costs and Benefits of Burundi's 2010 Elections." *Journal of Modern African Studies* 49 (2): 315–35.

War Murtiyeed. 2016. "Bayaanka Muwaadiniinta Madaxa-Banaan Ee Ku Aaddan Doorashada 2016-Ka." Axsaabta Siyaasiga ah ee Soomaaliya.

Williams, Paul. 2014. "Key Drivers of Violent Conflict in Africa: Myths and Reality. https://www.youtube.com/watch?v=pXN8_VIPcSQ (accessed September 3, 2016).

World Bank. 2005. *Conflict in Somalia: Drivers and Dynamics*. http://siteresources .worldbank.org/INTSOMALIA/Resources/conflictinsomalia.pdf (accessed on March 30, 2011).

———. 1989. Sub-Saharan Africa: From Crisis to Sustainable Growth. A Long-Term Perspective Study. Washington, DC.

Wright, Patrick. 2017. "South Sudan and the Four Dimensions of Power-Sharing: Political, Territorial, Military, and Economic." *African Conflict & Peacebuilding Review* 7 (2): 1–35.

Zanker, Franzisca, Claudia Simons, and Andreas Mehler. 2015. "Power, Peace, and Space in Africa: Revisiting Territorial Power-Sharing." *African Affairs* 114 (454): 72–91.

Chapter 4

Boko Haram Insurgency in Nigeria

Sylvester Odion Akhaine

Boko Haram, the Islamic insurgent group operating in Nigeria's northeast, has retained its currency in the news media. In March 2020, the insurgents launched a scorching attack on the Bohoma Army Base and killed about ninety-two Chadian soldiers. Correspondingly, the Chadian Army conducted a counteroffensive led by the country's President Idris Deby, a former rebel leader, that killed over one thousand insurgents around the islands of Lake Chad in April 2020 (Al Jazeera 2020). In a related incident, insurgents ambushed and killed about nineteen Nigerian soldiers on a counterterrorism operation along the Maiduguri-Damboa road in Borno on July 7, 2020. In yet another incident, Boko Haram fighters attacked a UN Humanitarian Air Service helicopter in Damasak, Borno state, without casualty on July 2, 2020 (Premium Times 2020). The cumulative consequence has been a decline of troop's morale underlined by young combatants producing YouTube videos denouncing the leadership of the military for its poor handling of the battlefield math (Sahara Reporters 2020).

Although there is continuing literature on the Boko Haram insurgency due to its prevalence (Madunagu 2011; Sani 2011; Toyo 2011), this chapter identifies and examines critically the drivers of the conflict, namely, internal and external factors. Although a combination of internal conditions, namely, poverty, power struggle, religion, and corruption, birthed the group, the overarching externality of the conflict, its sustaining logic, has yet to be critically examined. This chapter represents a modest effort in this regard. Its basic argument is that both internal and external factors constitute the sustaining logic of the conflict. It is concluded that both political will and strategic engagement with the external forces—the West and Arabs—would be invaluable to the resolution of the conflict. Firstly, I examine the internal factor;

secondly, the external factor; and thirdly, by way of conclusion, reflects on exit measures.

THE MAJOR CAUSES OF THE INSURGENCY

Internal factors

Power struggle

> Politics is about conflict, and about the ability of people to devise power struc-
> tures which, on the one hand, may work to the overall benefit or disadvantage
> of the individuals who are affected by them; but which, on the other hand, will
> invariably confer considerably greater benefits and costs on some people than
> on others. Not only is politics itself a contest, but the words and ideas which are
> used to describe it are contested too. (Clapham 1996:8)

Two related elements of the political content of Boko Haram can be discerned from available evidence. One is the control of Borno politics. The
second reason is connected with the demise of Sani Abacha in 1998 and
Nigeria's transition to democratic rule under the leadership of Olusegun
Obasanjo. To be sure, even before the end of Obasanjo's tenure in office in
2007, northern elites perceived themselves as marginalized. Consequently,
the struggle to return central power to the Northern Nigerian elites intensified
and provided fuel for the Boko Haram agitations. Alhaji Kashim Shettima
emerged as the candidate of the All Nigerian Peoples Party (ANNP) through
a second primary, after the murder of Modu Fannami Gubio, the party's flag
bearer for the 2011 gubernatorial election. However, he defeated the People's
Democratic (PDP)'s candidate, Mohammed Goni, under controversial circumstances. As noted by an observer,

> Around that inner circle is the manner in which the current administration in
> Borno was "elected" [sic] (Naija style) against the popular expectation (rightly
> or wrongly) that Goni was the legitimate winner. Rigging elections is a national
> pastime in Nigeria, but it is a dangerous game. (Personal Communication 2012)

Before the execution of Sheikh Mohammed Yusuf, the leaders of the Boko
Haram sect, Sani (2011: 28–29) quoting a Borno resident's viewpoint, noted
that during Friday prayers, Sheikh Yusuf received in audience powerful
people in society at his Railway Quarters, and the place was like a big party
summit in progress. His summary execution must have been a product of
power plays among these powerful individuals. It is in this connection that
the initial demand of the Boko Haram insurgents to effect the arrest and

prosecution of the former Governor of Borno State, Ali Modu Sheriff; the Shehu of Borno, Alhaji Abubakar Ibn Garbai El-Kanemi and former Minister of Police Affairs, Ibrahim Yakubu Lame, after the execution of Yusuf must be understood. As one individual noted:

> Around that concentric circle is the motive for justice and vengeance with regards to the extra-judicial murder of Yusuf. Until Chris Dega, the Police man, and Ali Modu Sheriff, the politician, clarify their roles in that unfortunate incident, the cycle of violence may continue. Patsies will not do. (Personal Communication 2012)

By 2007, power returned to the north with the election of President Umaru Musa Yar'Adua. Following his death in office, he was succeeded by President Goodluck Jonathan, a minority from Southern Nigeria. The intrigues of the succession process have been discussed elsewhere (Akhaine 2018). A section of the Northern elite did not countenance the power shift and felt that it had been shortchanged in the power equation in the country. Besides, the bid by Jonathan to officially run for the presidency did not go down well with this set of political actors, hence the supposition that these politicians supported the insurgent groups. As observed by Stephen Davis, an Australian negotiator with Boko Haram, who offered insight into the motives of the sponsors of the insurgents,

> The political sponsors of Boko Haram seem to think that they can use Boko Haram to terrorize Nigeria to demonstrate that the current government cannot ensure the security of Nigerian citizens both Muslim and Christian. Therein the sponsors assume they can undermine any efforts of the current government to be re-elected in 2015. Herein lies the flaw for the conflict and instability currently being fanned suits the aims of Al Qaeda and the architects of terrorism. Should the sponsors of Boko Haram win government in 2015, they will likely find that they cannot turn Boko Haram off or that Boko Haram will demand control of at least Borno State in return for reducing their attacks. Borno State may be just the beginning of an expanding caliphate. (Daniel 2014: 1 & 5)

Poverty

Poverty readily plays into the consequences of political miscalculation. As a condition of lack, it has been central to most conflicts. The Nigerian paradox has been that the country is rich but poor. The country is blessed with all forms of natural resources, many of which are unexploited. But the minders of the state have solely relied on the exploration and exploitation of its huge hydrocarbon reserve that at some point ranked it as the eighth oil-producing country in the world and the sixth in the Organization of Petroleum Exporting

Countries (OPEC). By some estimates, the country reportedly lost $400 billion to corruption between 1960 and 1999. Overall, there is nothing concrete to account for the huge earnings on the part of the citizenry except the outlandish consumption pattern of the ruling class hemmed within a cesspool of primitive accumulation, defined here as appropriation outside genuine production activities reducible to corrupt practices. Gurr's (1970) relative deprivation theory which posits that "the greater the discrepancy, however, marginal, between what is sought and what seems attainable, the greater will be the chances that anger and violence will result" has no explanatory value in explicating the Nigerian condition. The reason being that poverty is in the extreme and indescribable. World Clock ranked the country in 2018 as the global headquarters of poverty. With a pool of the impoverished, the absence of hope which leadership ought to inspire, such situation is easily exploitable by conflict entrepreneurs or those with the intent to destabilize the society for all manners of reason. As Barlow (2016:16) has rightly observed, "Boko Haram has exploited the loss of hope to influence and bolster its forces. It shows no interest in actually governing, developing the economy, or improving the standard of living of those living under its rule."

Religion

Religious extremism and intolerance, referred to as Islamic fundamentalism, have gained momentum in Northern Nigeria since the start of the century among some followers of the Islamic faith. These fundamentalists distort the teachings of Islam. They represent themselves as anti-imperialists opposing Western cultural influences while seeking to institute Islamic law, including strict codes of behavior.

Unarguably, the belief of the Boko Haram sect centers on a rejection of Western rational bureaucratic institutions such as banking system and legal jurisprudence. It sees Western education as anti-Islam and contrary to the Islamic worldview. Sheik Yusuf, the slain Boko Haram leader, and his followers shared this belief (Sani 2011:26). His emergence also coincided with the politicization of Islamic religion in Nigeria by the northern states, who declared sharia dispensation in flagrant violation of the secularity of the Nigerian state enshrined in Section 10 of the 1999 Constitution as amended. Relating to this point, Campbell (2014:1) noted that:

> In the past, the ruling elements have politicized religion and ethnicity to divert and confuse the peoples of Nigeria. The oligarchy in Northern Nigeria took the politicization of religion to a point where 12 Northern states are now under Sharia law. Boko Haram were (sic) pawns in a cold blooded game to control the state in Nigeria. Started in 2002 the movement exploded in the society after the death of President Yar'Adua in 2010.

Nonetheless, Sheikh Yusuf, who found a base in the north-eastern city of Maiduguri, had interfaced with political authorities in Yobe and Borno states. Indeed, many people from prominent families were said to be members of his sect. However, he was extrajudicially executed in 2009, following disagreement with political authorities over his threat to avenge seventeen of his followers, who were killed by a police patrol team known as *Operation Flush, while on funeral procession to bury four of their members who died in a motor accident. With increasing polarization, the group would later exploit its vast network to exact a toll on the state.*

Corruption

Corruption is endemic to the Nigerian political system. It has been severally ranked low on the Transparency International Corruption Perception Index (see, for example, CPI 2019). The institution of two major anti-corruption agencies, namely, the Economic and Financial Crimes Commission (EFCC) and the Independent Corrupt Practices and other Related Offences Commission (ICPC) by the Nigerian state points to a raging war against corruption. How well that war is doing is not the concern of this chapter. Its objective is to explain how issues like corruption among others constitute the driving force of the Boko Haram insurgency. There has been a continuous cry that the army needs more funding, but there is no balance sheet of how it has spent the money pumped into the conflict since its inception. Evidence suggests that the army is poorly trained and lacks tactical battleground hardware to fight increasingly well-armed insurgents. Barlow(2016: 18) of Special Tasks, Training, Equipment and Protection (STTEP) International Ltd noted that at the time of the private military company's intervention in late December 2014, it was "dismayed at the level and standard of training the Nigerian troops had received from their foreign trainers" and were equally poorly equipped. The point is what happened to the yearly appropriation and interventionist funding of the army? In 2017, the government of Goodluck Jonathan wrote the parliament to request approval of one billion dollars for military equipment upon its failure to suppress the insurgents. As Dorrie (2014: 1) has noted, the government's answer lay in

> [spending] more money on military equipment . . . President Goodluck Jonathan has asked parliament to approve a $1-billion loan to purchase new gear. In a letter to parliament, Jonathan wrote that he wanted "to bring to your attention the urgent need to upgrade the equipment, training and logistics of our armed forces and security services to enable them more forcefully [to] confront this serious threat . . . The letter is only a few paragraphs long and provides no details on how the government would use the funds. It also offers no explanation as to why the $6 billion in the existing 2014 military budget is inadequate. That sum is

already a marked increase over the $2.4 billion the Nigerian armed forces spent in 2013—and gives Nigeria one of the three largest defense budgets in Africa.

Equally, Dorrie (2014) has noted that the Nigerian Army was employing Boko Haram's threat to argue for budget increase and that the generals were not going to give up on the prebendal flow even if it meant the continuity of the conflict. The leader of the Nigeria's upper legislative chamber, Senator Ahmed Lawan, lent credence to the merchandization of the conflict. According to him, "Boko Haram has metamorphosed from a group of religious zealots into an industry. It is an industry because what they do is not religious. They have people from different faiths and countries who are part of Boko Haram" (Umoru 2020: 1).

External Factors

The West

To analyze the external factors in the Boko Haram insurgency in Nigeria, a brief highlight of the interests of the external actors would be invaluable. Clapham (1996) once observed the overarching externality of the African crisis. A major mistake of analysts of the African condition is to ignore how foreign influences have shaped the continent. The United Kingdom colonized Nigeria, and through all stratagems ensured the imposition of an "inheritance elite" at independence conducive to its neocolonial intent. It has continued to influence developments in the country to date. It would be recalled that under the authoritarian regime of General Sani Abacha, British influence was whittled down when the general played the French card by the sheer intention to introduce French language into Nigeria's education system, ban British Airways flights to Nigeria, and refusing audiences with British diplomats in Abuja to undermine its isolation by the international community (personal communication). A rattled London sought all devices to restore its relations with the country while playing the multilateral card. In his *The International Relations of Sub-Saharan Africa*, Taylor (2010: 24–34) explained US-Africa relations. The subtext, he underlined, is the continuation of the integration of the continent into the globalized orbit employing democracy promotion and the securitization of key areas of that relations through the combat of transnational security threat. As Taylor (2010: 33) has argued,

> What 9/11 arguably did do was to bring to close the "decade of disengagement" that had characterized American policies toward Africa became of greater significance as the continent was conceptualized within a securitization discourse that saw Africa as posing a possible threat to American interests.

Referencing the place of the US and UK in the broad canvas of the Boko Haram conflict, Barlow (2016:17) noted that the balkanization of the continent is a central goal of foreign powers. He cited the view of J. Peter Pham, who underlined the point that US interests were for the most part focused on the protection of the huge natural resources, including hydrocarbon that is in abundance and hedging out other foreign interlopers such as China, India, Japan, and Russia. Barlow (2016:17) further argued that the collapse of Libya boosted Boko Haram fighters who fought the Gaddafi regime with other Western-backed Islamic forces and were able to access Libyan military ordnance, which became handy in Nigeria (Barlow 2016:17).

Keenan (2012) has also provided illuminating details of the US connection to the terror networks in the Sahel Sahara. In his analysis of the invasion of Northern Mali by the Tuareg rebels in 2012, he noted that " the catastrophe now being played out in Mali is the inevitable outcome of the way in which the Global War on Terror has been inserted into the Sahara-Sahel by the US, in concert with Algerian intelligence operatives, since 2002" (Keenan 2012:1). As revealed by Keenan, Al-Qaeda in the Islamic Maghreb was a creation of Algerian intelligence, Département du Renseignement et de la Sécurité (DRS). And there was a convergence of interest between the United States and Algeria, which Keenan(2012:1) summed up:

> The Algerians wanted more terrorism to legitimize their need for more high-tech and up-to-date weaponry. The Bush administration, meanwhile, saw the development of such terrorism as providing the justification for launching a new Saharan front in the "Global War On Terror." Such a "second front" would legitimize America's increased militarization of Africa so as better to secure the continent's natural resources, notably oil. This, in turn, was soon to lead to the creation in 2008 of a new US combat command for Africa—AFRICOM.

The result is the birthing of Trans-Saharan Counter-Terrorism Initiative and the consequent "Operation Flintlock" military exercise across the Sahara.

Franco-African relations are accentuated by France's pervasive neocolonial presence in the continent, which the late Gabonese President Omar Bongo once approximated thus: "Africa without France is like a car without driver. But France without Africa is like a car without petrol" (Quoted in Taylor 2010: 52). This witty but deep expression of President Bongo speaks to the exploitative and asymmetrical nature of Franco-African relations, which Dr. Arikana Chihombori-Quao highlighted recently and earned her a place as the Nigerian Guardian "Man of the Year." She spoke about the exploitative French neocolonialism in Africa,

Today, France is taking out of Francophone Africa over US$500 billion. We, the Africans, the poor countries, are giving France US$500 billion year-in year-out. . . . France, the $500 billion you are taking out of Africa every year, no more. France needs to be the Third World developing country, not Africa. No more shall we continue to be exploited. France can no longer take $500 billion out of Africa." (Nigerian Guardian 2020:1)

Intriguingly, France has been indicted in the Boko Haram conflict to the extent of supporting the insurgents. The Movement Against Slavery and Terrorism (MAST) in Nigeria led a protest to the French embassy in Abuja, accusing France of "nefarious covert" activities in Nigeria (Mendy 2019).

The Arabs

The Arab states of Saudi Arabia, Turkey, and Qatar are implicated in the Boko Haram discourse. However, the pertinent question is: what is their interest in Nigeria? The most intelligible response is the expansion of the geography of global Islam. As is well-known, Boko Haram claims the establishment of an Islamic caliphate in Nigeria. The intermingling of these Arab states was accented by the former President of Benin Republic, Nicephore Soglo. At a conference organized by the US-based National Democratic Institute (NDI) on constitutional term limits in Niger Republic, former President Soglo pointed to Saudi Arabia and Qatar as sponsors of Boko Haram. According to him, "Boko Haram is funded by our friends from Saudi Arabia and our friends from Qatar. Are we friends or not? Let's tell ourselves the truth. We have to stand together. I'm optimistic we are going to win if we stand together" (The Cable 2019:1).

Earlier, CBN News also carried reports of arms shipment from Turkey to Boko Haram. It must be noted however that the Nigerian government has a cozy relationship with these countries that are central to the externality of the Boko Haram insurgency. The competing interests of these international actors could explain the sustaining logic of the insurgent groups that a five-nation coalition, comprising Benin, Cameroon, Chad, Niger, and Nigeria, ostensibly backed by the United States, United Kingdom, and France, has yet to defeat.

BOKO HARAM'S IMPACT ON NIGERIA
AND ITS NEIGHBORS

Nigeria is bordered by Cameroon, Benin Republic, Chad, and the Niger Republic on the four points of the compass. The activities of the Boko Haram insurgents have impacted these countries variously. The exception is Benin, which though has contributed troops to the multinational Joint Task Force against Boko Haram is not part of the Lake Chad Basin Countries (LCBC). To be sure, exertions of the insurgents have spilled over into northern Cameroon, parts of Chad around the Lake Chad Basin, and Niger, especially its Diffa region. The destabilization of Nigeria, the provider of stability in the West African subregion, is seen as the latent function of the insurgents. The strategic base of Boko Haram in Nigeria's northeast has served as a collaborating pad for the different terrorist groups in the central and West Africa subregions (Aduloju, Opanike, and Adenipekun 2014, cited in Aduku & Okolo 2019). This section briefly overviews the impact.

Cameroon

Cameroon has served as a buffer for the insurgents and Nigerian troopers besides being a target of insurgents' attacks. Insurgents easily seek refuge in its territory, while fleeing and deserting Nigerian soldiers have also sought refuge in its territory. Even more, its population has also come under attack by the insurgents. As noted by the International Crisis Group (2016: 1) between "March 2014 to March 2016, Boko Haram carried out more than 400 attacks and incursions in Cameroon, as well as about fifty suicide bombings that left 92 members of security forces dead, injured more than 120 others and killed more than 1350 civilians." As Opoku et al. (2017: 225) also noted, "Cameroon has suffered a lot of attacks from Boko Haram to its Extreme North after contributing military to the group." Like Nigeria and Niger, it has IDPs camps as a result of the conflict. Above all, insurgents' activities have strained its economy. This effect is appositely captured by Foyou, et al. (2018: 73):

> The trans-border incursions of Boko Haram into border towns and villages in Northern Cameroon has contributed to a depletion of the fragile economic base that sustained the three northern regions of Cameroon (the North, the Far North, and Adamawa) and threatened the security of helpless populations in these regions. Cameroon has had to deploy more forces and resources to its northern regions to contain the increasingly brutal and ruthless campaigns orchestrated by Boko Haram in those areas.

The point that economic activities have been affected due to perceived increase in taxes, low productivity, and exchange due to stricture on the movement of goods and services activities has also been affirmed by Opoku et al. (2017: 234). Indeed, the atrocities of the sect have nudged Cameroon into sharing intelligence with Nigeria while maintaining border surveillance.

Chad

Chad has been an active member of the regional war against Boko Haram insurgents. N'djamena, the capital city, has played host to the Multinational Joint Task Force. Like other coalition partners, it has borne the brunt of the war. Its troopers have been killed by the insurgents, the latest being the killing of 249 troopers by Boko Haram insurgents, resulting in a huge counteroffensive led by President Idris Derby which inflicted defeat on the insurgents and cleared them out of the Chadian side of the Lake Chad Basin (Al Jazeera 2020). In its efforts to rout the insurgents, it has to make incursions into both Niger and Nigeria. As the International Crisis Group (2017: 1) noted:

> At the start of 2015, the president authorized Chadian troops to enter Niger in their capacity as part of the MNJTF while on 6–8 February, Boko Haram launched violent attacks against the towns of Bosso and Diffa. In a way, the regionalization of both the threat and the military response fed each other. For many months, the front stabilized along the border with Nigeria. Its effect on the Chadian economy has been harrowing for those who rely on the trans-border trade.

The attacks on Chad by the insurgents have resulted in the death of hundreds and displacement of more than 100,000. Trade on the Chadian islands and shore of the lake has been severely affected, and above all, the regional economy of the Lake Chad basin has been undermined (International Crisis Group, 2017). And the official closure of the Nigerian borders has not helped matters.

Niger

The Niger Republic is drawn into the fray by the fact of a shared border and economic activities in the Lake Chad area. The country is part of the multinational force battling insurgents. The latter's activities have affected the effective control of its territory with a fair share of the IDPs. The Diffa community in its southeastern region is under the orbit of the insurgents who run an effective network of economic activities in ways that delegitimizes the Nigerien authorities. The International Crisis Group (2017: 1) has aptly summarized the plight of the Niger Republic thus:

> The Diffa region is suffering from both Boko Haram attacks and counter-insurgency measures taken by the Nigerien authorities, such as the extension of the state of emergency introduced in February 2015 that includes a ban on some commercial activities. Hundreds of thousands of refugees and internally displaced people only survive thanks to foreign aid. Recourse to local vigilante committees and reprisals by Boko Haram against anyone who

collaborates with the army have created a difficult atmosphere in which local score-settling, collective fear and informants are all ingredients of a dangerously toxic brew.

Nigeria

Since 2009 when the insurgency commenced, the country has been at the receiving end of the activities of the insurgents. Its impact is materially objectified in four key areas, namely, human casualties, food insecurity, capital expenditure, and image problem. The human cost is exceedingly frightening. Relying on data from Yar'Adua Foundation as of 2018, Akubo and Okolo (2018) noted that the group carried out 1,639 violent attacks with 14,436 fatalities, 6,051 injured victims, and 2,063 hostages across the northeast region of Nigeria. Indeed, the insurgents have recently attacked military formations in ways that call into question claims by the military that it was on top of the situation. As a result of a seeming scorched-earth policy of the insurgents, many villages have been destroyed in the northeast of the country with a consequent halt of production activities and related exchange of goods and services.

According to most recent reports, the impact on food production is also grave. About 78,000 farmers in Borno, Katsina, Taraba, Plateau, and other states in the north have abandoned their farmland as a result of attacks by Boko Haram terrorists and other forms of banditry. IDP camps are strewn all over the country and mainly concentrated in Monguno, Damboa, Gwoza, Pulka, Dikwa, and Gambouru, a border community with Cameroon, Bakassi, Gubio, and Dalori in Maiduguri metropolis in the northeast. The total number of farmers from 56,000 displaced Borno households is put at about 1.5 million people, quartered in twenty-four IDP camps. On aggregate, they used to cultivate about 95,000 metric tons of crops yearly, but have lost close to 504,000 metric tons of food since 2015. As a result of the siege, over 70,000 hectares of arable land have been abandoned in the area (Ibirogba 2020). Indeed, much of the displaced population has had to rely on food aids from international agencies (Kah 2017).

Beyond the economic impact, the current activities of the Boko Haram sect are threatening the corporate existence of Nigeria and its sovereignty. As Ovaga (2012: 31) has rightly noted:

The north and south of the country are in disharmony as a result of allegations and counter-allegations against each other. There is [an] established impression in the minds of the majority of the southerners that some northern leaders, disgruntled with the loss of leadership in the past nine years, have decided to precipitate crises using religious and sectarian platforms.

Besides, the crisis paints a picture of a destabilized country that suffers simultaneously negative sovereignty as a swath of its territory is under the control of non-state actors. The Chibok affairs, an incident in which over 276 schoolgirls were abducted by the insurgents in the town of Chibok in Borno in 2014, underlined the degree of the sect's damage to Nigeria.

CONCLUSION: REFLECTIONS ON EXIT STRATEGIES

In the foregoing, I have argued that a combination of the internal and external factors offer insights into the origin of Boko Haram and constitute the sustaining logic. A comprehensive appreciation of the factors could help chart a way out of the conflict. Many analysts, informed observers, and state actors have offered some insights on how to end the terror. While in the United States sometime in the middle of 2011, President Jonathan promised a "stick and carrot approach" to resolving the crisis. In apparent response to the president, the Boko Haram insurgents through an unverified letter written in Hausa and signed by Usman Al-Zawahiri gave conditions for dialogue, which included the prosecution of those implicated in the murder of their leader Sheikh Yusuf, namely, a former Governor of Borno State, Ali Modu Sheriff; the Shehu of Borno, Alhaji Abubakar Ibn Garbai El-Kanemi; former Minister of Police Affairs Ibrahim Yakubu Lame; former Borno State Commissioner of Police and Director of the State Security Service (SSS), and operatives of the *Operation Flush Joint Task Force* (JTF) based on sharia legal code. The leader of the Northern Civil Society Coalition, seems to affirm the predilection of the insurgents to dialogue. According to him:

> Boko Haram has agreed to a term of ceasefire, has agreed to dialogue, but has consistently been undermined by elements within the government who either choose to do so on the grounds that they believe the use of force can end the group or are sabotaging dialogue because they believe they are profiting from the system as it is. "Before now, I used to think that Boko Haram was completely opposed to peace or ceasefire, but in the few occasions that I have been involved in seeking a way out of this problem, I have seen that much of the sabotage came from the side of the government. (The Nation, 2012:1)

Similarly, a former Chairman of the EFCC, Mallam Nuhu Ribadu, recommended amnesty for the insurgents to avert a civil war. His view found support in the then Catholic Archbishop of Abuja Diocese, John Cardinal Onaiyekan, and the Sultan of Sokoto Caliphate, Alhaji Abubakar Sa'ad III. Onaiyekan in a detailed Easter message titled "God's Mercy and Human Pardon" called for amnesty based on the pricinple of forgiveness, which are repentance, making amends, and admitting guilt for killings. On his part, the sultan stressed the point that "government does well to reach out to all political forces and currents, so that the nation can be on the same political page and jointly address this common menace, which terrorism is" (Agba 2013:1).

Others have called for a sociological approach to dealing with crisis. According to one colleague:

> We will continue to stumble from disaster to disaster in the North East (and Nigeria in general) until there is a clear understanding of the nature of the BH grievance, and respect for the tenacity of those who are engaged in the insurgency - even if we disagree with their methods. In my view we are dealing with a complex mix of ethnic, religious and cultural dynamics. As far as BH proper is concerned (not the copy cats), it will mean beginning to think like an aggrieved Kanuri person, understanding the history and culture of that part of the country - in addition to an appreciation for the sense among many Kanuri that they were the first converts to Islam in what is now Nigeria, many centuries before the Fulani and the rest. You cannot fight someone if you do not know how he/she thinks. (Personal communication, 2012)

Chief Albert K. Horsfall, a former Director-General of the State Security Service (SSS), stressed the point that Boko Haram had sponsors who should be identified to initiate a dialogue (Hayford 2013). While these peace formulae appeared plausible, it is hard to understand how it will succeed without the collaboration of the external actors whose interests are antithetical to that of Nigerians. Perhaps, they need to be convinced on the point that instrumentalizing disorder for economic exploitation and global Islam is counterproductive to global peace in the long run.

Much earlier in 2012, twenty-one American scholars—A. Carl LeVan, Peter M. Lewis Jean Herskovits Daniel J. Smith, Adrienne LeBas, R. Kiki Edozie, Brandon Kendhammer, Susan Shepler, and John Campbell, and David Dwyer among others—opposed the designation of Boko Haram as a terrorist organization. They had argued in their letter to U.S. Secretary Hillary Rodham Clinton dated May 21, 2012, that

> As scholars with a special interest in Nigeria and broad expertise on African politics, we are writing to urge that you not designate Boko Haram a Foreign Terrorist Organization (FTO). We are acutely aware of the horrific violence perpetrated by Boko Haram, including attacks on both Muslims and Christians in Nigeria, whether government officials or civilian targets. We share your concerns about the impact of extremist violence on Nigeria's democratic progress and security in general. However an FTO designation would internationalize Boko Haram, legitimize abuses by Nigeria's security services, limit the State

Department's latitude in shaping a long term strategy, and undermine the U.S. Government's ability to receive effective independent analysis from the region.

On their part, the Israeli were disposed to assist Nigeria with their expertise in preventing terrorism. According to the Deputy Head of Mission of the Israeli Embassy in Nigeria, George Deek,

> We are willing to help Nigeria fish out and expose the aliens who are perpetrators of the heinous and inhuman acts of terrorism and the technical knowledge of how to prevent suicide bombing is intelligence because without intelligence you cannot prevent and pre-empt a suicide bomber. . . . The government and the people should exercise a very strong policy to prevent and pre-empt such occurrences with an iron face by not allowing terrorist determine its way of life. (Channels Television 2012)

In the Nigerian street language, otherwise called Pidgin English, there is an aphorism that runs thus: *Wetin you dey fain for Sokoto, dey for inside Sokoto.* Translated, it means: the solution to a problem is not elusive but within reach. Deducible from the preceding sections is that a "carrot and stick approach" is realistic. It would require political will on the part of the Nigerian leadership to confront the problem head-on. The Nigerian government must identify the sponsors and engage with them. As I have shown in the foregoing, they exist locally and internationally. Too, the Nigerian military has not demonstrated any battlefield superiority over ragtag insurgents; it is wedded to outdated European battle doctrine, poorly trained, and racked by corruption and ethnicization (Barlow, 2016: 18). Such an army cannot defend the territorial integrity of any country. Therefore, the military needs complete reorganization institutionally and philosophically to be on top of the situation and win the peace.

REFERENCES

Agba, George. 2013. "Boko Haram: Onaiyekan Backs Sultan Over Amnesty for Sect." April 3. https://allafrica.com/stories/201304030314.html. *Leadership* (Abuja). Accessed July 26, 2020.

Akhaine, Sylvester Odion. 2018. "Churg Strauss Syndrome, Death and the Politics of Succession in Nigeria." *Unilag Journal of Politics* 1 &2 (1): 193–214.

Akubo, Aduku A., and Benjamin Ikani Okolo. 2019. "Boko Haram Insurgency in Nigeria." *African Journal on Conflict Resolution* 19 (2): 1–17.

Aljazeera. 2020. "Chadian troops 'Kill 1,000 Boko Haram Fighters' in Lake." *Aljazeera.* April 9. https://www.aljazeera.com/news/2020/04/chadian-troops-kill

-1000-boko-haram-fighters-lake-chad-200409183528130.html. Accessed: July 26, 2020.

Barlow, Eeben. 2016. "The Rise and Fall—and Rise Again of Boko Haram." *Harvard International Review* 37(4): 16–20.

Campbell, Horace. 2024. "The Menace of Boko Haram and Fundamentalism in Nigeria." *Pambazuka*, June 4. https://www.pambazuka.org/governance/menace -boko-haram-and-fundamentalism-. Accessed June 24, 2020.

Cable. 2019. "Ex-President of Benin Rep Accuses Saudi Arabia of Funding Boko Haram." October 2. www.thecable/ng. Accessed October 1, 2021.

Channels Television. 2012. "Israel to Help Nigeria Tackle Terrorism." *Channels Television.* https://www.channelstv.com/2012/01/20/israel-to-help-nigeria-tackle -terrorism/. Accessed July 26, 2020.

Clapham, Christopher. 1996. *Africa and the International System.* Cambridge: Cambridge University Press.

Daniel, Soni. 2014. "Boko Haram Negotiator Explodes Again: How Shekau went wild, started beheading victims." *Vanguard* (Lagos). September 7, 1 and 5.

Dorrie, Peter. 2014. "A Billion Dollars Won't Help Nigeria Beat Boko Haram." https: //medium.com/war-is-boring/a-billion-dollars-wont-help-nigeria-beat-boko-haram -46b865e0e598. *Medium.com.* Accessed July 25, 2020.

Dorrie, Peter. 2014. "Nigerian Army Kills Boko Haram Leader Rounds Up Hundreds of Fighters." https://medium.com/war-is-boring/nigerian-army-kills-boko-haram -leader-rounds-up-hundreds-of-fighters-dfb58579fae7. *Medium.com*, September 5. Accessed July 25, 2020.

Foyou, Viviane E., Peter Ngwafu, Maribel Santoyo, and Andrea Ortiz. 2018. "The Boko Haram Insurgency and Its Impact on Border Security, Trade and Economic Collaboration Between Nigeria and Cameroon: An Exploratory Study." *African Social Science Review* 9(1): 66–77.

Gurr, Ted Robert. 1970. *Why Men Rebel.* Princeton: Princeton University Press.

Hayford, Lawson. 2012. "Boko Haram: Internal, Not International Threat—Horsfall." https://www.nigeriaa2z.com/2012/06/27/boko-haram-internal-not-international -threat-horsfall/. NigeriaA2Z. June 27. Accessed: 25 July 25, 2020.

Ibirogba, Femi, Njadvara Musa, Charles Akpeji, Danjuma Michael, and Isa Abdulsalami Ahovi. 2020. "78, 120 Farmers Abandon Food Production in Borno, Taraba, Others." *The Guardian.* August 24, 1.

International Crisis Group. 2016. "Q&A: Boko Haram in Cameroon." <https: //www.crisisgroup.org/africa/central-africa/cameroon/q-boko-haram-cameroon >Interview / Africa, April 6. Accessed August 28, 2020.

International Crisis Group. 2017. "Fighting Boko Haram in Chad: Beyond Military Measures." https://www.crisisgroup.org/africa/central-africa/chad/246-fighting -boko-haram-chad-beyond-military-measures. Report 246 / The Boko Haram Insurgency March 8. Accessed August 28, 2020.

International Crisis Group. 2017. "Niger and Boko Haram: Beyond Counter-insurgency." https://www.crisisgroup.org/africa/west-africa/niger/245-niger-and -boko-haram-beyond-counter-insurgency. February 27, Report 245 / Africa. Accessed August 28, 2020.

Kah, Henry Kam. 2017. "Boko Haram is Losing, But so is Food Production": Conflict and Food Insecurity in Nigeria and Cameroon." *Africa Development* 42 (3): 177–96.

Keenan, Jeremy. 2010. "How Washington Helped Foster the Islamist Uprising in Mali." *New Internationalist.* December 1. https://newint.org/features/2012/12/01/us-terrorism-sahara. Accessed January 18, 2021.

Kola, Olarewaju. 2020. "Nigeria: 19 Soldiers Feared Killed in Terrorist Ambush." July 8. https://www.aa.com.tr/en/africa/nigeria-19-soldiers-feared-killed-in-terrorist-ambush/1904068. Accessed July 25, 2020.

Madunagu, Edwin. 2011. "Reflections on Nigerian Terrorism." *The Constitution*, 11 (4): 1–16.

Mendy, Toney. F. 2019."Nigerians Protest Against France, Accuse Macron of Sponsoring Boko Haram Terrorist Group." *Eye Gambia*, December13..https://eyegambia.org/nigerians-protest-against-france-accuse-macron-of-sponsoring-boko-haram-terrorist-group/. Accessed July 24, 2020.

The Nation. 2012. "I Know Who Can End Boko Haram Menace, Says Sani." *The Nation* (Lagos) July. https://www.nairaland.com/983906/shehu-sani-know-end-boko/4accessed. Accessed June 14, 2020.

Opoku, Maxwell Pepreh, Bernard Nsaidzedze Sakah and Beatrice Atim Alupo. 2017. "The Impact of Boko Haram Threat on Economic Activities in Cameroon: Perceptions of People in Yaoundé." *Behavioral Sciences of Terrorism and Political Aggression*. 9 (3): 222–37.

Ovaga, Okey H. 2012. "The Socio-Economic Implications of Book-Haram Activities in Northern Nigeria." *Review of Public Administration & Management* 1(2): 19–37.

Premium Times. 2020."Buhari Condemns Boko Haram Attack on UN Helicopter in Borno." *Premium Times*. July 5. https://www.premiumtimesng.com/news/headlines/401309-buhari-condemns-boko-haram-attack-on-un-helicopter-in-borno.html. Accessed July 25, 2020.

Sani, Shehu. 2011. "Boko Haram: History, Ideas and Revolt." *The Constitution* 11 (4): 17–41.

Sunday, Nwafor. 2019. "Busted: Saudi Arabia, Qatar Allegedly Funding Boko Haram Terrorist Organization—Soglo" https://www.vanguardngr.com/2019/10/busted-saudi-arabia-qatar-funding-boko-haram-terrorist-organization/.*Vanguard.* October 3. Accessed July 25, 2020.

Okeregbe, Tony. 2020. "Arikana Chihombori-Quao: A Profile in Courage." *The Guardian* (Lagos) January 1. https://guardian.ng/news/arikana-chihombori-quao-a-profile-in-courage/. Accessed July 24, 2020.

Taylor, Ian. 2010. *International Relations of Sub-Saharan Africa*. New York and London: Continuum.

Toyo, Eskor. 2011. "Boko Haram and Western Education: A Comment." *The Constitution* 11(4): 42–57.

Umoru, Henry. 2020. "Boko Haram Now an Industry, Says Senate President." *Vanguard* (Lagos) June 1. https://www.vanguardngr.com/2020/06/boko-haram-has-now-become-an-industry-says-lawan/. Accessed July 26, 2020.

UNODC. ND. "Nigeria Corruption Busters." https://www.unodc.org/unodc/en/
frontpage/nigerias-corruption-busters.html/. UNDOC. Accessed July 25, 2020.
VOA News. 2020. "1,000 Boko Haram Fighters Killed in Raid, Chad Army Reports."
April 10. https://www.voanews.com/africa/1000-boko-haram-fighters-killed-raid
-chad-army-reports. Accessed July 25, 2020.

Chapter 5

Al-Qaeda

Scoping and Countering Jihadist Nebula in West Africa

Al Chukwuma Okoli

Globally, terrorist organizations thrive on tactical maneuverability, often based on operational opportunism and innovation (Okoli and Azom 2019). Their operational resilience and dynamism largely depend on their ability to adaptively sustain their cause through transnational networks, affiliates, and franchises. Transnational network means the operational syndicates, cells, and circuits of a terrorist organization abroad. Affiliates refer to localized indigenous extremist groups that identify with a mainstream terrorist organization that is based in another country. Franchises are mercenary commercial or criminal holdings that aid the endeavors of an established terrorist organization in any part of the world.

The tendency of mainstream terrorist organizations to spread their tentacles abroad has often coincided with the desire of some local extremist groups to seek international affiliations. Over the years, this has led to the multiplication and expansion of terrorist formations in various parts of the world. Alongside this multiplication comes the splintering of some indigenous extremist movements, thus adding to the evolving apocalyptic dynamics of global terrorism. This trend has complicated national and regional security situations in the affected areas (Blanchard and Cavigelli 2018; Blanchard and Husted 2019).

The growth and spread of jihadist extremism in the contemporary international system are based on asymmetric innovation and opportunistic logic. Both Al-Qaeda and ISIS have been involved in the internationalization of their operations through a variety of stratagems. They enjoy immense ideological association and tactical collaboration with different extremist groups around the world. More important, they have built and sustained a network of transnational alliances with local extremist groups in various localities and regions. The operational and ideological synergies between the mainstream jihadist organizations and their international cohorts and proxies, and the contingent asymmetric adaptations of the jihadist groups along the way, have presented a complex challenge here referred to as "jihadist nebula" (see Tables 5.2 & 5.3).

This chapter engages the phenomenon of jihadist nebula from the standpoint of the activities of Al-Qaeda in West Africa. The purpose of the chapter is to generate theoretical and practical insights relevant to understanding and countering the threat posed by Al-Qaeda's nebulous expressions and manifestations in the subregion. A discourse on jihadist nebula in West Africa is significant because of its potential to contribute to filling an apparent epistemic gap in the literature. Hitherto, academic and policy discourses on jihadist extremism in Africa have focused rather disproportionately on varying aspects of its origins, nature, contexts, drivers, funding, consequences, and mitigation (International Crisis Group 2017; Okoli 2017; Onuoha and George 2015). The present discourse takes a departure from the extant knowledge by exploring the sundry adaptational dynamics of jihadist extremism in West Africa in the context of the contemporary dialectics of local and international counterterrorism crusades. The purpose of the chapter would be justified if its outcome succeeds in engendering a corpus of knowledge capable of edifying existing scholarly and policy endeavors that counter the phenomenon of jihadist extremism in Africa and beyond.

The remainder of this chapter is structured around different themes; it starts with providing background issues, the conceptualization of terms, the contextualization of the focal setting, and the theoretical framework. This is followed by a brief exploration of relevant literature on the phenomenon of the jihadist nebula. A discussion on the counters and dynamics of the Al-Qaeda nebula in West Africa is presented, followed by a discussion on countering jihadist nebula in West Africa and then the conclusion.

THE FOCAL AREA: WEST AFRICA

West Africa is the locus of the discourse in this chapter. This refers to the westernmost region of Africa. The region comprises the sixteen countries of Benin, Burkina Faso, Cape Verde, The Gambia, Ghana, Guinea, Guinea-Bissau, Ivory Coast, Liberia, Mali, Mauritania, the Niger, Nigeria,

Senegal, Sierra Leone, and Togo, as well as the United Kingdom Overseas Territory of Saint Helena, Ascension, and Tristan da Cunha. The population of West Africa is estimated at 362 million people as of 2016, and at 381,981,000 as of 2017, of which 189,672,000 are female and 192,309,000 are male (Baten 2017).

Within the wider ambit of West Africa, the focus is on the manifestations of jihadist extremism in two important subregional axes: the Sahel and the Lake Chad Basin. The Sahelian axis consists of Mali, Burkina Faso, Niger, and Chad, while the Lake Chad Basin is made up of Nigeria, Cameroon, Niger, and Chad. The Sahel lies between North and sub-Saharan Africa, creating an expansive strip between Mauritania and Chad (Cherbib 2018; Gaye 2018). The Sahel-Sub-Sahara strip bears some significant geopolitical peculiarities, one of which being a critical hotbed of jihadist extremism in Africa. It is also the epicenter of the terror-organized crime convolution in the continent (UNODC 2013). As Gaye (2018: 7) succinctly captures it:

> Due to its geographic position, the Sahel has been and remains a hub of transit and trade between North Africa and Sub-Saharan Africa. Several communities coexist within the Sahel, which has some difficulty controlling their borders. The Sahel also contains vast areas that escape state control entirely. Within these spaces, jihadist groups flourish and multifaceted illicit trafficking rings, with connections to transnational crime in Europe, Asia and Latin America. The Sahel-Sahara continuum is a central hub in the geopolitics of organized crime.

The preferential focus on the Sahel-Sahara axis in the present discourse is predicated on its aforementioned geopolitical attribute, which has made it a veritable destination as well as a route for jihadism and allied organized crimes. It should be noted, however, that the phenomenon of jihadist nebula under consideration in this discourse has not manifested in the same pattern and measure in the focal areas. Hence, the discourse would leverage insights from select countries, namely Mali, Nigeria, and to a lesser extent, Niger, Cameroon, Chad, and Burkina Faso.

CONCEPTUAL CLARIFICATIONS

Seven key terms form the conceptual frame of this chapter, namely: Al-Qaeda, AQIM, Boko Haram, extremism, jihadism, jihadist nebula, and terrorism. This section considers these terms to situate their contextual meanings within the purview of the present chapter (see Table 5.1).

Table 5.1. Contextualization of Basic Terms

Term	Conceptualization
Al-Qaeda	"Founded in Afghanistan in 1988, Al-Qaeda ('the Base,' in Arabic) is a global jihadi enterprise composed of two major components: a 'core' (sometimes referred to as 'Al-Qaeda Central') and five major regional affiliates or 'franchises.' Al-Qaeda affiliates, as defined by one leading authority on terrorism, are 'those groups that have taken the Al-Qaeda name and/or whose leaders have sworn loyalty to the Al-Qaeda core leader who, in turn, has acknowledged that oath. Al-Qaeda militants dream of establishing a new Islamic state, modeled on the medieval caliphate. The restored caliphate would be ruled under sharia law and would include all current and former Muslim lands stretching from Southeast Asia to Western Europe. Ultimately, the caliphate would serve as a platform from which the entire world would be brought to Islam" (Rosenau and Powell, 2017: 3–5).
AQIM	"Al-Qaeda in the Islamic Maghreb (AQIM) is the leading transnational jihadist group in West Africa. Paradoxically, even as it has sown chaos by filtering into the uncontrolled spaces of north-eastern Mali and the Sahara, its leadership—based in Algeria's Kabylia region and reporting directly to the al-Qaeda high command in Afghanistan-Pakistan—has often proven weak and divided. Scraps of information that have emerged into the public domain show a weak organization beset by internal rivalries and largely unable to control its most effective battle commander, Mokhtar Belmokhtar. AQIM has planted itself in north-eastern Algeria while operating in neighboring countries, particularly Mauritania and Mali. It emerged out of the Salafist Group for Preaching and Combat (GSPC), itself a faction of the Armed Islamic Group (GIA), which was the most active terrorist group in Algeria's Islamist insurgency of the 1990s. Formed in 1998 and led by veterans of the war in Afghanistan, the GSPC gained its al-Qaeda affiliate status in 2006 and changed its name a year later to AQIM'"(MacIver, 2017: 8).
Boko Haram	"Boko Haram emerged in the early 2000s as a small Sunni Islamic sect in Nigeria advocating a strict interpretation and implementation of Islamic law and has evolved since 2009 to become one of the world's deadliest terrorist groups. The nickname *Boko Haram* was given by local communities to describe the group's narrative that Western education and culture are corrupting influences and *haram* ('forbidden'). The group called itself *Jama'a Ahl as-Sunna Li-da'wa waal Jihad* (roughly translated from Arabic as 'People Committed to the Propagation of the Prophet's Teachings and Jihad'). In 2015, its leadership pledged allegiance to the Islamic State (IS, aka ISIS/ISIL), and renamed itself the Islamic State's West Africa Province (aka ISWAP). The group, still widely referred to as Boko Haram, subsequently split into two factions" (Blanchard and Cavigelli, 2018: 1).
Extremism	"Extremism can be used to refer to political ideologies that oppose a society's core values and principles. In the context of liberal democracies, this could be applied to any ideology that advocates racial or religious supremacy and/or opposes the core principles of democracy

and universal human rights. The term can also be used to describe the methods through which political actors attempt to realize their aims, that is, by using means that 'show disregard for the life, liberty, and human rights of others" (Neuman, 2010: 12).

Jihadist nebula — Jihadist nebula refers to the tendency of jihadist movements or organizations to assume new and often nebulous forms and dimensions over time. It refers to the existential dynamics of a jihadi group in the course of its asymmetric evolution. The process is one of a dynamic transformation instantiated by a sort of "organizational learning, structural adaptation, and strategic maturation" (Lister, 2016: 7). Jihadist nebula manifests at the organizational, ideological, and operational levels of a jihadist movement.

Jihadism — "Jihadism is a discrete subset of Sunni Islamism with a unique approach to religion and politics. Indeed, jihadi identity is defined in opposition to the mainstream Islamism of the Muslim Brotherhood and AKP. The jihadis consider these groups deeply flawed in creed and methodology, too tolerant of 'wayward' Muslims such as Sufis, Shia, and autocratic rulers deemed heretics, and too willing to work within the structures of the state to achieve their aims. Against these flaws, the jihadis set their approach: a strict monotheism (tawhid) that brooks no deviation from a rigid theology and an unswerving commitment to armed struggle, or jihad, against the state and all they deem to be unbelievers. It is this 'rejectionism' that is their hallmark, framed around the creed of monotheism and the methodology of jihad" (Bunzel, 2017: 6).

Terrorism — "Although the term is not subject to a universally agreed definition, terrorism can be broadly understood as a method of coercion that utilizes or threatens to utilize violence to spread fear and thereby attain political or ideological goals. Contemporary terrorist violence is thus distinguished in law from 'ordinary' violence by the classic terrorist 'triangle': A attacks B, to convince or coerce C to change its position regarding some action or policy desired by A. The attack spreads fear as the violence is directed, unexpectedly, against innocent victims, which in turn puts pressure on third parties such as governments to change their policy or position. Contemporary terrorists utilize many forms of violence and indiscriminately target civilians, military facilities, and State officials among others" (UNODC, 2018: 1).

Sources: Author compiled with various authorities cited in-text.

THEORETICAL FRAMEWORK: BETWIXT EXISTENTIALISM AND "STATE FAILURE"

Existentialism is a nineteenth-century philosophical worldview that denies the assumption that the universe has any intrinsic meaning and purpose. Specifically, it repudiates "the existence of natural laws, an unchanging human nature, or indeed any objective rules" (McLean and McMillan 2003: 187). Pioneered by Soren Kierkegaard (1813–1855), the theory holds that each individual is cursed with freedom and must take responsibility for their actions and shape their destinies.

Existentialists see a human being as a self-willing agent living in an indifferent and perceptibly hostile environment where they must fend for themself (Okoli and Atelhe 2014). The violent campaigns of the jihadists, in a way, depict their existential struggle in what they perceive as an unfriendly apostate world that must be changed or destroyed. The violent struggle has been accentuated by the contemporary global counterterrorism campaign, which has further prompted the jihadists into more dire vindictive asymmetric violence and criminality.

But the jihadist onslaught is perpetrated within an enabling operational environment characterized, among other things, by "state failure." The notion of "state failure" does not essentially presuppose the absence of structure and authority of the state or the virtual state's collapse (cf. Okoli and Ochim 2016). Rather, it implies that the state in place does not have the requisite capacity to assume proper territorial control because of limited "regulatory capabilities, control and monopoly on legitimate violence" (Gaye 2018: 7). It is in this respect that the foregoing discourse finds David Kilcullen's competitive control theory both useful and plausible. The theory seeks to describe the territorial competition that occurs between the state and non-state groups in "ungoverned spaces" Fischer and Mercado 2014; Kilcullen 2013). It holds that in situations of armed conflict, non-state armed groups and the state are engaged in a contest for control of civil populations. In this context, powerful armed groups invoke support from the populations within their domain of control. As elucidated by Kilcullen (2013: 131), this "implies a competition among several actors who are all trying to control the population in a violent and contested environment."

The actors could be jihadists or organized criminal syndicates. The existence and prevalence of under-governed and ungoverned spaces within the territorial domains of most African states, coupled with the failure of the state to exercise firm coercive and legitimate control, has engendered the rise of non-state forces providing "alternative government," although through subversive means (Williams 2016). Over time, such types of parallel governance are entrenched in the locality, despite the stern disapproval of the central government. Incidentally, and despite the apparent illegitimacy of such governments, some sections of the local population are inclined to identify with them, either under duress or in sheer fatalism. The abusive ties between the jihadists and some tribal populations in the Sahel-Savannah strip demonstrate this arcane reality (Gaye 2018).

The theory of competitive control arose to make up for the inadequacy implicit in the theory of ungoverned spaces, which had assumed that "ungoverned spaces," strictly speaking, are wholly ungoverned. To be sure, territorial spaces assumed to be ungoverned in the "ungoverned spaces" theory are actually governed, albeit by some undesirable non/anti-state elements.

So what is lacking in such spaces is not governance per se, but a legitimate and authoritative central territorial control (Okoli and Ochim 2016). It is this vacuum that is being exploited by the various jihadist groups and their cohorts in Africa to perpetrate their nefarious acts of terrorism and allied organized crimes.

PERSPECTIVES ON JIHADIST NEBULA: EXPLORING RELEVANT LITERATURE

The notion of "jihadist nebula" presupposes the tendency of jihadist movements or organizations to assume new and often nebulous forms over time. It refers to the existential transformations of a jihadi group in the course of its asymmetric evolution. The transformation is a dynamic process instantiated by a sort of an "organizational learning, structural adaptation, and strategic maturation" (Lister 2016: 7). More fundamentally, it depicts a dialectical process characterized by "disintegration, reconfiguration and resilience" (Lounnas 2018: 1).

The phenomenon of the jihadist nebula has been occasioned by several factors relating to "individual zones of jihadist activity" (Lister 2016: 7). Some of these factors are external while others are internal. External factors relate to the developments in the international jihadi environment. Concerning this, Lister (2016: 7) opines of Al-Qaeda's asymmetric transformation thus: "Al Qaeda has evolved considerably over the past fourteen (14) years. Facing intense scrutiny and attack following 9/11, it expanded internationally through acquiring like-minded affiliates." This internationalization of jihadism has been further accentuated by the degrading of terrorists' sanctuaries and strongholds in the Arabian Peninsula as well as the forestallment of ISIS's global Caliphacy project consequent upon the group's sudden defeat in Syria (Wright et al. 2016/2017).

Internal factors relating to jihadist nebula refer to occurrences within the operational domains of specific jihadist organizations. They result from the organizational dynamics of such organizations, often in response to external pressures or critical changes within. This is often instantiated by systematic fragmentation and splintering (BCTR 2013; Perkoski 2015). In this respect, Perkoski (2015: iii) notes that:

> Militant organizations commonly break down and split apart, with new groups emerging from the ranks of existing organizations. From Syria to Iraq to Afghanistan, militant groups have splintered and proliferated in this way, creating fragmented oppositions that significantly complicate the conflict landscape. This process of organizational splintering historically has created some deadliest

and most well known organizations including Al Shabaab, Black September and the Real IRA.

Terrorist organizations the world over thrive on the logic of tactical opportunism and expediency (Okoli and Azom 2019). The jihadist nebula phenomenon depicts this strategic tendency, whereby a jihadist group under pressure or in crisis seeks to reinvent and reassert itself through some asymmetric adaptations. Options in this regard include even the use of hoaxes and subterfuge (cf. Tishler 2018). This tendency has been evidenced in a variety of ways in the various jihadi situations in Africa (cf. Hutte, Steinbery and Weber 2015; Wright et al. 2017).

The activities of Al-Qaeda in Africa and elsewhere in the world since 9/11, have borne fundamental trappings of the jihadist nebula. The post-9/11 global clampdown on Al-Qaeda has engendered and occasioned some decisive asymmetric transformations within the group's core and periphery. Among other things, as Rabassa et al. (2006:xx) argue,

> It (has) created a more disaggregated entity that is more difficult to predict and preempt. The emergence of numerous like-minded local organizations that strike at soft targets with deadly force . . . presents a substantial set of challenges for counter terrorism.

Incidentally, while the nebula phenomenon affords the jihadists the leverage to thrive, it has also posed new and more sapping asymmetric challenges that complicate national, regional, and global counterterrorism endeavors. The worst complication so far in this regard is the articulation of jihadism and criminality: the involvement of some jihadist elements in "the geopolitics of organized crime" (Gaye 2018: 7).

Jihadist nebula is evident in the organizational, ideological, and operational dynamics of terrorist movements. As Busher (2014: 2) notes,

> As is the case within any broadly conceived movement, across the myriad jihadist terrorist groups, there are competing interests, ideas, strategic priorities and tactical tastes. . . . For example, while there may be forms of association and collaboration between groups such as AQIM, Ansar Dine, Movement for Unity and Jihad in West Africa and the Islamic Movement for the Azawad, these groups have articulated different strategic priorities and have adopted subtly different tactical repertoires.

The jihadist nebula schema is an attempt to understand the opportunistic transformation often undergone by jihadist movements in a desperate bid to survive and sustain their operations. It affords analysts an enabling framework to explain and situate the gamut of disparate forms and manifestations an embattled jihadist organization could assume in pursuit of asymmetric advantage. The next section explores this jihadist phenomenon, with particular reference to the situation in West Africa.

SCOPING THE CONTOURS AND DYNAMICS OF AL-QAEDA NEBULA IN WEST AFRICA

Al-Qaeda nebula relates to the emergence of facets or facades of AlQaeda jihadism in new disparate forms. It is all about how the jihadist groups have "skillfully continued to evolve and proliferate" (Wright et al. 2016/2017: 5) in its dynamics of asymmetric transformation (see Tables 5.2 & 5.3). Al-Qaeda nebula in West Africa refers thus to the disparate and often nebulous networks and multifaceted expressions of Al-Qaeda jihadism in the subregion. They tend to assume diverse forms and manifestations over time in keeping with the situations in the local and international jihadi environment. Of this tendency, Rabasa et al. (2006: xxi) state that:

Table 5.2. Jihadist Groups in West Africa

Group	Operational Scope	Affiliation	Remark(s)
Boko Haram	Nigeria, Niger, Cameroon, Chad	Al-Qaeda, ISIS	Currently factionalized
Ansaru	Nigeria, Mali	Al-Qaeda, AQIM	Defunct
Ansaroul Islam	Mali, Burkina Faso	Al-Qaeda, AQIM, Ansaru	
Ansar Dine	Mali, Burkina Faso	Al-Qaeda, AQIM	
Al-Mourabitoun	Mali, Burkina Faso	Al-Qaeda, AQIM	
AQIM	The Sahel and coastal states	Al-Qaeda	
Islamic State in the Greater Sahara (ISGS)	Mali, Niger	ISIS	
Jama'at Nusrat al-Islam wal-Muslimin (JNIM)	Mali	Al-Qaeda, AQIM	
Movement for Unity and Jihad in West Africa (MUJAO)	Mali	Al-Qaeda, AQIM	
Islamic Movement in Nigeria	Nigeria	Shiite sects in Iran	Designated a terrorist group by Nigerian authorities in July 2019
Islamic State West Africa Province (ISWAP)	Northeast Nigeria, Chad	ISIS	

Source: Author's original compilation.

Jihadist groups in this category exhibit a dual nature: They are preoccupied with both local and regional jihads. They thus have a threat potential that goes beyond their immediate tactical environment. The hybrid ideological and operational nature of these organizations stems from their interaction with the international jihadist movement as currently constituted under the existing umbrella of al-Qaeda's global network. The scope and dimensions of the al-Qaeda nebula are both broad and complex. Ties among these groups run the gamut from logistical and financial support to combined operations and joint strategy meetings.

The phenomenon of the Al-Qaeda nebula in West Africa would be best understood against the backdrop of the changing complexion of jihadist extremism in the world since the 9/11 terrorist attacks on the United States. As Wright et al. (2016/2017: 5) posit, "Jihadism has evolved dramatically and traumatically since 9/11 attacks. Movements, leaders, targets, tactics, and operations have all proliferated in ways unimaginable in 2011." Essentializing this post-9/11 development in part is the continued internationalization of jihadist movements. In this context, Busher (2014:1) opines that: "We have seen the incorporation of what were initially national or sub-national terrorist groups into regional and even global networks of terrorists and insurgents and with this an apparent convergence of collective action frames and strategic goals."

But this internationalizing dynamics of jihadism is best conjectured as a strategic adaptation mechanism of the embattled mainstream terrorist groups that are seeking to reinvent and reassert themselves in the face of the post-9/11 global terrorism clampdown. In this situation, Al-Qaeda has sought to expand its operations internationally by "acquiring like-minded affiliates" (Lister 2016: 7) in West Africa and elsewhere. Besides the acquisition of affiliates, the group has explored sundry avenues for "fundraising and money-making" (Forest 2011: 78). This is in addition to its tactical alliances with local tribal, criminal, or insurgent groups (Cherbib 2018). In effect, "AQIM has proven to be a resilient entity, moving fighters across porous desert borders, kidnapping for ransom, mounting destabilizing attacks across a wide field, and adopting a fluid and adaptive political strategy that succeeds by attracting allies with appeals to highly localized grievances" (MacIver 2017: 9).

The dynamics of the Al-Qaeda nebula in West Africa have, over the years, presented a mosaic of jihadist asymmetric adaptations (see Table 3). How have these adaptations been manifested by Al-Qaeda and the universe of jihadi groups that are associated with or inspired by it within the subregion? It is to this important concern that we now turn.

The instrumental synergies between jihadists and local communities are a veritable factor in the Al-Qaeda nebula in West Africa. In effect, as Gaye (2018: 13) notes,

Table 5.3. Asymmetric Adaptations in Al-Qaeda Nebula

Manifestation	Mechanism(s)
Assimilation	Establishing communal ties with tribal and community systems through marriages and surrogacy.
Strategic alignments	Making alliances with local or regional extremist groups; tactical collaborations.
Commodification	Appropriating jihadist violence for fundraising and money-making: kidnapping for ransom, cattle rustling, smuggling, trafficking, etc.
Fragmentation	Splintering, fractionalization, or disintegration into subgroups.
Operational opportunism	The exploitation of domestic grievances and ethnic-religion-communal fault lines.
Territorial quest	Annexing, controlling, and even 'ruling' territories within a state.
Mutative translocation	Shifting operational and occupational bases from the mainland to frontiers to forests.

Source: Author's original compilation.

[A] number of Algerian AQIM leaders, such as Mokhtar Belmokhtar, have married into the Arab or Tuarey communities of northern Mali. He married a Malian woman from the Berabiche ethnic group. These matrimonial ties have helped strengthen the local anchoring of organized crime and terrorism in the Sahel. Through these marriages, alliances have been woven between jihadist leaders and tribal leaders, facilitating transactions in the community areas.

Assimilations by marriage are consolidated by strategic alliances with local or regional extremist groups in such a manner as to obfuscate the jihadist scenario in the subregion. For instance, AQIM worked with local groups, namely Ansar al-Din (AAD) and Movement for Oneness and Jihad in West Africa (MUJAO) to establish an Islamic Emirate in northern Mali in 2012/2013, in the immediate aftermath of the Tuareg's revolution (Belde 2018). As such, just like the typical situation in the Middle East, "The jihadist scene in the region is not dominated by a single large organization, but instead by changing alliances between numerous smaller groups" (Hutter, Steinberg, and Weber 2015: 69).

From the illustrative standpoint of Boko Haram, it is apparent that jihadist extremism in West Africa is thriving on the strategy of asymmetric mutations and alignments. Boko Haram has undergone many organizational transformations over the years. In 2012, the group witnessed a major splintering with the emergence of Ansaru. This was a result of disagreements over the operational tactics of mainstream Boko Haram. Leaders of Ansaru accused Boko Harm of orchestrating and condoning mass atrocities against Muslims and vulnerable civilians based on their indiscriminate strikes on soft targets. The group maintained close links with AQIM and Al-Qaeda, from which it derived its logistic and operational support (Guitta and Simcox 2014).

Ansaru went underground in 2016, following the capture of its leader by Nigerian forces in Lokoja, North-central Nigeria. It, however, started regrouping in 2019. It is believed that most of the Ansaru leaders and fighters have defected back to the Boko Haram fold during its organizational debacle. Besides Ansaru, Boko Haram again underwent another splintering in 2016, with the emergence of a faction named the Islamic State West Africa Province (ISWAP) within its fold. ISWAP currently operates in the wider Lake Chad Basin, with its base in Northeast Nigeria and Chad. Suffice it to note, however, that Boko Haram's destiny as an insurgent/terrorist group has largely been sustained by material and tactical support from Al-Qaeda. As Cummings (2017: 28) brilliantly avers, "Throughout Boko Haram's many transitional phases, al Qaeda has been in the foreground, assuming the purported roles of financier, interlocutor, and even divider of Nigerian jihadi groups as illustrated by the origin of Ansaru."

In addition to its diverse traversing synergies and alliances, Al-Qaeda jihadism in West Africa has been increasingly commodified. The commodification is in the fashion of "fundraising and money-making schemes" (Forest, 2011: 78). There is a bourgeoning underworld political economy that underpins jihadist extremism in the subregion. This embodies an assemblage of economic interests, actors, networks, and exchanges that oil the jihadist venture, providing it with requisite material sustenance and vitality. Jihadists work with a variety of commissioned agents, intermediaries, facilitators, and mercenaries, as well as local collaborators in their operational domains to foster a sort of economic relations (Gaye 2018). The imperative of survival has driven some jihadist groups in the subregion into a variety of criminal commercial franchises, including smuggling of counterfeit goods, human trafficking, drugs trafficking, arms trafficking, cattle rustling, illicit mining and lumbering, kidnapping for ransom, and the like (Gaye, 2018; Krech, 2011). Nigerian authorities, for instance, have fingered rural banditry and illicit mining as an enabling catalyst of insurgency in the country's Northeast (Okoli and Ogayi, 2018; Okoli and Lenshie, 2018). In August 2011, AQIM in Mali and Niger engaged in military confrontation "over the distribution of the profits made from drug trafficking" (Krech, 2011: 127).

The involvement of Al-Qaeda elements in organized crimes highlights the organization's inclination to operational opportunism. This is the tendency of the group to engage in extra-combat activities such as criminal, commercial, and allied operations (cf., Kamolnick, 2017). For instance, Gayes (2018: 16) asserts that,

Boko Haram works in connection and collaboration with criminal groups to control whole trafficking areas around the Lake Chad Basin through community support. Although it has been weakened somewhat, the movement still controls significant proportion of the routes travelled by heroine from Asia and used for trafficking of SALWs from Libya.

The ambience of transnational organized crime in the Lake Chad Basin has been bourgeoning. Jihadists allied to Boko Haram and Ansaru have infiltrated the theater of rural banditry and violence in the region. They have variously acted as mercenary assailants in the ongoing farmer-herder conflicts in the region. They have also featured as adversaries in the scourge of herdsmen militancy in Cameroon and Nigeria. Most importantly, they have been implicated in the menace of opportunistic rural banditry in northern Nigeria. In this context, they have been involved in the escapades of cattle rustling, kidnapping for ransom, highway robbery, and village raids (Okoli and Ogayi 2018). The incidence of rural banditry and violence in and around the Lake Chad Basin is essentially symptomatic of the prevalence of acute governance deficits in the affected states.

The territorial quest of Al-Qaeda jihadists in West Africa has led them into annexing and holding swaths of territory on the fringes and frontiers of their strongholds. The establishment of the Islamic Emirates of Northern Mali in 2012 by jihadists allied to AQIM is a case in point. Another relevant instance is the declaration of the Islamic Caliphate of Nigeria by Boko Haram insurgents (Belde, 2018). Although these projects were ultimately short-lived, the underlying quest underscores one of the most strategically ambitious but dicey agendas of the sect in its asymmetric transformation.

The dynamics of the Al-Qaeda nebula in West Africa have also thrown up the groups' tendency to fragmentation through splintering and fractionalization. The process has often come with ideological realignments whereby splintering bodies would switch alliances from one mainstream jihadist formation abroad to another. A veritable case in point is the emergence of Ansaru from the ranks of Boko Haram as well as Boko Haram's later defection from Al-Qaeda to ISIS (Guitta and Simcox 2014). Akin to the issue of organizational fragmentation is the one of mutative translocation. This refers to the shifting of the organizational or operational base of an Al-Qaeda affiliate from the mainland to the frontiers and from the frontiers to the forests. Ansaru Islam has been involved in predatory hit-and-run camping and attacks along the frontiers of Southern Mali-Burkina Faso-Côte d'Ivoire (Nseibia and Weiss 2018). The Boko Haram sect has also been at home with this tactical option of late. Capitalizing on a such pattern of operational pragmatism, the jihadists have remained diehard in the Sahel. They have survived various counterterrorism assaults in the region, apparently through their adaptive mutative translocation and dispersal. This trend is captured by an analyst thus:

> In the Sahel, they have proved to be extremely resilient. In spite of international and regional cooperation to fight jihadi organizations, and despite the French-led military Operation Serval and then Operation Barkhane, these groups have not only been able to absorb heavy losses both material and in terms of fighters but, worse, to strengthen themselves. Indeed, while jihadi violence was more or less limited to Northern Mali and the immediate border region of Niger in 2013—when the French launched Serval—the jihadists have now been striking in all the Sahel countries and in those never touched by jihadi violence before, such as Burkina Faso or Ivory Coast. (Luannas 2018: 11)

This pattern of survivalist adaptation has also been witnessed in the Lake Chad Basin. Under the pressure of the Multinational Joint Task Force (MNTJF), jihadist operations in the area have widened the scope of their operations by way of hit-and-run attacks in Cameroon, Niger, and Chad.

The contemporary trajectory of jihadism in West Africa has equally shown some traits of neo-sectarian extremism. In addition to the notable jihadist groups mentioned in the foregoing, there are emerging jihadi sects operating within the subregion. A case in point is the Islamic Movement in Nigeria (IMN). IMN is a Shiite-based sect based in northern Nigeria. It has been engaged in a series of confrontations with the Nigerian state owing to its extremist conduct, including blocking highways in the guise of a religious procession, attacking military and police personnel, and molesting the public (Anjide and Okoli 2016). In 2015, the sect assaulted a convoy of an army chief in the northern city of Zaria, triggering a massive retaliation by the state forces. Since then, the sect has remained embattled, with its leader Sheik El-Zazakky incarcerated by the federal government over charges amounting to treason and terrorism. In July 2019, the sect was proscribed and designated a terrorist group, following its renewed violent disturbances across some northern states, including Abuja.

Generally, jihadist extremists in West Africa have thrived based largely on their tactical opportunism. They have remained resilient owing to their "implanting and exploiting of local disorders in rural marginalized areas" (Cherbib 2018: 260). The most potent of the disorders in this regard are situations of crisis and/or instability. On this, the International Crisis Group (2016: 8) notes:

> Overall, therefore, jihadists' growing prominence over the past few years is more the product of instability than its primary driver. Movements have gathered force as crises deepen and violence escalates. In some cases, particularly Boko Haram's extremists have helped provoke the conflict they fight in.

The tactical opportunism of jihadists in West Africa is worth further exploration. This has ranged from exploiting existing conflict and identity fault lines to the deployment of women and children for combatant and allied operations. It is also evidenced in the indiscriminate civilian attacks, including Muslims in prayer sessions. The hijacking of the Tuareg's revolution in Northern Mali by jihadists in 2012 is a classic demonstration of this tactical approach. The jihadist infiltration and exploitation of the prevailing farmer-herder and banditry crises in Nigeria, but also elsewhere in West Africa, depicts the same reality. One of the most damming instances of this tactical opportunism is jihadists' instrumentalization of petty and organized crime in pursuit of the "jihadist cause."

Related to the question of instability are issues of socioeconomic malaise, state repression, and political exclusion. As correctly observed by the International Crisis Group (2016: ii), the Boko Haram insurgency is "rooted in the marginalized political economy of the structural violence of Northern Nigeria." These structural factors interact and intersect with a variety of other socio-contextual variables (see Table 5.4) to drive, catalyze, and complicate jihadist extremism as exemplified in the Al-Qaeda nebula in West Africa.

Of all the structural drivers of jihadist extremism in West Africa, the most salient and fundamental have been the complications arising from the state's functional ineptitude. Most of the Sahelian states are poor and fragile. Their fragility is a function as well as the effect of both underdevelopment and insecurity. It is also a product of vulnerabilities arising from the poorly regulated

Table 5.4. Contours of Jihadist Nebula in West Africa

Factor	Indicator(s)
Structural drivers	State fragility
	Weak political economy
	Livelihood crisis
	Social divisions
Prime actors	Jihadist groups and their networks
	Organized criminal syndicates
	National and foreign governments
	Interventionist domestic and foreign organizations
	Local tribal authorities and communities.
Critical catalysts	Armed conflict
	Transnational crime
	Religious/sectarian extremism
	State repression
Situational dynamics	Counterinsurgency drive
	Radical proselytism
	Insurgency-crime alignment
	Extremists' opportunism

Source: Author's original compilation

vast landmass, forestlands, and porous borders (Gaye 2018). This situation is also to a reasonable extent true of the coastal states within the subregion. The gross governance deficits in most states in the area, exemplified in swaths of "ungoverned" or "ungovernable" spaces, have provided an enabling pretext for criminal franchise and impunity, encouraging organized transnational criminal networks to have a field day (Okoli and Lenshie 2018). The crime-terror nexus in these states has been one of the most critical contextual force multipliers of extremist violence in the subregion.

COUNTERING JIHADIST NEBULA IN WEST AFRICA

Jihadism is transnational violence; so also are other organized crimes allied to or associated with it. As transnational phenomenon jihadism requires an equally transnational mitigation strategy. Events in West Africa have demonstrated the futility of national and interventionist efforts at counterterrorism. This has recommended an institutionalized transnational approach to the problem. So far, most West African states have shown commitment to counterterrorism by adopting laws aimed at combating violent extremism. They have also collaborated with various international organizations in implementing the "multiple Sahel strategies": the United Nations Integrated Strategy for the Sahel, the European Union Strategy for the Security and Development in the Sahel, the ECOWAS Sahel Strategy, etc. (Gaye 2018: 26).

In terms of military operations, there have been national and subregional interventions in the affected areas. In the Lake Chad axis, the repeated failures of the respective states in finding a lasting solution to the Boko Haram insurgency necessitated the formation of the Multinational Joint Task Force (MNJTF). The MNJTF option appears to have been replicated in the Sahel with the creation of the G5 Sahel (Gaye 2018). Both MNJTF and G5 Sahel have made some significant progress in degrading the operational strengths of jihadists in their respective jurisdictions. Nonetheless, their successes have also been associated with unanticipated and untoward outcomes. For example, the military campaigns of the MNJTF have pushed jihadists out of the front lines in northern north East Nigeria to new theaters in the frontiers of Chad, Cameroon, and Niger. This is also true in the Sahel, where the activities of G5 Sahel have contributed to dispersing jihadist cells and circuits into Burkina Faso and Côte d'Ivoire. This is not to say, however, that the operations of such subregional strike forces have been wholly futile or counterproductive. Perhaps what is needed is a pragmatic re-strategization of the extant mechanisms to match the emerging terror/counterterror asymmetries.

By and large, national efforts at combating jihadist terrorism in West Africa have, at best, been precarious. Even when complemented by foreign intervention, as in the case of Mali, the result has not been a resounding suc-cess. The major challenge in this regard has been barriers arising from ter-ritoriality as well as a lack of synergy among extant national strategies. The learned experience of MNJTF and G5 Sahel has indicated that the prospect of effective and sustainable counter-jihadism in West Africa lies with a transna-tional mechanism capable of transcending territorial barriers while leveraging multilateral synergies.

It is in light of the foregoing that this chapter makes a case for a wider trans-regional counterterrorism strategy whereby countries within the Western Sahel and Lake Chad axis would synergize efforts in countering the jihadist menace in the region. This presupposes a functionalist collective security mechanism that prioritizes strategic collaboration in the spheres of intelligence, logistics, tactics, personnel, and shared mandate. The mandate of the collaboration should encompass both military and nonmilitary dimen-sions of the counterterrorism agenda: eliminating the jihadi fighters, dislodg-ing their transnational networks, de-radicalizing and demobilizing extremists, and subverting the syndicates of criminal/communal franchises allied to their operations.

The framework being advocated must take the crime-terror nexus seriously. In this regard, there must be a concerted effort at mitigating the incidence and prevalence of organized crimes in the subregion. Transnational crimes, such as cattle rustling, kidnapping, human trafficking, drug trafficking, arms traf-ficking, and smuggling, have been variously implicated in the convolution of a jihadist uprising in West Africa (Belde 2018; Bushar 2014; Zimmerer 2019). Apart from boosting the operational resilience of extremist groups, transnational organized crimes further aggravate the vulnerability of the state and civil population in situations of armed violence. Hence, any meaningful endeavor at countering jihadism in West Africa must recognize and prioritize the associated criminal complications. The same degree of priority should be accorded soft counterterror drives, such as de-radicalization and demobiliza-tion (cf. Borum 2011).

Furthermore, there is a need to creatively address domestic fault lines, including local grievances, socioeconomic vulnerabilities, socioreligious divisions, and political repression (Lister 2016). Such fault lines provide extremists with an enabling pretext to revolt. As Lister (2016: 30) observes, jihadists often "exploit domestic anger, frustration, and disfranchisement by offering to punish authorities to replace their systems of control." Exploitable domestic fault lines are rife in most countries of West Africa. Managing these fault lines through good, inclusive governance is, therefore, a desideratum in the fight against jihadism in the subregion.

Essentially, combating jihadist extremism in West Africa requires a proactive strategy that embodies strategic domestic intelligence, counter-radicalization, and sustainable peace-building. This is against the limitations of the subsisting pro-military approach that has been often proven counterproductive. In effect, as Wright et al. (2016/2017: 39) posit,

> Defeating jihadi extremism and preventing its return requires a long-term policy that not only eliminates fighters but also undermines the legitimacy of violence as a means of obtaining political ends. Eliminating an extremist group physically does not defang its ideology or change the underlying circumstances that allowed the group to gain traction in the first place. Reconstruction, rehabilitation, and particularly reconciliation are just as important as any military counter-terrorism campaign in building societal resilience against the appeal of extremism.

CONCLUSION

Global jihadism is currently in recession, yet it is still holding out resiliently. Embattled by sustained national and international counterterrorism endeavors, mainstream jihadist organizations have refused to concede defeat. In an apparent retreat, they have resorted to some tactical asymmetric maneuvers to reassure strength, resilience, and continuity. Through structural fragmentation and adaptation, the organizations have reproduced themselves in disparate nebulous networks of affiliates, proxies and allies internationally. This phenomenon, designated in this chapter as "jihadist nebula," has presented a Herculean challenge to the global counterterrorism campaign.

Using the example of Al-Qaeda in the West African subregion, it has been demonstrated in this chapter that the exigencies of survival in the face of global counterterrorism pressure have driven jihadist organizations into desperate asymmetric transmutations. From the standpoint of the contemporary expressions of Al-Qaeda jihadism in the Sahel-Sahara strip as well as the Lake Chad area, the chapter showed how the prevailing dynamics of jihadi manifestations and alignments have complicated the comprehension and mitigation of terrorism in that context. The multiplicities of alliances between disparate jihadist groups, the collusion between jihadism and organized criminality, and the opportunistic synergies between the jihadists and local extremist groups point to the complicated and obfuscated jihadi scenario in the focal area. The failure of the state to wield firm territorial control in the area has further provided an enabling environment for extremist violence. The way forward lies in the trans-regional mechanism whereby the wider Sahelian and West African authorities collaborate on an institutionalized multilateral functionalist basis toward bringing about enduring collective security.

REFERENCES

Anjide, S. T., and A. C. Okoli. 2017. "New Trajectory of Islamic Extremism in Northern Nigeria: A Threat-Import Analysis of Shiite's Uprising." *International Journal of African and Asian Studies* 32: 41–51.

Baten, J. 2017. European Trade, Colonialism and Human Capital Accumulation in Senegal, Gambia and Western Mali, 1770 – 1900. CESifo Working Papers. Stockholm, Swden.

BCTR. 2013. *Splinter Terrorism Groups: Emerging Trends of Terrorism in Bangladesh.* Dhaka: Center for Terrorism Research.

Belde, D. 2018. Salafi-Jihadist Evolution Since the Arab Spring, What Has changed? A Critical Analysis of AQIM and the Anzawad Case. MA Dissertation, Ghent University.

Blanchard, L. P., and K. T. Cavigelli. 2018. *Boko Haram and Islamic State's West Africa Province.* Washington, DC: Congressional Research Service.

Blanchard, L. P., and T. F. Husted. 2019. *Nigeria: Current Issues in U.S. Policy.* Washington, DC: Congressional Research Center.

Borum, R. 2011. "Radicalization into Violent Extremism I: A Review of Social Science Theories." *Journal of Strategic Security* 4(4): 7–35.

Bunzel, C. 2017. Jihadism on its Own: Islamism and International Order— Understanding a Movement. Hoover Institute Essay. Stanford: Stanford University.

Busher, J. 2014. "Introduction: Terrorism and Counter-terrorism in Sub-Saharan Africa." *Journal of Terrorism Research* 5(1): 1–4.

Cerbib, H. 2018. Jihadism in the Sahel: Exploiting Local Disorders (Strategic sectors/ Security and politics). In *IEMed Mediterranean Yearbook.* Barcelona, 260–64.

Cummings, R. 2017. "A Jihadi Takeover Bid in Nigeria? The Evolving Relationship Between Boko Haram and A-Qaeda." *CTC Sentinel* 10(11): 24–29.

Fisher, D., and C. Mercado. 2014. " 'Competitive Control': How to Evaluate the Threats Posed by 'Ungoverned Spaces." *Small Wars Journal.* September. www. smallwarsjournal/printpdf/16159. Accessed August 2, 2019.

Forest, J. F. 2011. "Al Qaeda's Influence in Sub-Sub-Saharan Africa: Myths, Realities and Possibilities." *Perspectives on Terrorism* 5(3/4): 63–80.

Gaye, B. S. 2018. *Connections Between Jihadist Groups and Smuggling and Illegal Trafficking Rings in the Sahel.* Dakar: Friedrich-Ebert-Stiftung.

Guitta, O., and R. Simcox. 2019. *Terrorism in Nigeria: The Threat from Boko Haram and Ansaru.* Briefing. London: Henry Jackson's Society.

Hutter, M., G. Steinberg, and A. Weber. 2015. "Jihadism in Africa: An Introduction." In *Jihadism in Africa: Local Causes, Regional Expansion, International Alliances.* Edited by G. Steinberg and A. Weber. SWP Research Paper. Berlin: German Institute for International Affairs. 7–29.

International Crisis Group. 2016. *Exploiting Disorders: al-Qaeda and the Islamic State.* Brussels: International Crisis Group.

Kamolnick, P. 2017. *The Al-Qaeda Organization and the Islamic State Organization: History, Doctrine, Modus Operandi, and U.S. Policy to Degrade and Defeat*

Terrorism Conducted in the Name of Sunni Islam. Carlisle, PA: Strategic Studies Institute/U.S. Army War College Press.

Kilcullen, D. 2013. *Out of the Mountains: The Coming Age of the Urban Guerilla.* New York: Oxford University Press.

Krech, H. 2011. "The Growing Influence of Al-Qaeda on the African Continent." *African Spectrum* 46(2): 125–37.

Lister, C. 2016. *Jihadi Rivalry: The Islamic State Challenges al-Qaeda*. Washington, DC: Brookings Institute.

Lounnas, D. 2018. *Jihadist Groups in Northern Africa and the Sahel: Between Disintegration, Reconfiguration and Resilience.* MENARA Working Papers No. 16, .1–17.

MacIver, D. 2017. *Migration and Jihadism in the Sahel: Trade Routes to a New World.* Oslo: Hate Speech International.

McLean I., and A. McMillan. (eds). 2009. *Oxford Concise Dictionary of Politics*. Oxford: Oxford University Press,

Neuman, P. 2010. *Prisons and Terrorism Radicalization and De-radicalization in 15 Countries.* Policy Report. London: International Center for the Study of Radicalization and Violence (ICSR).

Nsaibia, H., and C. Weiss. 2018. "Ansaroul Islam and the Growing Terrorist Insurgency in Burkina Faso." *CTC Sentinel* 11(3): 21–26.

Okoli, A. C. 2019. "Boko Haram Insurgency and the Necessity for Trans-national Forestland Governance in the Lower Lake Chad Basin." *African Journal on Conflict Resolution* 19(1): 37–56.

———. 2017. "Nigeria: Volunteer Vigilantism and Counter-insurgency in the North-East." *Conflict Studies Quarterly* 20: 34–55.

Okoli, A. C., and   S. N. Azom. 2019. "Boko Haram Insurgency and Gendered Vctimhood: Women as Corporal Victims and Objects of War." *Small Wars and Insurgencies* 30(4): 1214–32.

Okoli, A. C., and E. N. Lenshie. 2018. "Nigeria: Nomadic Migrancy and Rural Violence in Nigeria." *Conflict Studies Quarterly* 25: 68–85.

Okoli, A. C., and C. O. Ogayi. 2018. "Herdsmen Militancy and Humanitarian Crisis in Nigeria: A Theoretical Briefing." *African Security Review* 27(2): 129–43.

Okoli, A. C., and G. Atelhe. 2014. "Nomads Against Natives: A Political Ecology of Herder/Farmer Conflicts in Nasarawa State, Nigeria." *American International Journal of Contemporary Research* 2: 76–88.

Okoli, A. C., and P. Iortyer. 2014. "Terrorism and Humanitarian Crisis in Nigeria: Insights from Boko Haram Insurgency." *Global Journal of Human Social Sciences. F: Political Science* 14 (1:1.0): 39–50.

Okoli, A. C., and F. I. Ochim. 2016. "Forestlands and National Security in Nigeria: A Threat-Import Analysis." *International Journal of Political and Administrative Studies* 2(2): 43–53.

Onuoha, F. C., and T. A. George. 2015. Boko Haram's Use of Female Suicide Bombing in Nigeria. Doha: Aljazeera Center for Studies.

Perkoski, E. 2015. Organizational Fragmentation and the Trajectory of Militant Splinter Groups. Publicly accessible Penn Dissertations, 1943; http://repository .upenn.edu/dissertations/1943.

Rabasa, A. et al. 2006. *Beyond Al Qaeda (1): The Global Jihadist Movement.* Arlington, VA: RAND Corporation.

Rosenau, W., and A. Powell. 2017. *Al-Qaeda Core: A Case Study.* Arlington, VA: CAN Analysis and Solutions.

Tishler, N. A. 2018. "Fake Terrorism: Examining Terrorist Group's Resort to Hoaxing as a Mode of Attack.' *Perspectives on Terrorism* 12(4): 3–13.

UNODC 2013. *Transnational Organized Crime in West Africa.* Vienna: United Nations Office for Drugs and Crime.

UNODC 2018. *Education for Justice: University Module Series* (counter-terrorism). Vienna: United Nations Office on Drugs and Crime.

Warner, J., and C. Hulme. 2018. "The Islamic State in Africa: Estimating Fighter Numbers in Cells Across the Continent." *CTC Sentinel* 11(7): 21–28.

Williams, Phil. 2016. "The Global Crisis of Governance." In *Beyond Governance: World Without Order.* Edited by Michael. Miklaucicia and Hilary Matfess. Washington DC: Center for Complex Operations, 21–45.

Wright, R. et al. 2016/2017. *The Jihadist Threat: ISIS, Al Qaeda, and Beyond.* Washington, DC: United States Institute of Peace/Wilson Center.

Zimmerer, M. 2019. "Terror in West Africa: A Threat Assessment of the New Al Qaeda Affiliate in Mali." *Critical Studies in Terrorism,* 12(3): 491–511.

Chapter 6

The Rise and Influence of ISIS in Sub-Saharan Africa

Angela Ajodo-Adehanjoko

The emergence of the Islamic State of Iraq and the Levant (ISIL), also known as the Islamic State of Syria and Iraq (ISIS) is the most significant development in Islamist extremism since the bombing of the twin towers of the World Trade Center in New York on September 11, 2001, by Al-Qaeda (Allison 2014). ISIL, also known as Daesh, a formerly unrecognized proto-state, emerged in 2004 from the remnants of Al-Qaeda in Iraq (AQI), a transnational terrorist group created and led by Abu Musab al Zarqawi a militant Islamist from Jordan (Kirda 2011; Wilson Centre 2019). In 2010, Abu Bakr al-Baghdadi was announced as the leader of the group and he subsequently assumed leadership of the organization and was named the new Caliph Ibrahim. The announcement demanded the loyalty of all Muslims around the world and specifically from other jihadist groups (Stern and Berger 2017). In April 2013, the group rebranded itself as the Islamic State in Iraq and Syria, engendering conflict with other terrorist actors in the region, such as the Nusra Front in Syria. In June 2014, ISIS proclaimed itself a worldwide caliphate and began referring to itself as the Islamic State (IS); it claimed religious, political, and military authority over all Muslims worldwide (African Defense Forum 2015).

For much of its existence, ISIS had its operational base in the Middle East, notably Syria and Iraq. Its emergence undermined stability in Iraq, Syria, and the broader Middle East and posed a threat to international peace and security, including to Africa. Since its emergence, ISIS has declared branches and established networks in other countries and attracted an international network of supporters; launched acts of violence and terrorism in various countries throughout the world; and to control territory, and steadily consolidate and expand its position, as part of an ideology to create a government where Muslims can live under Islamic law (Byman 2015; GAO 2017).

Following the humanitarian crisis that resulted from ISIS's conquests, the US began air strikes and subsequently deployed foot soldiers, which eventually led to the defeat of the group. In response to territorial losses on the ground in Iraq and Syria, ISIS turned its attention to Africa, which has for some time been of particular interest to the group (Cochi 2016). At the end of 2016, ISIS leader Abu Bakr al-Baghdadi announced that the group had expanded and shifted some of its command, media, and wealth to Africa. And in ISIS' *Dabiq* magazine, the group divided Africa into different regions as part of its "caliphate." For example, it referred to Sudan, Chad, and Egypt as the province of Alkinaana; Eritrea, Ethiopia, Somalia, Kenya, and Uganda as the province of Habasha; and the North African region encompassing Libya, Tunisia, Morocco, Algeria, Nigeria, Niger and Mauritania as the Maghreb, the province of the caliphate (Siegle 2017). While the group's influence is pronounced in four countries in Africa, namely Algeria, Libya, Morocco, and Tunisia, there are genuine concerns that with its defeat in Syria, thousands of ISIS' African fighters, with access to the group's considerable war chest, will return home to enflame existing conflicts in sub-Saharan Africa (Mohammad 2017). The biggest danger for African countries, according to Allison (2014:.3), is the "potential impact of thousands of well-trained, battle-hardened fighters choosing to return, or being ordered home after stints with ISIS or other jihadist groups in Syria." And, as Woldemichael (2019) notes, the return of terrorist fighters is nothing new in Africa as records show that in the 1990s, terrorist fighters returned mostly to Algeria, Morocco, Egypt, Libya, and Sudan engaged in elaborate transnational criminal networks. And while most of the returnees from North Africa joined the jihad against the Soviet Union in Afghanistan in the 1980s, alongside al-Qaeda; others created affiliate terrorist organizations in their respective countries. The affiliate organizations became the platforms for carrying out the intent and goals of the jihadists — overthrowing governments and establishing an elaborate transnational criminal network that smuggled goods, natural resources, people, and drugs, and kidnapped people for ransom.

On October 26, 2019, al-Baghdadi died following a raid on his hideout by US Special Forces, and a day later, the spokesman for the group, Abu al-Hassan al-Muhajir, was also killed in an air strike in northern Syria. Despite this, it does not signal the death of the group, as the Pentagon states that "we're under no illusion that ISIS will go away" (CNN 2019). In the same vein, announcing its new leader, Abu Ibrahim al-Hashemi al-Qurayshi, ISIS sent a warning to the United States that the end of the group had not come as it was evolving. This statement was buttressed by Hennigan (2019), who observed that despite the loss of its territorial caliphate in Iraq and

Syria, ISIS has expanded its reach to include fourteen separate affiliates in countries across Asia and Africa strengthened by a cadre of battle-hardened young leaders who are climbing toward the top echelons and establishing themselves in the terror group's global network. He opined that ISIS is not a crippled organization because Baghdadi's gone. Khatib (2019: 2) shared a similar view when she stated that; "The killing of Abu Bakr al-Baghdadi does not mean the automatic end of ISIS (Islamic State of Iraq and Syria). But the immediate future of ISIS depends more on local dynamics in Syria than on whether it still has a leader or not." ISIS' "sleeping cells" of "equipped fighters" remain active in several places in Syria, with enormous "hidden assets, thought to be either in Iraq and Syria or smuggled into neighboring countries for safekeeping" (Mashaly 2019:.2). A recent Defense Department Inspector General report shows that ISIS has between 14,000 and 18,000 members who have pledged allegiance to al-Baghdadi. This is in addition to more than thirty detention camps that hold about 11,000 ISIS fighters, sympathizers, and other associated detainees across northern Syria. Similarly, another recruiting source includes a camp for internally displaced persons known as al-Hol, in northeastern Syria that holds nearly 70,000 people, including thousands of ISIS family members.

While the death of its leader is no doubt a significant blow to the sect, the world is not yet a safer place because of ISIS' operative strategy and the presence of "lone wolves." ISIS' operative strategy is said to be "resilient" enough to be "decentralized" away from its supposed "core leadership" in Iraq and Syria. Specifically, after its collapse in 2017 and, even though al-Baghdadi was the main designer of the strategy of war of attrition that helped to regroup and revive the group's fighters after its defeat in Syria, the group's franchises and branches have proved capable of carrying out his violent ideology remotely on their own; e.g., in Libya and several countries in West Africa, (Mashaly 2019). Besides, lone wolves in sub-Saharan Africa could pose a grave threat after al-Baghdadi's death.

To be sure, ISIS remains a worldwide threat because the group has affiliates in sub-Saharan Africa. ISIS affiliates in the sub-Saharan African region make it, in a general context, a region where Islamist extremism is becoming vividly active. With al-Shabaab, Boko Haram, Al-Qaea in the Islamic Maghreb (AQIM), MUJAO, Ansar Dine, and other extremist groups already established in sub-Saharan Africa, the region is already ripe for ISIS to spread its ideology. Sub-Saharan Africa has achieved notoriety for the presence of extremist groups in the region, which is the result of weak institutions, porous borders, poor governance, socioeconomic factors, and the prevalence of conflict, among others. For decades, the activities of Boko Haram, al-Shabaab, and AQIM in no small ways caused instability and humanitarian crisis in the region and despite efforts to tackle these groups, the region has been reeling from jihadist activities. Sub-Saharan Africa has thus become the focus of extremist incursion not only as the threat from violent extremism appears to be worsening but also as the strategic African and non-African coalition response has not been able to adequately tackle the challenge.

This chapter will address several major issues. First, what are ISIS' major strategies and modes of propaganda? Second, what factors contributed to the rise of ISIS in sub-Saharan Africa? What steps need to be taken to counter ISIS' activities in sub-Saharan Africa?

ISIS' STRATEGIES AND PROPAGANDA TOOLS

ISIS has adopted several strategies and propaganda tools in its conquests. As it conquered territory, it often took control of critical infrastructure, like dams that gave the group control over water supplies in parts of Iraq and Syria, and oil fields and refineries that made oil one of the group's primary sources of revenue. In the territory it controls, the Islamic State uses mass executions, public beheadings, rape, and symbolic crucifixion displays to terrorize the population into submission and "purify" the community, and at the same time provides basic (if minimal) services (Byman 2015). ISIS has also sought to expand its reach and influence in various ways; while its core membership consists of Iraqis and Syrians, it has drawn on an extensive network of foreign fighters estimated at 40,000 from more than 120 countries. The group has also developed a highly professional online presence and messaging approach referred to as cyber jihad, with messages intended to intimidate globally, encourage terrorist attacks, gain followers, and attract recruits. In 2014 it launched the most advanced, massive, and probably the most efficient cyber jihad campaign ever, whose releases online resulted in *shock and awe* among Western audiences (Lakomy 2017a). Images and recordings of brutally decapitated shot or burned hostages, professionally recorded and directed, instantly proliferated over the web environment, reaching millions of internet users in addition to advanced releases of battle footage, "documentaries," online magazines, and *nasheed* music videos. Lakomy (2017b) has classified the Islamic State's propaganda tools into four major categories:

- Audio (radio broadcasts, *nasheed* music) such as the radio al-Bayan, which broadcasts locally in many provinces or *wilayahs: Nasheed* songs and radio broadcasts were usually designed to encourage Muslim audiences to enter the path of jihad and to reinforce the attitudes of ISIS supporters. Some also provided false information to audiences. *Nasheed* songs often refer to themes of war and fighting, which inspire listeners, while radio broadcasts covered a much wider spectrum of issues, including religious programs.

- Visual (memes, pictures, banners, symbols, infographics): Ordinary pictures, symbols, and banners played rather decorative or informative roles, despite their high quality, as they are extensively used in online bulletins, social media, articles, magazines, and movies released on the internet, while memes and infographics employed persuasion techniques and appealed to qualitatively different groups of receivers. Memes composed of pictures combined with a short text message are designed to reach younger, less educated, and less aware audiences and contain references to mass culture canons, such as popular movies, music, ideas, gestures, or symbols that exploit humor and aimed to infect ignorant receivers with jihadist concepts; to recruit them or only to improve the organization's image among the youth. Infographics, on the other hand, are designed to reach more demanding and conscious audiences, who usually need illusionary facts and statistics, to strengthen or change their attitudes.
- Audiovisual (execution recordings, battle footage, "documentaries," interviews, *nasheed* music videos, short advertisements, and reportages, such as *mujatweets*). The most influential and successful pieces of propaganda posted online in 2014 and 2015 were videos that showed the sheer brutality of the Islamic State's executioners. The brutal beheading of Western journalists and humanitarian aid workers by the IS group dominated the headlines in 2014. Images of captives in orange jumpsuits, forced to read out statements criticizing Western government policy towards the Middle East before being decapitated, have earned the Sunni terrorist group a reputation for barbarity (Political Insight 2015). Although this was unusual and exceptionally disturbing, when compared to the "mainstream" *jihadi* releases, they spread instantly over the Web, reaching millions of Internet users, and thus becoming the greatest success in the history of cyber jihad. Audiovisual content in the form of *nasheed* music videos, similar to the best American and Western European pop stars' productions, was also hugely successful. This music encouraged recipients to conduct terrorist attacks against the "disbelievers." One of its sources, posted on the popular video hosting service LiveLeak, has been viewed more than 120,000 times since April 2015. Other productions such as "documentaries," interviews, and reports (e.g. *mujatweets*, *Windows* episodes) designed to look like the best programs from global TV networks contained sophisticated manipulation techniques glorifying IS members' heroism and dedication to jihad and thus encouraging recipients to follow in their footsteps. Texts, including

primarily online magazines (*Dabiq, Islamic State News, Islamic State Report, Dar al- Islam, Konstantiniyye, Istok,* and *Furat Press*), Internet bulletins, as well as declarations and statements posted on the web also exploited similar, advanced manipulation methods, although their roles were narrower, as they usually aimed to enlist or strengthen the attitudes of jihadist supporters.

* Other channels of distribution include traditional websites and blogs, frequently located on the most popular blogosphere platforms (e.g., BlogSpot) which are secondary, backup channels of distribution and much more difficult to find via conventional search engines, online communication applications, such as Skype, Signal, Whatsapp, and Snapchat usually used for more confidential forms of contact and frequently used for recruitment purposes at the later stages of selection, as it provided a high degree of privacy and security for terrorists.

Early propaganda strategy of the Islamic State in cyberspace that greatly contributed to its initial success employed methods of distribution similar to viral marketing, to generate a "viral effect," that is, to attract receivers' interest to "infect" them with an idea, to which they can subsequently share with other users through social networks; an approach designed to enable Western audiences to fully embrace manipulated messages (Lakomy 2017a).

ISIS's cyber jihad has led to diverse opinions from scholars. Siboni, Cohen, and Koren (2015) believe that ISIS uses social media for two reasons; the first is psychological warfare targeting the morale of the enemy's soldiers while the second involves gaining support from Western Islamic groups while unifying the Islamic State's soldiers behind one goal." In contrast, Williams (2015) argues that "Islamic State's media effort has several aims that target both sympathetic and hostile audiences; one of which is to recruit supporters and the second, to generate fear among its opponents, which has very specific advantages on the battlefield while a third goal is to assert its legitimacy and gain acceptance of its status as a state." The bulk of Islamic State's releases target Muslim societies around the world; although they also attempt to influence "disbelievers" or lone wolves.

According to Byman (2015), ISIS' impressive social media efforts and overall appeal also make it better able to mobilize "lone wolves" to attack the West. Many of these individuals with little or no contact with the group will find its ideology and methods appealing and will act on their own. While some of these individuals may have preferred to go to Iraq and Syria, Western disruption efforts make it easier for them to attack at home. Several instances of this abound; a French national who returned from Syria killed four people at a Jewish mosque in Brussels, and a lone actor in Ottawa left a video recording of his ideological and political grievances before an attack on Parliament that left a soldier dead, and a young teen who claimed to have been paid by ISIS to commit an attack in Vienna (Stern and Berger 2015). According to recent translations of propaganda videos and audio records, ISIS elements steadily promote "the wheel of attrition" as their operations are running "smoothly" and "daily and on different fronts," regardless of the death of its leaders (Mashaly 2019).

THE ISLAMIC STATE'S RISE IN SUB-SAHARAN AFRICA: REASONS FOR EMERGENCE

An estimated 36,500 foreign fighters have joined the Islamic State since the start of the Syrian war with most of these coming from the Arab world, and close to eight thousand from the four countries of the Maghreb, namely Algeria, Libya, Morocco, and Tunisia (Zitouny 2016). Since 2013, ISIS has recruited from the Maghreb and sought to build a presence there in multiple ways — from the creation of recruitment and operational cells to seizing and governing territory. Tunisia has the highest number of foreign fighters (an estimated six thousand) the highest for any country in the world, Morocco (1,623 plus an estimated two thousand who hold European citizenship), and Libya (an estimated six hundred) while Algeria has seventy-eight with an estimated two hundred who hold a second nationality and came from Europe (International Crisis Group 2017). Although global attention toward the Islamic State has generally focused on the Middle East while their influence abroad has focused on these four African countries, the group is finding adherents throughout sub-Saharan Africa as well. Extremists are penetrating sub-Saharan Africa at an alarming rate, threatening states ill-prepared to deal with the resulting complex social and security challenge (Daragahi 2018; International Crisis Group 2017). A mix of ungoverned spaces, poverty, injustice, local conflicts, existing extremist networks, and ideology in many parts of sub-Saharan Africa has presented a chance for ISIS to regroup and recruit millions of young people in the region (Bukarti 2017; Ellis 2018). This encroachment poses unique challenges for policymakers and government officials struggling with limited resources. Some of the factors that encourage ISIS's incursion into sub-Saharan Africa are discussed in this section.

The loss of territories in Syria and Libya and the resultant insecurity and proliferation of Small and Light Weapons (SALW) coupled with the movement of mercenaries from these territories to the sub-Saharan region account partly for the presence of ISIS in the region to establish a world caliphate; a defeat in Syria for ISIS is an opportunity to achieve this goal.

Conflict and insecurity remain principal causal factors for ISIS's rise in sub-Saharan Africa. The International Crisis Group (2017) observed that in the Middle East, jihadists' expansion is more a product of instability than its primary driver; and Abubakar (2017) argued that political and leadership vacuums are created when people are insecure, allowing insurgent groups, such as ISIS, a place to thrive. Insecurity in sub-Saharan Africa no doubt provides a breeding ground for ISIS to grow. In Africa, there has been an increasing number of violent conflicts, especially following the end of the Cold War, and, although internal violent conflict is not new to Africa, post–Cold War civil conflicts in the continent have become so phenomenal that they have been described as "new wars" by Mary Kaldor (Ajodo-Adebanjoko 2018). In sub-Saharan Africa, these new wars have been characterized by civil wars, ethnic and religious conflicts, resource-based conflicts, and electoral violence, and these have resulted in insecurity on the continent. In 2015 alone, the first two months recorded about 8,300 deaths from conflict in sub-Saharan Africa, with five countries Nigeria, Cameroon, Sudan, Somalia, and Niger accounting for roughly 90 percent of these deaths (De Villiers 2015). These conflicts have made the region insecure and created an environment for extremism to thrive.

Consistent with research findings by the Institute for Security Studies (ISS), perceived injustice is another factor at the root of ISIS's rise in sub-Saharan Africa. In a survey of Islamist militants in Kenya, 65 percent claimed that they joined radical Islamist groups because of injustices at the hands of Kenyan security forces, specifically referring to "collective punishment" (Botha 2014 cited in Allison 2014). In other words, heavy-handed counterterrorism tactics became a powerful recruiting tool for Islamist groups in the country. Also, a research finding by UNDP (2017) observes that, where there is injustice, deprivation, and desperation, violent extremist ideologies are a challenge to the status quo and serve as a form of escape. Ogundiya (2009), and Omeje, (2009) (cited in Yusuf 2013) argue that the Boko Haram insurgency, like many others before it is deeply rooted in a legacy of gross deprivation, violations of human rights, and social dislocation that is most acute in the northeastern part of the country.

Preexisting networks also constitute another factor. Recruitment networks feed on well-established, preexisting jihadist networks. These are often in historically marginalized areas with a history of dissidence and alienation from the central state, where the role of the informal or criminal economy is strong, and the rule of law relatively weak. Allison (2014:4) notes that:

> the prevalence of radical Islamist groups within Africa makes the continent particularly vulnerable to new threats driven by the rise of the Islamic State. There are plenty of existing fault lines on the continent for the Islamic State to exploit,

and plenty of radical Islamist groups that know how to exploit them. The rise of the Islamic State does not represent a completely new threat to Africa rather, its potential impact will be in exacerbating existing tensions and conflicts. There is no suggestion that the Islamic State will expand alone into Africa. Instead, it will seek to ally with or co-opt similarly minded organizations in Africa.

Boko Haram, Al Murabitoun, Ansar Dine, Al-Shabaab, Al-Qaeda in the Islamic Maghreb (AQIM) and the Movement for Oneness and Jihad in West Africa (MUJAO) are existing networks that have made the incursion of ISIS into the region easy. Some sect leaders and members have also trained with various militant groups in Afghanistan. Thus, ISIS takes advantage of existing militant jihadist organizations to promote defections, recruit local fighters, and adapt to local conditions.

Based on a common extremist view of Islam, ideology is another factor that has provided a fertile ground for ISIS. Most extremist groups currently active in sub-Saharan Africa largely define themselves in religious terms, sharing a common ideology that aligns with ISIS' ideology (Slayton 2015; UNDP 2017). The nexus between religion and terrorism has a long genealogy in Western scholarship; among others, religious terrorists have anti-modern goals of returning society to an idealized version of the past and are therefore necessarily antidemocratic and anti-progressive (Agbiboa 2014). Groups such as ISIS have selectively interpreted Islamic teachings, and their only unifying vision is for a world in which sharia is implemented at the point of a gun. In a video of an ISIS killer dubbed "Jihadi John," before beheading American journalist James Foley in August 2014, he declared; "You are no longer fighting an insurgency, we are an Islamic army" (Fromson and Simon 2015). While ideology is a factor in ISIS's incursion into the region, extremists are driven less by a simple lust for destruction and killing than by various ideological constructs (Rich 2013). In contrast, Joseph Siegle indicates that ISIS' ideology holds little appeal but instead the highly conservative Wahhabi model of Islam, which continues to exert a strong influence supported by ample funding, social media, and other forms of communication (Pagano 2017). Whatever the argument, different jihadists and affiliates draw strength from an extreme view of Islam.

Socioeconomic factors such as state neglect, unemployment, poverty, and illiteracy, perceived to be a result of structural injustice, are prevalent in the region and provide an enabling environment for the Islamic State to operate. According to UNDP (2017), while there is agreement that poverty alone is not a sufficient explanation for violent extremism in Africa, it is accepted that violent extremist groups exploit perceptions of disproportionate economic hardship. A key indicator for measuring poverty level is education. Countries in sub-Saharan Africa have a huge number of out-of-school children. For instance, Nigeria has the highest number of out-of-school children, globally estimated at 13.2 million in 2018, with 69 percent of this in the north, where extremism is rife (Eze 2018; Ibrahim 2008). Research also shows that a significantly larger percentage of those who voluntarily become members of the Boko Haram sect are often those with the lowest levels of secular schooling. Those with less secular education are predicted to be more susceptible to recruitment and influence by jihadists (UNDP 2017). This also applies to other countries in sub-Saharan Africa where poverty and illiteracy are rife. The promise of employment by extremist groups is a huge motivation for recruitment.

Research finding identifies employment as the single most frequently cited 'immediate need' at the time of joining a sect (UNDP 2017). Unemployment remains high in sub-Saharan Africa. For example, in 2019, of the 38.1 percent estimated total working poor, young people accounted for more than 30 percent. During the same period, the national unemployment rates ranged from 1.8 percent in Ethiopia, 6.0 percent in Nigeria, and 18.2 percent in Botswana, to 27.3 percent in South Africa according to the International Labor Organisation (ILO 2019). According to Atta-Asamoah (nd: p.1), "the history of insecurity in Africa [is] associated [with] high youth unemployment with the numerous situations of instability on the continent ranging from mass killings in the Great Lakes region and other parts of Africa and contemporary extremism." This statement was confirmed during an email interview with Ugwumba Egbuta, who states that the large population of unemployed, economically and politically excluded youths has provided foot soldiers to be recruited as fighters, informants, and suicide bombers, among other roles (Egbuta 2019, personal communication, October 5). The United Nations Office of the Special Representative of the Secretary-General for Children and Armed Conflict stated that more than 2,500 boys were recruited and over 1,600 children abducted by al-Shabaab in 2018; a majority of these being out-of-school children and unemployed youth (Van and Ngachanja 2019).

Amongst other factors, ungoverned spaces or territories explain ISIS's presence in sub-Saharan Africa. Such territories serve as hideouts, or as Freedom Onuoha puts it, during an interview, permits for training and hiding (Onuoha 2019, personal communication). Ungoverned territories are areas in which a state faces significant challenges in establishing control or areas of limited or anomalous government control inside otherwise functional states (Keister 2014). They can be failed or failing states, poorly controlled land or maritime borders, or areas within otherwise viable states to which the central government's authority does not extend. Keister (2014) believes the term "ungoverned spaces" is a misnomer, because these areas are not ungoverned in the real sense of it but are simply ruled by subnational authorities or by alternative authorities. Large areas of Africa, such as remote rural areas, entire regions of so-called fragile states, and urban slums, are barely touched by any state presence and are regarded as black holes and security threats (African Studies Center Leiden nd). Since the end of the Cold War, failed or failing states and ungoverned territories within otherwise viable states have become a more common phenomenon. These territories generate all manner of security problems, such as civil conflict and humanitarian crises, arms and drug smuggling, piracy, and refugee flows. The events of 9/11 demonstrated how terrorists can use sanctuaries in the most remote and hitherto ignored territories of the world to mount devastating attacks against the United States and its friends and allies (Bai and DeSmet nd). While ungoverned territories occur throughout the world, not all such territories become terrorist sanctuaries. Beyond the natural tendency of terrorist groups to operate in their home areas, several factors make a territory conducive to such groups, and these include; access to infrastructure, local financing, a local population favorably disposed to the terrorists, and invisibility, or those characteristics to a local environment that render terrorists hard to find by the authorities. Al-Qaeda and other groups in the global jihadist movement use ungoverned territories as financial, logistical, and training bases or as operational bases and each of these activities poses a different set of requirements (Rabasa and Peters 2007). Ungoverned territories pose an increasingly urgent threat to Africa's security. Terrorism experts have long feared that parts of the Sahel, beyond the control of any government, could become nurseries for radical Islamic terrorism that would focus on Western interests and security. This fear partly compels the United States to provide limited military assistance to the states in the region, notably Niger, and to sell military equipment to Nigeria (Campbell 2018).

ISIS has also taken advantage of the security vacuum caused by weak or absent governance in sub-Saharan Africa to increase its influence and expand its network. Governance in the region is weak and this is evidenced by lax laws and porous borders. This is made worse by the ECOWAS Transhumance Protocol of 1998 and the ECOWAS Protocol of Free Movement of Goods and Persons in West Africa, which has made the region more or less a borderless society and has eased the influx of extremists into the region. Yusuf (2013) argues that the institutionalization of a governance gap has become a common experience in many developing countries, especially in sub-Saharan Africa, where there exists a gulf between citizens and the state because of the lack of credible leadership and implementation of programs that bear little or no positive impact on the social development of the people. This gap leads to social disillusionment and produces large numbers of citizens who become disconnected from the state and its institutions and become easy recruits in the hands of extremists. The failures of successive governments in sub-Saharan Africa characterized by decaying infrastructure, deteriorating democratic accountability, and inadequate capacity of the security forces to

protect the people have led to the failed state theory in which several countries in the region are classified.

Also, another factor is the significant expansion of internet access across
the continent; with it, social media has led to increased ISIS presence
in sub-Saharan Africa. In 2014, 100 million people in Africa were using
Facebook each month with the figure projected to be more than 120 million
(Ward 2017). While there is a positive development of improved connectivity,
ultimately, the democratization of access to the internet also benefit IS as it
uses the same internet for its online communication and propaganda.

ISIS' AFFILIATES IN SUB-SAHARAN AFRICA

Despite the news of the defeat of the Islamic State in Iraq, the group's ideo-
logical hold in sub-Saharan Africa has been quietly growing. ISIS leader Abu
Bakr al-Baghdadi always showed interest in establishing new provinces in
Africa; claimed new oaths of allegiance from extremists in Mali and Burkina
Faso in the Sahel region, and displayed a report on the group's "Central
Africa province." ISIS has thus had a varying degree of success in making
inroads into sub-Saharan Africa jihadist groups linked to al-Qaeda; the latter
still exerts a strong influence, especially in the Sahel and the Horn of Africa.
Though North Africa has been a greater priority from the perspective of
counterterrorism, jihadist ideology has for some years been gaining adherents
farther south. There are three jihadist hotspots: northern Nigeria and the Lake
Chad basin region; the Horn of Africa; and Mali and its neighbors in the Sahel
region. In most of these areas, al-Qaeda has had a hold over jihadist movements and remains hard to shift. There are also examples of the influence of
ISIS in other areas such as Sudan, where in October 2015 the government
confirmed that seventy of its nationals had joined ISIS in Syria or Libya, and
in South Africa where more than twenty people, including eight families with
children, were reported to have traveled to the "caliphate."

The Islamic State has specifically gained support from some important
jihadist groups; Islamic State in West Africa Province or Boko Haram in
Nigeria, Islamic State in Somalia (ISS), and the Islamic State in Somalia,
Kenya, Tanzania, and Uganda (ISISKTU). In May 2015 Adnan Abu Walid
Sahrawi pledged allegiance to ISIS leader Baghdadi, and Baghdadi, in turn,
mentioned Sahrawi while acknowledging pledges of allegiance from Mali
and Burkina Faso, calling on them to "intensify their strikes on Crusader
France and its allies," and starting in May 2019, Islamic State began to attribute insurgent activities in the Mali-Burkina Faso-Niger tri-border area to
its West Africa Province affiliate. This region is far to the west of ISWAP's
normal operational area around Lake Chad, but rather than a westward

expansion by that Nigerian-led group, these claims appear to represent the promotion of the actions of the Islamic State in the Greater Sahara under the West Africa Province brand (The Defense Post 2019). Islamic State Central Africa Province was also confirmed in 2019 after ISIS attributed an attack on Congolese soldiers at Kamango in the Democratic Republic of Congo to it.

There are currently four ISIS affiliates in sub-Saharan Africa that form the focus of its operations in the region. These affiliates are the Islamic State in West African Province (ISWAP) in northeast Nigeria and the three new Islamic State affiliates; Islamic State in the Greater Sahara (ISGS), Islamic State in Somalia (ISS), and Islamic State in Somalia, Kenya, Tanzania, and Uganda (Jahba East Africa). The section will assess their areas of convergence or divergence ideologically, operationally, strategically, and explain what their presence in the region might mean in the future.

The Islamic State in West Africa Province (ISWAP) is regarded as the largest ISIS affiliate in sub-Saharan Africa. ISWAP emerged as a splinter group from the Jama'at ahl al-sunna li-Da'wah wa-l-qital wal-Jihad "People Committed to the Propagation of the Prophet's Teachings and Jihad," also known as Boko Haram, in 2016, and is primarily a Nigerian organization, with few foreign fighters. Boko Haram, literally translated, means *Western education is forbidden.* Boko Haram was founded in Maiduguri, Borno State, in 2002 by Mohammed Yusuf to establish a sharia government in all the northern states and the Federal Capital Territory (FCT), Abuja. Following the death of Yusuf in 2009, Abubakar Shekau became the leader of the group. Under Shekau, the group became notorious for a series of bombings and killings, and was responsible for the abduction of 276 schoolgirls from Chibok village in Borno state in 2014; an act which led to international protests against the group's activities. In 2015 Shekau pledged allegiance to Abu Bakr al-Baghdadi and ISIS and thereafter became Islamic State West Africa Province. This alliance led to an outcry from the international community, and some people referred to it as a "marriage from hell" (Warner and Hulme 2018). In its operations, ISWAP's effective use of technology and media made its operations difficult for governments and the international community to decode and mount a counter operation (Egbuta 2019, personal communication).

In 2016 tension rose between ISWAP and Islamic State Central, primarily due to the latter's dislike for ISWAP's hard-line approach or the justification to target and kill apostate Muslims and, as a result, in August of that year Shekau was replaced by Abu Musab al-Barnawi, who is believed to be the son of the group's founder, Mohammed Yusuf. As a consequence of Shekau's rejection of the change in leadership, claiming that he remained in charge of both groups, ISWAP splintered into two factions: the al-Barnawi-led faction that controls territory in the Lake Chad Basin area in northern Borno state and the Shekau-led faction, which controls land in central and southern Borno state, including in the group's stronghold of the Sambisa forest (Warner and Hulme 2018). Another ISIS-orchestrated leadership change occurred once again when Abu Abdullah Ibn Umar al-Barnawi was reportedly appointed the new governor of the Wilayah of West Africa.

Estimates from the U.S. Department of Defense, in April 2018, put the membership of the Barnawi faction at 3,500.11 (added to Shekau's faction, this would add another 1,500 fighters). As of July 2018, Barnawi's ISWAP faction was the largest Islamic State grouping in Africa, with three and half times as many fighters as the next largest Islamic State cell in Africa, Islamic State-Sinai (in Egypt), and more fighters than all other Islamic State cells in Africa combined (Warner and Hulme 2018). Despite its influence in West Africa, ISWAP attacks have been limited to the Lake Chad area of eastern Niger, western Chad, northern Cameroon, and northeastern Nigeria, with the majority of the attacks in Nigeria. The group attempts to win over residents in the area as it pushes into northeastern Nigeria and Niger (Miller 2015). Based on ISWAP's tactics, the local nature of ISIS affiliates and the group's overall decentralized nature is similar to the local affiliate in Libya where ISIS took advantage of the post-Qaddafi situation when authorities marginalized the city of Sirte, Muammar Qaddafi's hometown, which he used as a base of support for his regime. Some of Sirte's residents welcomed militant jihadist groups that promised stability and services that the government failed to provide. As the Islamic State is forced out of its self-proclaimed caliphate in the Middle East, ISWAP appears to be growing even stronger (Obaji 2019) and despite its lack of propagandistic and technical resourcefulness compared to ISIS, its recent setbacks remain as deadly as ISIS (Nwankpa 2015). The expansion of ISWAP demonstrates that ISIS is not only a formidable threat in sub-Saharan Africa but continentally and globally.

The Islamic State in the Greater Sahara (ISGS) is the second Islamic State in sub-Saharan Africa. ISGS gained prominence with a string of deadly attacks in 2016. It was formerly known as the Islamic State in Mali, a group formed by Adnan Abu Walid Sahraoui, a senior leader for an al-Qa'ida-aligned group known as al-Mourabitoun with allegiance to al-Baghdadi in 2015. Sahraoui and dozens of fighters left and formed their own Islamic State grouping, the Islamic State in Mali, after being rejected for pledging allegiance to IS (Warner and Hulme 2018). The group emerged from the merging of two jihadi groups; the Movement for Oneness and Jihad in West Africa (MUJAO) and the Masked Men Brigade, which created a third group, al-Mourabitoun, in 2013. In 2016, it carried out three notable attacks near the borders of Burkina Faso, Niger, and Mali. The first attack led to the killing of two guards, while in a second operation, the group attacked a police outpost in Intoum, Burkina Faso, just kilometers from the Mali border, which killed three police officers; and in a third and most sophisticated attack, ISGS orchestrated an attempted jailbreak of the high-security Koutoukale prison in Niamey, Niger but was repelled by the guards, who killed one of the assailants (Warner 2017). The group also carried out an ambush near Tongo Tongo that left twenty-eight Niger soldiers dead. The capacity of ISGS to carry out deadly attacks signaled to the Islamic State that the sect was more than just a nominal fighting force and welcome addition to forward its ideology.

Despite its announced affiliation with the Islamic State, there has been little evidence that either of the ISWAP factions (Shekau's or al-Barnawi's) has had any interaction with ISGS. ISIS has grouped ISGS with the Wilayah of West Africa, but that doesn't mean there is a definitive link between ISGS and ISWAP, and there remains the potential for ISIS central to give ISGS control of its province. However, while seemingly remaining separate, there are potential connections between the two groups.

The Islamic State in Somalia (Abnaa ul-Calipha) is the third Islamic State affiliate in sub-Saharan Africa. ISS, as a splinter group from al-Shabaab, emerged in 2015, and was led by Abdulqadir Mumin who pledged *bay`a* to al-Baghdadi and the Islamic State in October 2015; and in that same month, began recruiting soldiers among the disenchanted population. From twenty followers in the early days, it is now believed that the group has between one hundred and two hundred fighters (Warner 2017). Although ISIS has not officially acknowledged Mumin's pledge of *bay`a*, nor is ISS an official wilaya operationally, ISS has arguably been the most powerful of the new Islamic State affiliates in sub-Saharan Africa. Like the parent group IS, Jahba East Africa emerged when fighters previously loyal to al-Shabaab sought to realign with the Islamic State. In 2016, about fifty members of ISS seized the port town of Qandala in the Bari region of Puntland, making the town the first territory the Islamic State has held inside Somalia. This was particularly worrisome as Qandala's location would have given the group port access on the Gulf of Aden, and potentially afforded it proximity to linkages with Yemen. Although Qandala was later captured by the Somali maritime forces, ISS's holding of the town, even for a short time, could be interpreted as an important symbolic victory for the group (Warner and Hulme 2018). Two locals were sentenced to death for suspected links to the group, while seven of its members were killed by Somali forces in the Bari region. Although, operationally, ISS has proven to be more of an ideological threat than a physical one, its most notable attack was on a convoy from the African Union Mission in Somalia (AMISOM) in April 2016, which was the first time that an Islamic State affiliate had claimed an attack in Somalia. The group's activities made the African Union-led meeting of security chiefs from around East Africa warn that the ISS was "aggressively seeking to establish its influence in northeastern Somali" (Warner and Hulme 2018).

The fourth and newest ISIS affiliate in sub-Saharan Africa is the Islamic State in Somalia, Kenya, Tanzania, and Uganda (Jahba East Africa). Jahba East Africa or the Islamic State in Somalia, Kenya, Tanzania, and Uganda (ISISKTU) pledged allegiance to the Islamic State in 2016, hailing a "new era" in the region (Dearden 2016). Like the Islamic State in Somalia, ISISKTU is a splinter group of al-Shabaab and the group is alleged to have been initiated by Mohamed Abdi Ali, a medical intern from Kenya, along with his wife. ISISKTU has among its ranks, citizens from Somalia, Kenya, Tanzania, and Uganda, and given that the group is composed of East African citizens who had previously been part of al-Shabaab, ISISKTU is thought to contain elements of al-Shabaab that were once described as the group's "foreign fighters."

The various sub-Saharan affiliates of ISIS have some areas of convergence. In the first place, except for ISISKTU in 2016, all the groups emerged as affiliates around the same time in 2015, which is when the Islamic State was at the height of its power. Second, the groups emerged as breakaway groups. Third, apart from ISWAP, none of the groups is particularly large, nor are they very well-understood; and fourth, ideologically all the groups share a similar extremist view of Islam and a hardline approach or the justification to target and kill apostate Muslims.

And, despite their similarities, there are notable differences among the groups. ISWAP is the largest Islamic State group in Africa and has more fighters than all other Islamic State cells in Africa combined. But ISGS is thought to be slightly more institutionalized than the other two new affiliates because it is the only one of the three new Islamic State affiliates whose *bay'a* to the Islamic State has been acknowledged, and the only one of the groups to have carried out multiple attacks. The Islamic State in Somalia is, however, the only group to have held and occupied territory in the form of the town of Qandala (not desert) (Warner and Hulme 2018). Conversely, ISWAP is the most sophisticated and effective in terms of the employment of technology in its operations and effective use of media. Operationally, ISWAP attacks have been limited to the Lake Chad area of eastern Niger, western Chad, northern Cameroon, and northeastern Nigeria, with the majority of the attacks in Nigeria; while ISGS has operated and carried out attacks near the borders of Burkina Faso, Niger, and Mali. Although ISS is not an official wilaya, operationally it is regarded as the most powerful of the new Islamic State affiliates and operates in Somalia, while ISISKTU has members from Somalia, Kenya, Tanzania, and Uganda and thus, in theory, has a wider operational base.

Through these affiliates, ISIS has significant operational capability and influence in some of the countries where they operate, despite expansion challenges from competing extremist groups. The expansion of ISWAP and the emergence of these new affiliates demonstrate that ISIS is not only a formidable threat in sub-Saharan Africa, but continentally and globally, and unless its effort to expand is tackled, ISIS' presence and influence in the region may increase and expand with time.

SECURITY IMPLICATIONS OF ISIS' PRESENCE IN SUB-SAHARAN AFRICA

ISIS' presence in sub-Saharan Africa has serious implications for security in the region. Collaborative efforts by governments in the region have deployed several tactics to rid the region of extremism with relative success. However, the Al-Shabaab, AQIM, Ansar Dine, MUJAO, and ISWAP sects continue to unleash terror on the continent has led to the loss of lives and destruction of property.

Thus, the presence of ISIS and its affiliates continues to pose security challenges to a continent that has been reeling from the effects of these terrorist groups since early 2000. There are genuine concerns that the Islamic State's thousands of African fighters will return home to inflame existing conflict and these returnees may provide ideological, tactical, and strategic reinforcement to extremist groups in Africa, and this will pose a new challenge in the effort to counter terrorism on the continent (Muhammad 2017). Théroux-Bénoni and Dakono (2019) observed that there have been several attacks on civilians in the Sahel and violence related to local conflicts in the area reached unprecedented levels in 2019 when attacks on January 1, in Yirgou village, in north-central Burkina Faso killed forty-nine people. On the same day, an attack in Koulogon village in central Mali left thirty-nine people dead; and on March 23, nearly 160 people died in an attack in Ogassagou village in Mali's Mopti region. That was followed by another attack on April 1, in the northern Burkinabe commune of Arbinda, which killed about sixty people; and subsequent attack on Sobane Da, a village in central Mali, bordering Burkina Faso, on October 4 killed thirty-five people; and another attack in Arbinda left more than twenty people dead. According to Théroux-Bénoni and Dakono, while the rising violence can be attributed to local tensions that are exploited by terror extremists, analysts and policymakers should not lose sight of the structural dynamics that underpin such violence. A case in point, ISGS exploits the Fulani's frustrations against the Daoussahaq in a border conflict that has existed between Mali and Niger since the 1980s; and by supporting one group in an existing divide within communities, ISGS intensifies frustrations and insecurities across communities and states.

Another major concern is the fear that the Islamic State could become a source of funding for Islamist groups in sub-Saharan Africa. For example, Boko Haram was one of the major beneficiaries of US$3 million sent to terror groups in Africa by the founder of Al-Qaeda, Osama bin Laden, in 2002 (Attah 2019). Estimates suggest that the Islamic State is the richest terrorist organization in the world whose assets are more than US$2 billion and is alleged to be generating as much as $1 to $3 million per day (Policy Brief 2014; Stern and Berger 2015). The sect's sources of funding include ransom-taking, bank robbery, "charitable" donations, looting and selling antiquities, and oil smuggling (considered the most important revenue source) among others. Thus, external funding of terrorist organizations by ISIS in the region will affect strategies aimed at cutting off sources of financial support and other counterterrorism efforts against extremist groups.

ISIS affiliates' strategy of attacking military targets — a country's first line of defense — hitting tourist hotels and resorts, and killing foreigners poses a significant risk to African states' capacity to protect their people and territories (Onuoha 2019, personal communication October 15). The implication is that it may open up sub-Saharan Africa to the kind of onslaught by foreign governments witnessed in Syria, Libya, and other countries where ISIS has been operating. Innocent citizens have been killed as a result of foreign troops' deployment and launching of air strikes. It is a fact that drones fail to hit their intended target 96.5 percent of the time, and this is devastating for the civilian population (Kotze 2013). Besides, the militarization of the continent will not augur well for the practice of democracy, liberty, and freedom as counternarratives against Islamic jihadists.

Militarization of the polity could result in the resurgence of praetorian regimes in sub-Saharan Africa, which was under military rule for several decades until the post–Cold War democratization projects. Despite the allure of democracy, African countries continue to witness coups d'état in the twenty-first century with the most recent attempted coup, in an otherwise relatively peaceful Ghana, occurring on September 24, 2019. From 2001 to date, there have been a total of ten successful coups out of twenty-one coups in Africa, an occurrence which may not be divorced from the prevalence of weak institutions and conflicts on the continent. The success rate of these coups (48 percent) is not only disturbing but demonstrates an untiring effort by the military to intervene in domestic politics (Ajodo-Adebanjoko 2019).

The presence of ISIS in Africa will also discourage foreign direct investments which the continent is in dire need of at the moment. The environment of insurgency and insecurity in Africa has deprived the continent of the funds needed for development and this situation will become worse if ISIS's presence becomes dominant. This is because many foreign nationals will see sub-Saharan Africa as a terrorist den and as unsafe for their businesses, and consequently, will be forced to relocate to economies that are considered more stable. This will further compound Africa's development problems.

Tackling ISIS will require that more funds be budgeted for the military at the expense of other sectors such as health and education that have traditionally suffered from low budgetary support. A lower budget for education for instance will lead to an increased number of out-of-school children who are likely to become vulnerable to extremist recruitment and radicalization. Furthermore, more funding for the military at the expense of economic development projects is likely to increase the rate of poverty and unemployment in various countries in the region. Sub-Saharan Africa currently ranks as one of the poorest regions in the world, with many people living below the poverty line. Increased poverty will likely lead to an increase in conflict and insecurity, thus continuing the cycle of insecurity.

Another challenge is the humanitarian crises that will arise from the activities of the sect. Already sub-Saharan Africa is faced with the challenges of refugees and Internally Displaced Persons (IDPs). It is estimated that IDPs currently make up about two-thirds of the total population of 40 million displaced by armed conflict globally, while the Norwegian Refugee Council's internally Displaced Monitoring Center states that as of the end of 2014, there were at least 1.5 million IDPs across eight West African countries: Cameroon, Côte d'Ivoire, Liberia, Mali, Niger, Nigeria, Senegal, and Togo with Nigeria (IDMC 2015; Olowokere 2016 cited in Ajodo-Adebanjoko 2018:12; UNICEF 2002). The presence of ISIS in sub-Saharan Africa is leading to the increased internal displacement of populations and insecurity.

Furthermore, ISIS is notorious for enslaving women and girls as seen in the case of hundreds of women and girls who have been captured from Yazidi and Christian villages as sex slaves. This practice of enslaving the female gender and making them sex slaves will further worsen the record of sub-Saharan Africa in the area of gender-based violence. The region has recorded cases of violence against women by the Boko Haram sect whose practice has been to turn abducted women into sex slaves, similar to the Sierra Leone warlords, who during the Civil War in the country from 1991 to 2002, turned young girls to ''bush wives'' (Ajodo-Adebanjoko and Tinuola 2015). Efforts have been ongoing to stop these practices, and as part of these efforts, countries in sub-Saharan Africa have adopted the Sustainable Development Goals (SDGs) of the United Nations, which are aimed at eliminating gender-based violence. The presence and activities of ISIS will make this difficult to achieve knowing that the sect targets women indiscriminately.

In addition, the practice of enslaving people in ISIS-conquered/dominated towns and regions has negative psychological impacts on the people who have had to deal with enduring enslavement under extremist groups. Sub-Saharan Africa was one of the worst victims of the slave trade that existed from the sixteenth to the nineteenth centuries and the impacts remain in the oral narratives of various communities. The historical trauma experienced can predispose society toward violence, identity politics (in the form of hatred of an outgroup), and the rise of paranoid leadership and ideologies (Stern and Berger 2015). The activities of ISIS affiliates in the region are a source of concern; and allowing ISIS to take root in the region can lead to the destabilization of communities and the festering of other organized criminal activities, like drug and human trafficking that are already part of the anti-government activities.

CONCLUSION

Over the past two decades, the threat posed by violent extremist groups that espouse fundamentalist religious narratives has grown substantially across Africa (Buchanan-Clarke and Lekalake 2016). In sub-Saharan Africa, several groups have emerged advocating conservative religious rule as a cure for modern societies' social ills. Terrorism is never static; it evolves all the time, and wherever the war on terror is being won, the threat moves away and mostly into new battlegrounds (Kotze 2013). As the Islamic State continues to lose territories in Syria, Iraq, and Libya, sub-Saharan Africa becomes an important strategic region for the group. Many extremist groups in the region such as ISWAP, ISGS, ISS, and ISISKTU have publicly declared allegiance to ISIS leader Abu Bakr al-Baghdadi. With some of the fighters returning home and bringing ISIS' ideology with them, the sect's presence in Nigeria, Niger, Cameroon, Chad, Kenya, Mali, Burkina Faso, Somalia, and South Africa could mean that sub-Saharan Africa may become the next caliphate if nothing is done to reverse this trend. ISIS has taken advantage of the security vacuum caused by weak or absent governance in these countries to increase its influence and expand its network (Ellis, 2018).

The fight against extremism in the sub-Saharan African region has been based largely on security-led approaches such as the African Union-backed regional force from Lake Chad Basin Commission (LCBC) countries including Cameroon, Chad, Niger, Nigeria, and the Republic of Benin, the Multinational Joint Task Force (MNJTF) and Operation Barkhane by France, among others. This approach has been found to have largely failed to con-tain violent extremists in the region and has led to the emergence of more development-oriented approaches, such as countering violent extremism (CVE) and preventing violent extremism (PVE) initiatives, which seek to address root political and socioeconomic causes of extremism (Buchanan-Clarke and Lekalake 2016). To prevent the Islamic State from gaining and sustaining its influence in sub-Saharan Africa, the following measures are therefore recommended:

1. Many of the drivers of terrorism remain local; thus combating the spread of the Islamic State will require long-term domestic solutions that will address the underlying causes of extremism such as discontent, conflict, injustice, poverty, nonexistent democracy, endemic corruption, low education, and unemployment, among others.
2. Denying ISIS safe haven in the region. This will require identifying and dismantling the sect's current operational cells in the region. To do this, there is a need for intelligence gathering and information sharing, which could be provided through local policing. In this regard, governments need to partner with affected communities and private organizations for intelligence sharing.
3. Identifying and disrupting ISIS's finances. This will also be necessary for an effort to eliminate their presence in the region. This may require denying the group access to its main funding sources, such as oil, and its ability to access the international financial system.
4. It will also be necessary to disrupt the flow of foreign fighters to and from the battlefield. Agencies will need to work collaboratively with coalition partners to improve information sharing and other efforts to detect and counter foreign terrorist fighters at the borders before they arrive. Also, there is a need for a database on foreign fighters returning from the battlefield, and while those who return should be monitored closely, defectors who return should be rehabilitated and reintegrated into society.
5. There is also the need to directly counter IS' propaganda tool, social media. One way to do this is for governments to partner with foreign governments and other organizations to conduct their messaging campaigns, and deny the sect a messaging platform.
6. The porous nature of the borders of countries in sub-Saharan Africa must be addressed. Border security efforts and activities must be put in place to counter homegrown violent extremism and protect the region from the threats posed by ISIS. An enhanced interface between state actors and border communities is necessary to achieve this.
7. Governments within the region should, as a matter of urgency, convert ungoverned spaces to productive use. Ungoverned spaces have become the den of extremists and as such are sources of threats. These territories exist and persist because integrating them offers few benefits and may pose high costs to host regimes. It will therefore be necessary to integrate them by extending state control into these areas and improve the government's provision of services and political representation through reforming them, outcompeting ISIS for local loyalty, hearts, and minds, and coopting and using them as local governance contractors (Keister 2014)

8. Regional counterterrorism frameworks should be strengthened. At the regional level, there is the 2002 AU Plan of Action on Prevention and Combating Terrorism and other frameworks; but despite these, ISIS has remained a formidable threat to the stability and development of the region. The counterterrorism frameworks need to be synchronized and go beyond tackling threats within individual borders. Although the Nigerian military with the African Union-backed regional force from Lake Chad Basin Commission (LCBC) countries has recorded some substantial success in its counterterrorism effort against ISWAP, there is a need for a counterterrorism effort that will have a wider coverage that will include the entire sub-Saharan African region.

9. Regional coordination of counterterrorism efforts is also important to enable vital security and intelligence cooperation and reduce the risk of various countries fueling proxy wars that, in turn, create an enabling environment for jihadist movements. The African Union and the Economic Community of West African States (ECOWAS) need to therefore play a better-coordinated role in this regard.

10. There is also the need for greater collaboration between state agencies in Africa and greater intelligence sharing between foreign countries and African states if extremist groups and terrorists are to be checkmated.

REFERENCES

Attah, Ejura Christiana. 2019. "Financing Terrorism in Nigeria: Cutting Off the Oxygen" *Africa Development* 44 (2): 5–26.

Abubakar, Atiku. 2017. *"Great Job Beating ISIS In Syria—Now Let's Keep Them Out Of Africa.* Available at: https://www.washingtonexaminer.com/great-job-beating -isis-in-syria-mdash-now-lets-keep-them-out-of-africa. Accessed October 4, 2019.

African Defense Forum, 2015. "ISIS Moves Into Africa," Available at: http://www .defenceweb.co.za/index.php?view=article&catid=49%3ANational+Security&id =40109%3Afeature-isis-moves-into-africa&tmpl=compon. Accessed on August 4, 2019.

Agbiboa, Daniel E. 2014. "Boko-Haram and the Global Jihad: 'Do Not Think Jihad is Over, Rather Jihad Has Just Begun.' " *Australian Journal of International Affairs* 68 (4): 400–417.

Ajodo-Adebanjoko, Angela, and Tinuola Femi. 2015. "Violence Against Women And Its Implication For Development: A Case Study of Women in Kogi State." *Jos Journal of Conflict Management and Peace Studies* (2): 5–13.

Ajodo-Adebanjoko, Angela. 2017. "Armed Conflict, Insecurity and the Rights of the Nigerian Child: A Study of Northeastern Nigeria." *FULafia Journal of Contemporary Political Science* (FJCPS). 1 (1): 170–89.

Ajodo-Adebanjoko, Angela. 2019. "Another Military Intervention? Exploring The Role of the Military in the 2019 General Elections and its Implications for Nigeria's Democratic Consolidation." Paper Presented at the 2nd National Conference Organized by the Faculty of Social Sciences, Federal University Lafia, September 22–24, 2019.

Allison, Simon. 2014. "The Islamic State: Why Africa Should Be Worried." Policy Brief 68. Institute for Security Studies, 3–4.

Atta-Asamoah, Andrew. nd. "Youth of Africa: Unemployment, Social Cohesion and Political Instability." Available at: https://www.unicef-irc.org/article/1060-youth -of-africa-unemployment-social-cohesion-and-political-instability.html. Accessed October 13, 2019.

Bai, Jane, and DeSmet David. nd. "Ungoverned Territories: A Unique Front in the War on Terrorism." Research Briefs. Available at: https://www.ascleiden .nl/research/projects/governance-ungoverned-spaces; https://www.rand.org/pubs/ research_briefs/RB233/index1.html. Accessed October 4, 2019.

Buchanan-Clarke, Stephen, and Lekalake Rorisang. 2016. "PP32: Violent Extremism in Africa: Public opinion from the Sahel, Lake Chad, and the Horn." Policy Papers. Available at: https://www.bicc.de/publications/publicationpage/publication /towards-a-continental-strategy-for-countering-violent-extremism-in-africa-in -global-peace-operation/. Accessed October 12, 2019.

Bukarti, Audu Bulama. 2017. "Embattled ISIS May Turn To Africa," Available at: https://institute.global/insight/co-existence/embattled-isis-may-turn-africa. Accessed October 4, 2019.

Byman, Daniel. 2015. "Terrorism in Africa: The Imminent Threat to the United States." Prepared Testimony Before the Subcommittee on Counterterrorism and Intelligence of the House Committee on Homeland Security, United States of America. April 29, 2015

Campbell, John. 2018. "Terrorists Are Not the Only Ones Exploiting Ungoverned Spaces Across Nigeria." Council on Foreign Relations, Available at:https://www .cfr.org/blog/terrorists-are-not-only-ones-exploiting-ungoverned-spaces-across -nigeria. Accessed October 4, 2019.

Cochi, Marco. 2016. "Africa, the Islamic State's New Stronghold?" Sub-Saharan African Monitor, available at: https://eastwest.eu/en/opinioni/sub-saharan-monitor /africa-the-new-islamic-state-s-stronghold. Accessed October 4, 2019.

Daragahi, Borzou. 2018. "Sub-Saharan Africa Becoming New Battleground Against Violent Extremism As Jihad 'Goes South." Available at: https://www.msn.com /en-xl/africa/top-stories/sub-saharan-africa-becoming-new-battleground-against -violent-extremism-as-jihad-%E2%80%98goes-south%E2%80%99/ar-BBRaewX. Accessed October 4, 2019.

De Villiers, Shirely. 2015. "FACTSHEET: Conflict-Related Deaths in Sub-Saharan Africa/" Africa Check, Available at: http://africacheck.org>factchecks>conf.... Accessed February 20, 2017.

Dearden, Lizzie. 2016. "ISIS: New Terrorist Group Jahba East Africa Pledges Allegiance to 'Islamic State' in Somalia, the Jihadist Group Hailed a 'New Era' in East Africa," Available at: https://www.independent.co.uk/news/world/africa

/isis-new-terrorist-group-jahba-east-africa-pledges-allegiance-to-islamic-state-in -somalia-a6974476.html. Accessed October 6, 2019.

Ellis, Sam. 2018. "How Islamist Militant Groups are Gaining Strength in Africa," Available at https://www.vox.com/2018/6/21/17484188/isis-islamist-militant -terrorism-qaeda-africa-boko-haram. Accessed October 4, 2019.

Eze, Fred. 2018. "Nigeria Ranks Highest in Out-Of-School Children Globally, Says FG" Available at https://www.sunnewsonline.com/nigeria-ranks-highest-in-out-of -school-children-globally-says-fg/. Accessed February 12, 2019.

Fromson, James, and Steven Simon, S. 2015. "ISIS: The Dubious Paradise of Apocalypse Now." *Survival* 57 (3): 7–56.

GAO, 2017. "Countering ISIS and its Effects: Key Issues for Oversight," Report to Congressional Addressees, United States Government Accountability Office

Hennigan, William J. 2019. "Abu Bakr al-Baghdadi Is Dead. Where Does that Leave ISIS?" Available at https://time.com/5711828/al-baghdadi-dead-isis-future/. Accessed October 31, 2019.

Ibrahim, Mohammed. 2018. "69 Per Cent Of Nigeria's Out-Of-School Children in the North—UNICEF." Available at: https://www.premiumtimesng.com/news/ top-news/288344-nigeria-now-has-13-2-million-out-of-school-children-ubec.html. Accessed February 12, 2019.

IDMC 2015. Global Overview 2015: People Internally Displaced by Conflict and Violence. Geneva: Norwegian Refugee Council.

ILO 2019. "Africa's Youth Unemployment Rate to Exceed 30% in 2019: ILO." Available at https://7dnews.com/news/africa-s-youth-unemployment-rate-to -exceed-30-in-2019-ilo. Accessed October 13, 2017.

International Crisis Group 2017. How the Islamic State Rose, Fell and Could Rise Again in the Maghreb. Crisis Group Middle East and North Africa. Report No. 178. July 24. Available at: https://www.crisisgroup.org/middle-east-north-africa/north -africa/178-how-islamic-state-rose-fell-. Accessed October 4, 2019.

Keister, Jennifer. 2014. "The Illusion Of Chaos: Why Ungoverned Spaces Aren't Ungoverned, and Why That Matters," Policy Analysis Number 766. Washington DC: CATO Institute.

Khatib, Lina. 2019. Abu Bakr al-Baghdadi: What His Death Means for ISIS in Syria. Chattam House. Available at: https://www.chathamhouse.org/expert/comment/abu -bakr-al-baghdadi-what-his-death-means-isis-syria. Accessed October 31, 2019.

Kirdar, M. J. 2011. Al Qaeda in Iraq. Aqam Futures Project Case Study Series. Case Study Number 1. Center for Strategic And International Studies (CSIS), Homeland Security & Counterterrorism Program Transnational Threats Project

Kotze, Jacobus. 2013. *The Egg Breakers - Counter Terrorism in Sub Saharan Africa.* CreateSpace Independent Publishing Platform

Lakomy, Miron. 2017a. "Cracks in the Online 'Caliphate': How the Islamic State is Losing Ground in the Battle for Cyberspace." *Perspectives on Terrorism* 11 (3): 40–53.

Lakomy, Miron. 2017b. "Lessons Learned from the 'Viral Caliphate': Viral Effect as a New PSYOPs Tool?" *Cyber, Intelligence, and Security* 1(1): 47–65.

Mashaly, Marwa. 2019. "After Baghdadi's Death: Can Isis Escalate its War of Attrition?" Available at https://7dnews.com/news/after-baghdadi-s-death-can-isis-escalate-its-war-of-attrition. Accessed October 31, 2019.

Miller, Elissa. 2015. "ISIS is Expanding in North and West Africa." *The Arab Weekly.* Available at https://thearabweekly.com/isis-expanding-north-and-west-africa), Accessed October 4, 2019.

Muhammad, Dan Suleiman. 2017. "Deadly Reinforcement: ISIS Fighters Return to Africa." Available at: https://www.foreignbrief.com/africa/deadly-reinforcement-isis-fighters-return africa. Accessed October 4, 2019.

Nwankpa, Michael. 2015. Boko Haram: Whose Islamic State? James A. Baker III Institute for Public Policy, Rice University.

Obaji, Phillip, Jr. 2019. "ISIS West African Offshoot Is Following Al Qaeda's Rules for Success." Available at https://foreignpolicy.com/2019/04/02/isiss-west-african-offshoot-is-following-al-qaedas-rules-for-success-nigeria-niger-chad-terrorism-islamic-state/ .Accessed October 4, 2019.

Pagano, S. 2017. "Impact of The Presence of ISIS in Africa." Available at https://nsiteam.com/sma-reachback-impact-of-the-presence-of-isis-in-africa/. Accessed October 4, 2019.

Rabasa, Angel, and John E. Peters. 2007. "Dimensions Of Conduciveness." In *Ungoverned Territories: Understanding And Reducing Terrorism Risks.* Edited by Angel Rabasa et al. Santa Monica: RAND Corporation, 15–21.

Rich, Paul B. 2013. "Understanding Terror, Terrorism, and their Representations in Media and Culture." *Studies in Conflict & Terrorism* 36 (3): 255–77.

Siboni, Gabi, Daniel Cohen, and Tal Koren. 2015. "The Islamic State's Strategy in Cyberspace." *Military and Strategic Affairs* 7(1): 127–44.

Siegle, Joseph. 2017. ISIS in Africa: Implications from Syria and Iraq, Africa. Center for Strategic Studies.

Slayton, Caleb. 2015. "Underselling Islamist Extremism in Sub-Saharan Africa." *Defense & Security Analysis 31(2):* 123–36.

Stern, Jessica, and J. M. Berger. 2015. *ISIS: The Islamic State of Terror.* New York: HarperCollins Publishers.

Théroux-Bénoni, Lori-Anne, and Baba Dakono. 2019. "Are Terrorist Groups Stoking Local Conflicts in the Sahel?" Available at https://issafrica.org/iss-today/are-terrorist-groups-stoking-local-conflicts-in-the sahel?utm_source=Benchmar kEmail&utm_campaign=ISS_Weekly&utm_medium=email. Accessed October 17, 2019.

UNDP 2017. Journey to Extremism In Africa. New York: United Nations Development Program.

Van, Zyl Isel and Ruth Juliet N. Ngachanja. 2019. "How Is Africa Dealing with Young Extremists?" Available at: https://issafrica.org/iss-today/how-is-africa-dealing-with-young-extremists. Accessed October 17, 2019.

VOA 2018. View on Africa: How to Stop ISIS' Expansion in Africa. African Studies Center, Leiden University. Available at: https://www.ascleiden.nl/research/projects/governance-ungoverned-spaces. Accessed October 4, 2019.

Ward, Alex. 2017. "Why Africa Could Provide An 'ISIS Renaissance'". Available at https://nationalinterest.org/feature/why-africa-could-provide-isis-renaissance-23199 Accessed October 4, 2019.

Ward, Alex. 2019. "Jackpot: Inside The US Military Raid to Kill ISIS Leader Baghdadi." Available at: https://www.vox.com/2019/10/28/20936137/isis-baghdadi-raid-military-dog. Accessed October 31, 2019.

Warner, Jason, and Charlotte Hulme. 2018. *The Islamic State in Africa: Estimating Fighter Numbers in Cells Across the Continent,* Available at https://ctc.usma.edu/islamic-state-africa-estimating-fighter-numbers-cells-across-continent/. Accessed October 4, 2019.

Warner, Jason. 2017. "Sub-Saharan Africa's Three 'New' Islamic State Affiliates." Available at https://ctc.usma.edu/islamic-state-africa-estimating-fighter-numbers-cells-across-continent/. Accessed October 4, 2019.

Williams, Lauren. 2015. Islamic State Propaganda and the Mainstream Media. Iowa Institute for International Policy Analysis.

Wilson Center 2019. "The Islamists Research Timeline: The Rise, Spread, and Fall of the Islamic State." Available at: https://www.wilsoncenter.org/article/timeline-the-rise-spread-and-fall-the-islamic-state. Accessed October 4, 2019.

Woldemichael, Shewit. 2019. Africa Needs a Continental Strategy on Foreign Terrorist Fighters. Available at https://issafrica.org/iss-today/africa-needs-a-continental-strategy-on-foreignterroristfighters?utm_source=BenchmarkEmail&utm_campaign=ISS_Weekly&utm_medium=email. Accessed October 31, 2019.

Yusuf, Hakeem O. 2013. "Harvest Of Violence: The Neglect of Basic Rights and the Boko Haram Insurgency in Nigeria." *Critical Studies on Terrorism* 6(3): 371–91.

Zitouny, Ismail. 2017. Exploiting Disorder: Al-Qaeda and the Islamic State. Report 178. Middle East & North Africa Crisis Group. International Crisis Group.

PART III

COUNTERTERRORISM

Chapter 7

Assessing the Economic Community of West Africa (ECOWAS) Counterterrorism Strategy

Clayton Hazvinei Vhumbunu

Since the September 2001 attacks, there has been an increase in the adoption of pro-active measures and strategies across the globe by countries to both protect and defend their territories from possible terrorist attacks. More noticeable has been the fundamental shift toward collectivity as opposed to individuality as countries are resorting more to regional and continental approaches in countering and combating terrorism given the trans-boundary nature of terrorist activities. Just like other regional groupings in Africa, Asia, Europe, and Latin America, the Economic Community of West African States (ECOWAS) adopted its Counter-Terrorism Strategy in Yamoussoukro, Cote d'Ivoire, in February 2013 that establishes a common framework for intergovernmental action and regional cooperation among West African states to jointly prevent and combat terrorism for the maintenance of regional peace, stability, and security.

Given the dynamism of terrorist activities, and the evolution of regional political security, it is always prudent to assess the appraise the effectiveness of regional security strategies in order to keep track of the emerging challenges and complexities that obstruct progress, while also identifying possible areas that require interventions. The persistence and prevalence of terrorism in the West Africa region has motivated this assessment, considering that this continues against a background of a regional counterterrorism strategy that has been in existence for over half a decade now. The assessment focuses on evaluating the extent to which the agreed interventions as outlined in the ECOWAS Counter-Terrorism Strategy have been implemented, and how these interventions have assisted to contain and eliminate terrorist threats within the subregion. In terms of organization, the first section of the chapter presents a brief background to the ECOWAS Counter-Terrorism Strategy. The second section is dedicated for a discussion of the conceptual framework and literature review. A detailed discussion of the successes achieved in implementing the ECOWAS Counter-Terrorism Strategy is presented in the fourth section, while the challenges and complexities facing ECOWAS member states in implementing the Counter-Terrorism Strategy are presented in the fifth section. The future prospects and recommendations building from the analysis constitutes the last section before conclusion.

CONCEPTUAL ISSUES AND LITERATURE REVIEW

Given the social and political emotions attached to the concept and practice of terrorism, together with the inherent bias within different organizations, government agencies, and bodies driven by their individual interest, it has now become difficult to define terrorism in a universally accepted manner. As Mannik (2009: 152) argues,

> The task of defining terrorism is complicated, but absolutely necessary in order to develop a sufficient understanding of this phenomenon and to deal with it effectively. The complexity of defining terrorism has many aspects. It arises from the variety of parties who have used violence to instil terror. There have also been many different justifications given for the use of this violence (that we may intuitively define as "terrorism"), and there have been many different interested parties defining terrorism, each having own views and in many cases vested interests in a particular way of defining "terrorism."

This lack of definitional consensus has led to what Best and Nocella (2004: 1–2) term "semantic chaos" and "abuse of the term." However, the United Nations defines terrorism as a form of transnational organized crime. It defines terrorism as follows:

> Criminal acts intended or calculated to provoke a state of terror in the general public, a group of persons or particular person for political purposes are in any circumstance unjustifiable, whatever the considerations of a political, philosophical, ideological, racial, ethnic, religious or any other nature that may be invoked to justify them. (Best and Nocella 2004: 1–2)

The causes of terrorism range from ideological extremism and religious fundamentalism to the pursuit of radical political objectives. Botha (2007:4–5) identifies the root causes of terrorism as the nurturing of draconian or closed political systems; existence of weak or failed states with governments that cannot exercise control over their respective territories which creates safe havens for transnational terrorists; existence of nationalist, separatist, or ethnic movements; conflict over natural resources and marginalization of certain groups of the society; religious fundamentalism; and poverty, unemployment, and the growing gap between the rich and the poor. Mercenarism, quest for wealth especially through kidnapping-for-ransom, and perpetuation of trans-organized crimes' networks are also factors behind terrorism. It is also argued by scholars such as Hassan (2012) that terrorism breeds when citizens are frustrated by national or local politics, and opportunities for economic survival are limited. Given the multiplicity of causes and objectives of terrorism, it is not surprising that political movements have used the term to label their opponents so as to demonize and render them unattractive on the political marketplace.

Terrorism takes place in many forms such as assassinations of political leaders; taking targeted citizens or leaders as hostage; bombing political and military targets or civilians using conventional, biological or chemical weapons; and destruction of tourist attractions or centers of heritage or symbolic buildings; with state and non-state actors employing it as a weapon to achieve various goals such as political, social, and even religious goals. Counterterrorism has now become a very complicated exercise that would require concerted efforts at subnational, national, regional, and international levels. States are transformatively leaning more towards the cooperative security approach, as argued by De Castro (2004: 193–217), given the regional and international dimension of terrorism especially after the September 11 attacks in the United States.

Several studies have been conducted on regional approaches being undertaken in Asia, Latin America and Europe to prevent, counter, and combat terrorism. In EU Counterterrorism Policy: A Paper Tiger?, Bures (2006: 72) examines the European Union's Counter-Terrorism Strategy adopted in 2005 and accompanying counterterrorism initiatives. He argues that while the strategy has assisted to fight terrorism in Europe through strengthened interstate cooperation, the policy suffers from an "implementation deficit" due to a number of political, legal, and cultural challenges that include weak enforcement capabilities, lack of coordination between the EU member states and the relevant EU institutions, and a disturbing tendency by several member states' governments to opt for bilateral cooperation instead of a regional collective approach.

One of the key challenges confronting the EU in implementing its counterterrorism strategy, as Bures (2006) posits, is that more often than not, decisions adopted at the EU level relating to counterterrorism are not been fully implemented by the member states, and in some cases agreed measures are interpreted differently while at the same time agencies in charge of intelligence and law enforcement do not cooperate with the European Union Agency for Law Enforcement Cooperation (Europol) all the time (Bures 2006). Similarly, studies in Argomaniz et al. (2015: 6) that have analyzed the successes and failures of the European Union's Counter-Terrorism Strategy and the EU Counter-terrorism Action Plan have also revealed capacity challenges at the national and supranational level, which are undermining the efficacy of the strategy despite notable successes as evidenced by the fact that a number of terrorist cells have been dismantled and thwarted across the EU, as a result of coordinated collaborative efforts facilitated through the strategy. If these are not addressed together with the root causes of terrorism, underpinned by "genuine pro-integration thinking," the EU counterterrorism policy will be rendered "less of a paper tiger," instead of being an effective "counterterrorism device" (Argomaniz, Oldrich, and Kaunert 2015: 72–73).

Emmers (2009: 159) explored approaches adopted by the Association of Southeast Asian Nations (ASEAN) to counter terrorism since the 9/11 and 2002 Bali terrorist attacks. The ASEAN approach, as Emmers (2009:159) notes, combines security, law enforcement, socioeconomic, ideological, and educational policies at the national level with regional resilience against the threat of terrorism promoted via synergies through a comprehensive security agenda. Whilst the region has in place the ASEAN Declaration on Joint Action to Counter Terrorism of 2001, the ASEAN Convention on Counter-Terrorism of 2007 and the ASEAN Comprehensive Plan of Action on Counter-Terrorism of 2017 both aim at enhancing regional cooperation among the ten member states to counter, prevent, and suppress terrorism; scholars like Borelli (2017: 16) have averred that these ASEAN policy and accompanying legislative frameworks are mere "soft laws" that use vague language and impose "uncertain obligations" on member states without any clear implementation time frames and enforcement mechanisms for monitoring and evaluation. To Borelli, such frameworks have "weak concrete impact" since in the end there are varying levels of interpretation and implementation commitment, which is further worsened by lack of political will for collective security and responsibility within the region. The ASEAN counterterrorism strategy has also been criticized for being reactive rather than being proactive or preventive, with member states lacking not only the mordent ICT infrastructure to prevent radicalization and recruitment of terrorists in the region but also research on vulnerabilities and regional risk assessments which are key in counterterrorism (Borelli 2017: 17–19).

Based on comparative analysis of how other regions implement their approaches towards counterterrorism in Europe, North America, Latin America, and Asia, it can be observed that coordinated and collective efforts in preventing and combating terrorism entails cross-border enforcement of anti-terrorist laws; intelligence and information sharing on terrorist threats; joint cross-border management, controls, and surveillance; joint military operations; joint investigations of terrorist attacks; regional capacity building; collective strengthening of criminal justice systems; and close coordination of anti-terrorist initiatives among others.

In *The Center Can Hold: Towards a Regional Approach to Combating West Africa's Terrorists,* Salihu (2015: 1) argues that while ECOWAS has managed to establish institutional and legal frameworks to undertake the "three-pronged approach to counter-terrorism: [to] prevent, pursue and reconstruct," with most West African states now pursuing "national, bilateral and regional efforts to counter-terrorism," there have been "mixed outcomes." To Salihu (2015: 1), one of the greatest challenge is that "there is a wide gap between policy rhetoric and the reality on the ground especially in terms of legislation related to foreign terrorist fighters (FTF) in West African states." In an examination of the challenges to peace and security in the West African subregion, Tejpar and de Albuquerque (2015: 4) argue that despite having made significant inroads in preventing different forms of conflict in the region, ECOWAS' conflict prevention tools suffer from deficiencies in logistical and financial capabilities especially in the deployment of armed forces. The effectiveness of the regional body's institutional capacity, however, is dependent upon the active support and implementation of the regional body's organizational agenda.

The first step in ensuring more impactful implementation of regional approaches to counterterrorism measures may be the alignment of national counterterrorism laws, policies and strategies with those at the regional level. Using absolute data catch-up and convergence estimation techniques for the period 1980 to 2012, Asongu and Nwachukwu (2018: 237–59) assessed the feasibility of policy harmonization by African countries in the fight against terrorism. The authors' empirical findings augment the view that policy harmonization is needed in fighting transnational crimes in the form of terrorism while also emphasising the importance of strengthening country-specific harmonization and coordination of counterterrorism policies. Thus, well-coordinated national and regional synergies and complementarities are a necessary, though not sufficient, condition for the success of any regional approach to address regional problems.

ECONOMIC COMMUNITY OF WEST AFRICAN STATES (ECOWAS) COUNTERTERRORISM STRATEGY: TARGETS AND ASPIRATIONS

ECOWAS, itself a regional grouping comprising fifteen member states geographically located in the West African subregion, namely Benin, Burkina Faso, Cape Verde, Cote d'Ivoire, The Gambia, Ghana, Guinea, Guinea Bissau, Liberia, Mali, Niger, Nigeria, Senegal, Sierra Leone, and Togo, has for some time now placed regional peace and security as a priority on the agenda especially at the turn of the millennium. More specifically, strategies to combat, counter, and eliminate terrorism have since become the critical issues of focus in the region's conflict prevention and management framework, largely due to the terrorism dynamics within the region.

The adoption of the ECOWAS Counter-Terrorism Strategy was preceded by numerous policy decisions that aimed at combating, countering and eliminating terrorism in the West-African subregion. The ECOWAS Treaty lists as one of its fundamental principles the adherence to the collective maintenance of regional peace, stability, and security, whilst undertaking, in Article 58 of the Treaty, to cooperate in establishing appropriate mechanisms and systems for the management of peace and security within the region (ECOWAS 2010:36). In addition, the ECOWAS Protocol Relating to the Mechanism for Conflict Prevention, Management, Resolution, Peacekeeping and Security, 1999; under Article 3, the objective is to cooperate at regional level in various areas of peace and security including preventing and combating of international terrorism (ECOWAS 1999). The ECOWAS Conflict Prevention Framework of January 2008 also lays down the foundation for collaborative approaches in dealing with conflicts in the region (ECOWAS 2008).

Building on all the above legal and policy frameworks, the ECOWAS Political Declaration on a Common Position against Terrorism of 2013, which embodies a Counter-Terrorism Strategy and Implementation Plan detailing implementation measures and strategic policy direction, seeks to prevent and combat terrorism and terrorism-related acts in West Africa through a combination of military and nonmilitary measures and tools so as to create a peaceful and stable environment that is conducive for socioeconomic development, while also providing a common operational framework for the implementation of continental and international counterterrorism strategies and policies. Other supporting legal frameworks include the Protocol on Non-Aggression of 1978; Protocol Relating to Mutual Assistance and Defense Matters of 1981; the Convention on Mutual Assistance in Criminal Matters of 1992; the ECOWAS Convention on Mutual Assistance in Penal Matters of 1992; the ECOWAS Convention on Extradition of 1994; Protocol on Democracy and

Good Governance of 2001; Protocol on the Fight Against Corruption of 2001; Protocol on the Establishment of a Bureau of Intelligence and Investigation on Criminal Matters of 2006; and the ECOWAS Convention on Small Arms and Light Weapons, the Ammunition and Other Related Materials of 2006. Together with these frameworks, the ECOWAS Counter-Terrorism Strategy aims at addressing all forms of terrorism, including kidnapping, hijacking, hostage-taking, ransom demand practices, bombing of public and private properties and critical infrastructures, sabotage acts, and the desecration of religious and other cultural sacred places.

In terms of aspirations and targets, the ECOWAS Counter-Terrorism Strategy implores its member states to institute justice mechanisms to deal with people who finance, plan, direct and perpetrate terrorism activities. The broader objectives are to enhance coordination and harmonization of counterterrorism efforts among member states, strengthen national and regional capacities to prevent and combat terrorism, promote a democratic criminal justice approach in counterterrorism, and promote regional and international cooperation on terrorism-related matters (ECOWAS 2013). It calls on member states to freeze accounts and confiscate assets and other economic resources belonging to terrorist groups or those facilitating, inciting, or funding such activities. In the spirit of collective action, the ECOWAS Counter-Terrorism Strategy also calls upon member states to refrain from tolerating safe havens for terrorists' recruitment and training within their territories. In addition, the strategy also targets that all member states should ratify all the ECOWAS conventions and protocols relating to combating terrorism as well as similar legal frameworks at the African Union (AU) and United Nations (UN) levels (ECOWAS 2013: 5).

Through the ECOWAS Counter-Terrorism Strategy, member states also commit to institute operational measures to facilitate the effective implementation of all the regional and continental legal counter-terrorism instruments through the enactment of appropriate and restrictive national legislations which criminalize terrorism with accompanying national coordinating mechanisms. There was also an undertaking within the ECOWAS Counter-Terrorism Strategy to strengthen cross-border cooperation and synergies in the areas of information sharing, intelligence gathering, investigation, prosecution, and law enforcement so as to prevent and combat terrorism. However, in enforcing such laws, member states are called upon in the strategy, to adhere to the dictates of rule of law and international law, specifically continental frameworks such as the African Charters on Human and People's Rights and global conventions such as the Universal Declaration on Human Rights, Convention Against Torture and Other Cruel, Inhuman or Degrading Treatment or Punishment (ECOWAS 2013: 6).

In terms of institutional framework, the ECOWAS Counter-Terrorism Strategy envisaged the establishment of an ECOWAS Counter-Terrorism Coordination Unit, ECOWAS Arrest Warrant, ECOWAS Black List of Terrorist and Criminal Networks, and a subregional Counter-Terrorism Training Center. The resource requirements for the implementation of the counterterrorism strategy in the form of technical assistance, personnel, and funding were anticipated to be sourced from member states while development partners and relevant international organizations would assist to bridge the capacity gaps (ECOWAS 2013: 7). An encouragement is also made in the strategy, for the civil society to work in collaboration with member states in mutually reinforcing and coordinating their efforts in preventing and combating terrorism within communities.

In terms of approach, the ECOWAS Counter-Terrorism Strategy is anchored on three main pillars: (1) Prevent, (2) Pursue, and (3) Repair. In "Prevent," ECOWAS seeks to detect and prevent terrorism before it emerges through adopting policies that address and eliminate conditions conducive to terrorism such as poverty, unemployment, economic and political marginalization, human rights abuses, corruption, and insecurity, among others. Prevention would then be actualized through eliminating these conditions, developing proactive and operational capabilities to detect and disrupt terrorism in the form of early warning systems, suppressing terrorism financing, developing measures to prevent extremism and radicalism, and promoting democratic practices (ECOWAS 2013: 25–31).

On the other hand, in "Pursue," the regional group intends to take measures to minimize the impact of terrorism on communities through rapid responses whenever it occurs. This, according to the ECOWAS Counter-Terrorism Strategy, will be achieved through the ratification and implementation of all regional, continental and international conventions and legal frameworks relating to terrorism; enhancing democracy and rule of law; improving cross-border cooperation, border control, and surveillance; suppressing and criminalizing terrorism funding; protecting critical infrastructure and soft targets of terrorism; and building capacity for preventing terrorism (ECOWAS 2013:31–38). The "Repair" or "Reconstruct" Pillar sets the strategy for member states to rebuild societies in the aftermath of terrorism. Thus member states commit to put in place measures to protect the victims of terrorism and uphold their rights, reconcile communities, repair the social contract with citizens, and develop counterterrorism strategies to address future threats (ECOWAS 2013: 38–39).

In order to translate plans into actions, as well as facilitating effective coordination of efforts at regional level, the ECOWAS Counter-Terrorism Strategy lays down an implementation mechanism that consist of an institutional as well as monitoring and evaluation framework. With regard to the institutional framework, the strategy envisaged the development of national taskforces in all ECOWAS member states charged with the responsibility to serve as a focal point for counterterrorism matters at the national level. At the regional level, the strategy entails the involvement of several institutions, namely the ECOWAS Commission (to coordinate the implementation of the strategy through the Regional Security Division), ECOWAS Court of Justice (to enforce the rights of terrorism victims), Committee for the Coordination of Security Services (to coordinate intelligence cooperation in implementing the strategy), ECOWAS Early Warning and Response Mechanism (to gather information for predicting and detecting terrorism activities), ECOWAS Counter-Terrorism Training Center (to provide training, technical assistance, research, analysis and information dissemination on counter-terrorism), Counter-terrorism Coordination Unit (to monitor the implementation of the strategy, undertake technical functions within the Regional Security Division and recommend measures to strengthen the strategy), and the Inter-Governmental Group Against Money Laundering (to coordinate activities related to the suppression of terrorist funding and undertake vulnerability assessments) (ECOWAS 2013: 40–42). International organizations and the civil society would assist to implement the strategy in a complementary fashion while an ECOWAS Counter-Terrorism Training Manual would be developed for counterterrorism training. The strategy provides for regular and periodic assessments and reporting of progress and challenges, on a biannual basis, with the outcome of the evaluations informing any revisions of the strategy as and when necessary.

What can be noted from the aspirations and targets of the ECOWAS Counter-Terrorism Strategy is that it lays a very broad framework for the regional grouping to fight terrorism, with the supporting institutional and implementation mechanisms. For a regional grouping of fifteen countries, at different levels of economic development, in addition to distinct political economies and socio-religious structures, the implementation of the ECOWAS Counter-Terrorism Strategy is bound to have different outcomes.

Since 2013 when the strategy was adopted, there has not been any detailed assessment of the strategy in terms of its challenges, successes and progress. Meanwhile, there are now several terrorist groups operating in the West African subregion such as Jama'at Ahl al-Sunna li al-Da'wa wa al-Jihad (popularly known as Boko Haram), Movement for the Emancipation of Niger Delta (MEND), and Islamic State West Africa Province (ISWAP), mostly in Nigeria, Al-Qaeda in the land of Islamic Maghreb (AQIM), the Movement for Oneness and Jihad in West Africa (MOJWA), Group for the Support of Islam and Muslims (GSIM), Jumaat Nusrat al-Islam wal Muslimeen (JNIM), Islamic State Greater Sahara (ISGS), Ansar Dine/Ansar al-Din (AAD), Movement for Unity and Jihad (MUJAO), al-Mouwakoune

Bi-Dima/Signed-in-Blood Battalion/Signatories-in-Blood Battalion, Islamic Movement of Azawad (IMA), and Al Murabitoun, as well as several terrorist cells involved in transitional criminal activities and terrorism. It is therefore timely to undertake a comprehensive assessment of the ECOWAS Counter-Terrorism Strategy, in order to determine its successes, challenges, complexities, and opportunities at a time when several West African countries are suffering from terrorist attacks that are causing heavy loss of life and property (Akanji 2019: 2–11). For instance, the United Nations Office for the Coordination of Humanitarian Affairs (OCHA) reported that over 2.3 million people had been displaced by terrorist activities of Boko Haram across Nigeria, Niger, Cameroon, and Chad as of November 2017, with 7.2 million resultantly threatened by food insecurity (United Nations 2017). All this is impeding socioeconomic development in the region.

EVALUATING SUCCESSES, FAILURES, AND CHALLENGES IN IMPLEMENTING THE ECOWAS COUNTER-TERRORISM STRATEGY

Whilst it has to be acknowledged that a sure-proof evaluation of the successes and challenges of any policy strategy may be debatable given the inherent limitations of all qualitative and quantitative approaches that may be deployed, this evaluation of the ECOWAS Counter-Terrorism Strategy attempts to assess the successes, failures, and challenges of the strategy in light of the objectives, targets and aspirations of the strategy itself as articulated above. Granted, some of the objectives are broad generalizations, and they do not sufficiently satisfy the quality of being "measurable" as espoused in the SMART criteria (that is embodying the qualities of being *specific, measurable, achievable, relevant*, and *time-bound*). However, the effort is made to contextualize such objectives and targets within reasonable and standard expectations.

Institutional Framework and Regional Coordination in Counterterrorism

As discussed above, ECOWAS envisaged the establishment, or use of already existing, institutions in order to facilitate implementation of the ECOWAS Counter-Terrorism Strategy. These are the Regional Security Division of the ECOWAS Commission, ECOWAS Court of Justice, Committee for the Coordination of Security Services, ECOWAS Early Warning and Response Mechanism, ECOWAS Counter-Terrorism Training Center, ECOWAS Counter-terrorism Coordination Unit, and the Inter-Governmental Group

Against Money Laundering. To its credit, ECOWAS has managed to establish the relevant institutions for the intended purpose.

However, it is the operational capacities and capabilities of these institutions that have been considered to be affecting their delivery potential (see for instance Tejpar, Johan and de Albuquerque 2015:5). Inadequate financial and technical resources limit the impact of ECOWAS' coordination capacity; yet counter-terrorism measures require a well-oiled and technically capable institutional framework. The ECOWAS counterterrorism institutions are performing below expectations in terms of coordinating concerted efforts to achieve set goals across the region (Maiangwa 2017:112). There is the persistent failure of the region to disrupt, dismantle, and defeat the ever-proliferating terrorist groups within the ECOWAS subregion, such as Boko Haram, MEND, ISWAP, AQIM, MOJWA, GSIM, JNIM, ISGS, AAD, MUJAO, IMA, al-Mouwakoune Bi-Dima/Signed-in-Blood Battalion/Signatories-in-Blood Battalion, and Al Murabitoun, among other insurgency groups especially in Nigeria, Mali and Niger. For this reason, foreign troops from France and the United Nations are now a dominant and more visible feature in the region, undertaking counterterrorism operations to bridge the capacity gaps.

Further, the lack of effective coordination has also been cited with the evidence of the absence of smooth cross-border cooperation of the relevant counterterrorism institutions at the regional level with those at the various national levels in the member states. For instance, the police force institutions of the various ECOWAS member states are uncoordinated in their counterterrorism activities, despite the existence of the Regional Security Division of the ECOWAS Commission and the ECOWAS Counter-terrorism Coordination Unit. Another challenge is that the International Police Organization (INTERPOL) does not fully work in liaison with the West African Police Chiefs Committee (WAPCCO) for regional coordination and cooperation of police force in border security as envisaged in the ECOWAS Counter-Terrorism Strategy and ECOWAS Conflict Prevention Framework (Maiangwa 2017:114).

Strengthening of National Capacities to Detect, Deter, Intercept, and Prevent Terrorism

It is incontrovertible, that real counterterrorism starts at the community and state level. If states do not possess the requisite ability and capability to detect, deter, intercept and prevent terrorism, then it will be unfathomable to imagine that they can manage to develop a solid regional counterterrorism machinery. Most of the ECOWAS member states have ailing economies that cannot sustain a capable public administration machinery in the form of a well-skilled, motivated, and competent police force, intelligence unit, border management authorities, army, judiciary, parliament, media, and civil society. The African Development Bank reports that almost half of the West African population of over 300 million people is living below the international poverty line, with their governments ridden in heavy debts and burgeoning budget deficits (African Development Bank 2018: 9–12). Even the relatively better economically performing countries in the subregion, such as Nigeria and Côte d'Ivoire are not immune from such macroeconomic challenges (African Development Bank 2018: 23).

To make matters worse, a number of the countries are more often than not confronted with unpeaceful transitions, civil strife, and pockets of instability as is the case for Nigeria, Liberia, The Gambia, Sierra Leone, Côte d'Ivoire, Mali, Burkina Faso, and Niger. Most of the critical departments of police, intelligence, army, justice administration, border control, and others are therefore either understaffed or ill-equipped to deal with terrorist groups that are now using more sophisticated weaponry and advanced digital information communication technology devices for communication and liaison as they undertake terrorist activities. All this erodes the national capacities of the ECOWAS member states to domesticate and implement the counterterrorism strategy as this requires strong institutions, financial resources, technical resources, and skills. For instance, Nigeria's Civilian Joint Task Force struggles to implement its long-term counterterrorism plan against Boko Haram, which killed 6,612 people in 2012 and 1,254 in 2017 (Institute for Economics and Peace 2018:17) through high-impact bombings, explosions, and suicide bombs, whilst Fulani extremists caused almost 1,700 deaths between January and September 2018 (Institute for Economics and Peace 2018: 56). On the other hand, Mali experienced 141 deaths and 171 terrorist incidents (Institute for Economics and Peace 2018: 52), mostly as a result of JNIM's terrorist attacks, despite the Malian government being assisted by the United Nations Multidimensional Integrated Stabilization Mission in Mali's (MINUSMA) soldiers to provide security and peacekeeping.

What has to be noted is that even if some ECOWAS member states have established national mechanisms such as counterterrorism units and other structures to coordinate national counterterrorism measures, the absence of the same in other countries would ultimately weaken the coherence of the regional counterterrorism machinery. This is because terrorist groups always take advantage of loopholes or weaknesses in anti-corruption or tax laws within some countries in the region and establish their havens and/or mechanisms to access their illicit finances (United Nations Economic Commission for Africa 2018: 47). For instance, despite being a member of the Inter-Governmental Action Group Against Money Laundering in West Africa, Senegal does not criminalize the provision of funds to terrorist organizations or to individual terrorists in the absence of a link to a specific terrorist act (US

Department of State 2018: 39). Nevertheless, other countries in ECOWAS such as Burkina Faso have instituted financial intelligence units—Cellule Nationale de Traitement des Informations Financières (CENTIF)—charged with tracking terrorist financing (US Department of State 2018: 14).

It is also a reality that most member states in ECOWAS do not have sufficient human resource capacity and hard infrastructure for managing effective border control systems. Most of the states in ECOWAS have poor control of their borders to the extent that terrorists take advantage to launch cross-border attacks (Pujol-Mazzini 2018). With terrorist groups allowed free movement through the porous borders, it is easy for them to expand their networks and zones of influence and operation, which makes them very difficult to detect, deter, and intercept. For example, in Niger, there is the MUJAO, Boko Haram, ISIS in the Greater Sahara (ISIS-GS), ISISWA, and JNIM, among many others. These are reported to easily transit across Niger's porous borders into Nigeria and Chad with weapons and contrabands to carry out attacks on their targets (US Department of State 2018: 32). The existence of several active terrorist groups in most ECOWAS countries is a clear sign that they are lacking capacity to detect and interrupt them.

Whilst West Africa is generally endowed with a demographic dividend, having over 300 million people in ECOWAS, which should logically translate to overwhelming army, intelligence and police recruitment, the limited military and security budgets at both the national and regional levels obviously limit the personnel deployed to fight against terrorism along national borders, ports of entry, and other areas of deployment; and the availability of skilled personnel also remains a challenge. It extends beyond numbers to quality training and technical as well as tactical abilities. Translating demographic dividend into larger military establishments through larger conscriptions would need more financial and logistical support for the armed forces. Nigeria is the most populous country not only in ECOWAS but also in Africa, and it has one of the largest militaries on the continent. According to the World Bank, in 2016, Nigeria had a total of 200,000 personnel in its armed forces (World Bank 2019). This was far much larger than the number of personnel in the military of other African countries, with larger area size, and whose borders and/or coastlines are relatively longer. The countries include Niger (10,700), Mauritania (20,850), Tanzania (28,400), Mali (15,800), Chad (39,850), South Africa (82,150), and the Democratic Republic of Congo (134,250) (World Bank 2019). Despite this huge military, Nigeria's counterterrorism efforts in collaboration with other ECOWAS states to fight Boko Haram was, and is still, faced with financial and technical challenges. Apparently, it is not just mere numerical supply and size of the military. In the end, the challenge is compounded by poor logistical and transport infrastructures, which make counterterrorism surveillance difficult.

However, one may also need to acknowledge the efforts invested toward strengthening national capacities to detect, deter, intercept, and prevent terrorism through the ECOWAS Counter-Terrorism Strategy, especially through training and capacity building. ECOWAS has managed to conduct training programs for all member states, with participants from departments that are more relevant in the fight against terrorism. For instance, the regional body has been collaborating with the Institute of Security Studies (ISS)—a Pretoria-based think tank - to conduct Counter-Terrorism Training Courses for members of the police, intelligence, national guard, gendarmerie, ECOWAS Interpol, counterterrorism, organized crime units, and border control units from all member states so as to build their respective capacities to address the threat of terrorism. The focus of the training course has been on aspects such as intelligence and counterintelligence, legal aspects of terrorism, border control and surveillance, terrorism incidents investigation, and operational responses to terrorism, among others.

Military assistance has also been extended to address capacity shartfalls. For example, most of the Joint Task Force (JTF), Multinational Joint Task Force (MNJTF), and Civilian Joint Task Force (CJTF) activities directed at fighting terrorism in Nigeria, Benin, Niger, Chad, and Cameroon have been made more efficient and effective through the provision of capacity-building assistance from Western countries. The United States has been training Nigerian soldiers in counterinsurgency, counterterrorism, and bomb disposal (Ray 2016), while in August 2017, the country adopted its Policy Framework and National Action Plan for Preventing and Countering Violent Extremism which had been developed through funding from the United Kingdom's Department for International Development (DFID) (United States Department of States 2018: 37). In addition, the United States has also been assisting several West African countries to build their counterterrorism capacity. For instance, from 2012 to 2017, the US Departments of Defense and State provided approximately US $240 million in security assistance, counterterrorism, and countering violent extremism (CVE) programming, while the US Agency for International Development (USAID) also provided US $30.9 million for CVE programs (US Department of State 2018: 32).

Countries like Senegal also lack adequate national capacities for counterterrorism despite the objective of enhancing national capacities as espoused in the ECOWAS strategy. While Senegal has specialized units to detect, deter, and prevent acts of terrorism in the form of its gendarmerie and national police, these face challenges in executing interagency cooperation and information sharing (US Department of State 2018: 38). It is also reported that the country lacks border resources and does not have systems to ensure travel document security, terrorist screening facilities, and biometric screening capabilities at the country's major ports of entry, which makes the country vulnerable to terrorist intrusion due to failure to detect and intercept suspects (United States Department of States 2018). Likewise, while Niger's legislation, law enforcement, and border security authorities, especially the National Police, National Guard and Gendarmerie, are actively engaged in detecting, deterring, and preventing terrorism acts within their country, their work is impeded by insufficient manpower, funding, and equipment (US Department of State 2018: 33).

Prevention and Combating of Violent Religious Radicalism/Extremism

Preventing and combating violent extremism and radicalism is always a wearisome and elephantine task. This is first due to the nonconventional methods that are used by terrorist groups as they are usually invisible and employ surprise attacks as well as suicide attacks. It is second due to the fact that the existing conditions of unemployment, poverty, inequality, and poor service delivery in most ECOWAS states create fertile ground for extremism, fundamentalism, and conflict. In the end, terrorists find it easy to recruit as they easily manipulate community grievances while also taking advantage of prevalent corruption to benefit from illicit trade in weapons and arms.

ECOWAS member states have therefore encountered serious challenges in ensuring that religious radicalization and extremism are prevented as envisaged in the ECOWAS Counter-Terrorism Strategy. This is evidenced in the proliferation of terrorist groups and report of several terrorist attacks in all but five of the fifteen ECOWAS member states as depicted in Table 7.1. The Global Terrorism Index (GTI) reports, since 2014, after the ECOWAS Counter-Terrorism Strategy was put into place, clearly show that eliminating terrorism in the West African subregion is proving to be difficult, although there is a noticeable reduction in terrorist attacks.

The GTI provides a summary of key trends and patterns in terrorism across the world based on data from the Global Terrorism Database (GTD) collected by the University of Maryland's National Consortium for the Study of Terrorism and Responses to Terrorism (START). It scores countries based on the number of terrorist incidents, number of terrorism-induced fatalities, number of terrorism-induced injuries, and approximate level of property damaged as a result of terrorist incidents, all for a given year. All this is ranked on a scale of 1–10, with *0* representing no impact of terrorism, *1–2* representing lowest impact of terrorism, and *8–10* representing highest impact of terrorism.

While Sierra Leone, Togo, The Gambia and Benin have had no reported terrorist attacks in the period under review, from 2014 up to 2018, the ECOWAS member states of Nigeria, Niger, Mali, Liberia, and Burkina Faso

Table 7.1.

Country	Ranking on 2014 GTI (out of 124 countries)		Ranking on 2016 GTI (out of 130 countries)		Ranking on 2018 GTI (out of 138 countries)		Performance in Global Ranking & Terrorism Impact from 2014
	Rank	Rank	Rank	Score	Rank	Score	
Benin	124	0	130	0	138	0	No impact
Burkina Faso	87	0.7	63	2.623	37	4.811	Worsening
Cape Verde*	-	-	-	-	-	-	-
Cote d'Ivoire	40	3.76	72	2.177	63	3.276	Improvement
The Gambia	124	0	130	0	138	0	No impact
Ghana	124	0	106	0.346	138	0	Improvement
Guinea	81	1.12	85	1.403	112	0.324	Improvement
Guinea Bissau	97	0.35	122	0.077	138	0	Improvement
Liberia	113	0.08	110	0.25	119	0.210	Worsening
Mali	22	5.29	25	6.03	22	6.015	Worsening
Niger	58	2.59	16	6.682	23	6.004	Worsening
Nigeria	4	8.58	3	9.314	3	8.660	Worsening
Senegal	45	3.55	64	2.598	96	1.012	Improvement
Sierra Leone	124	0	130	0	138	0	No impact
Togo	120	0	130	0	138	0	No impact

have been struggling to disrupt, dismantle, and defeat violent extremism and fundamentalism, which has bred terrorism.

What can be deduced from this trends and patterns is that the affected ECOWAS member states' respective national authorities, parliaments, law enforcement agencies, and military, judiciary, educational, and social institutions are not managing to effectively detect, intercept, and disrupt terrorist activities within their national borders. Whilst the ECOWAS Counter-Terrorism Strategy provides that every member state should implement a zero-tolerance policy to terrorism, and treat it as a serious crime, mostly through eliminating conditions conducive to terrorism, this is not being implemented fully on the ground. One of the greatest mistakes that is being made by most of the countries is to put more resources toward, and emphasis on, military approaches to counterterrorism instead of also deploying, with more or less equal measure, complementary nonmilitary approaches. This is despite the fact that empirical evidence has proved that military force rarely ends terrorism (Institute for Economics and Peace 2018: 56).

In Burkina Faso, for instance, the government has been adopting a heavy-handed military approach, through a special terrorism detach-ment, Groupement des Forces Anti-Terroristes (GFAT), in collaboration with the G-5 Sahel Joint Force to fight the JNIM terrorist group mostly in the Northern border with Mali (US Department of State 2018: 13). The Burkinabe security forces have been accused of using torture, extrajudicial killings, burning of property, and arbitrary detention in their counterterrorism responses (US Department of State 2018: 14). Given the fact that poverty, unemployment, and marginalization are not addressed in the communities, the terrorist organizations continue to successfully recruit marginalized, poor, and historically disadvantaged Fulani people (US Department of State 2018: 13). The government of Burkina Faso continue does not have any programs to rehabilitate or reintegrate terrorists into the society which may assist if complemented with de-radicalization strategies and community education and empowerment initiatives (US Department of State 2018).

On the other hand, some ECOWAS member states such as Mali are mak-ing progress in implementing strategies to combat violent extremism as envisaged in the Counter-Terrorism strategy although the impact of such interventions is minimal given the increasing terrorist activities and attacks. In June 2017, Mali adopted a national strategy for the prevention of radical-ization to violence and terrorism, and it involves the Ministry of Religious Affairs working in collaboration with the High Islamic Council and other religious associations while efforts are being made to formulate the "Program for Accelerated Development in the Northern Regions" to decentralize the North so as to initiate development (US Department of State 2018: 29–30). If implemented in a comprehensive manner, with genuine commitment for

people-centered and broad-based socioeconomic development, such interventions may be fundamentally transformative in ending extreme radicalism and fundamentalism. All in all, however, it can be noted that most of
the ECOWAS countries are not promoting national reconciliation, interfaith
dialogue, and peaceful resolution of conflicts that harden fundamentalists
and extremists, especially with the various groups that are opposed to governments and expressing themselves through terrorist attacks (United States
Department of State 2018).

Promotion of Criminal Justice in Counterterrorism

The ECOWAS Counter-terrorism Strategy aims at promoting a criminal
justice approach to counterterrorism that stresses strict adherence to the
rule of law, respect for human rights, and protection of civilians from
counterterrorism activities. An assessment of the ECOWAS' regional performance to date would reveal that whilst a number of countries have managed
to put in place the relevant justice delivery systems within their jurisdictions,
there is still a plethora of cases of reported incidents where basic human
rights of terrorist suspects are violated, including ill-treatment and detention
without trial. In the mean, civilians are left vulnerable without protection
from imminent terrorist attacks.

Some ECOWAS member states have developed institutions in pursuit of
the criminal justice objective. An example is Burkina Faso, which, in January
2017, created a Special Judicial Interagency Working Group based on best
practices across the region that will have jurisdiction over terrorism-related
legal cases (US Department of State 2018: 14). A number of countries are
also improving in terms of civilian protection from terrorist attacks through
boosting security presence in strategic areas, and also via efficient training of
their emergence response teams. An example is Mali's Gendarmerie Crisis
Response Team, which tactically and timely responded to the Campement
Kangaba terrorist attack in June 2017 and saved people from potential death
(US Department of State 2018: 28). The Gendarmerie Crisis Response Team
had been trained through assistance from the US Department of State's
Anti-Terrorism Assistance (ATA) Program (United States Department of
State 2018).

Nevertheless, there are cases of miscarriage of justice in dealing with terrorists or terrorist suspects. For instance following the arrest of 250 terrorist
suspects in Niger in 2017, there were reports that security officials were
sometimes abusing or harming detainees suspected of terrorist activities,
despite the fact the standing law in Niger prohibits torture and degrading
treatment (US Department of State 2018: 33). In Nigeria, there have also

been reports about the military denying terrorist suspects their rights to legal representation, due process, and right to be heard by a judicial authority (US Department of State 2018: 36). Such acts, although often justified on the basis of displaying a "zero-tolerance attitude" toward terrorism, definitely undermine the intentions of the regional counterterrorism strategy, given the inviolability and inalienability of human rights.

Promotion of Regional and International Cooperation on Terrorism-Related Matters

As the ECOWAS Counter-Terrorism Strategy aspires, responses to terrorism should be harmonized and there should be regional and international cooperation on terrorism-related matters including extradition and mutual legal assistance. In assessing the extent to which member states are pursuing this objective, it may be difficult to ignore the fact that almost all the ECOWAS member states have soldiers participating in joint forces fighting terrorism within the sub-region. Burkina Faso has forces in the G-5 Sahel Joint Force and provides forces to improve security along shared borders to fight ISIS-GS and AQ, whilst at the same time maintaining two peacekeeping battalions in Mali within the framework of the MINUSMA (United States Department of State 2018: 15). Similarly, the Malian military participates in multinational border security operations under the G-5 Sahel Joint Force. Niger is also part of the G-5 Sahel Joint Force, and the country also deployed an infantry battalion to MINUSMA, as well as the Multinational Joint Task Force along with Benin, Cameroon, Chad, and Nigeria (US Department of State 2018: 34).

However, while the implementation of the ECOWAS Counter-Terrorism Strategy has been a collective effort, the member states that are less affected by terrorism—Liberia, Sierra Leone, Togo, The Gambia, Benin, and Ghana—are less active in terms of regional and international cooperation on matters relating to counterterrorism. Conversely, those member states that are heavily affected by terrorist activities such as Nigeria, Mali, Niger, and Burkina Faso participate more in the fight against terrorism. This is evident in their contribution of forces to the G-5 Sahel Joint Force, Multinational Joint Task Force, and MINUSMA. This may affect the spirit of cooperation within the regional grouping, which may adversely impact the achievement of the strategy's goal.

FUTURE PROSPECTS AND RECOMMENDATIONS

From the assessment of the ECOWAS Counter-Terrorism Strategy, it can be noted that the implementation of the strategy has assisted the region to pursue its aspirations and determination to disrupt, dismantle, and defeat terrorism so as to create a conducive environment for regional integration, peace, security, stability, and development. Indeed, the Counter-Terrorism Strategy creates opportunities for a regional approach in preventing and combating terrorism at a time when cross-border terrorist networks and cells are too complex and intricate to address as individual countries.

In pursuit of the objective of enhancing coordination amongst member states in the field of intelligence, law enforcement, and the investigation and prosecution of terrorist crimes, the assessment reveals that ECOWAS has managed to put in place the institutional framework to facilitate regional coordination of counterterrorism efforts. However, the greatest challenge has been translating the plan into action as there is no evidence of greater coordination between and among counterterrorism institutions in member states. In light of this, capacity challenges have been identified as well as lack of smooth cross-border cooperation of the relevant counterterrorism institutions at the regional level with those at various national levels. It is suggested that regional institutions be capacitated mostly through funding to attract better skills, infrastructure and action plans to carry out their functions.

The ECOWAS Counter-Terrorism Strategy's second objective seeks to strengthen national and regional capacities to detect, deter, intercept, and prevent terrorist crimes. An assessment of the Counter-Terrorism Strategy against this objective suggests that the capacities (institutional, personnel, financial, and technical) are very weak to the extent that they struggle to effectively detect, deter, intercept, and prevent terrorism. ECOWAS itself does not have sufficient capacity to build these national capacities; rather, it relies on international partners and donors to fund capacity- building initiatives. This is despite the fact that without sufficient national and regional capacities, the ECOWAS Counter-Terrorism Strategy will remain a "paper tiger." The recommendation from the analysis is that mechanisms that are inward-looking should be explored in order to reduce the overreliance on donor funding for vital and sensitive operational undertakings that involve state security.

An assessment of the ECOWAS Counter-Terrorism Strategy vis-à-vis its objective of promoting a criminal justice approach that emphasizes the rule of law, due process, respect for human rights, and the protection of civilians in counterterrorism activities; brings to the fore the reality that despite the existence of laws, conventions and declarations that affirm the inviolability of basic human rights, a number of countries are committing acts that are inconsistent with the strategy insofar as protecting arrested terrorist suspects is concerned. There are reports alleging the abuse of human rights, including illegal detention and inhuman treatment, among others. What may be refreshing, however, is the fact that some countries such as Burkina Faso have established criminal justice institutions to facilitate the implementation of counterterrorism measures agreed to at the regional level. In addition, it is also noteworthy that there are some member states that are improving in terms of ensuring justice by protecting not only terrorist suspects but also efficient tactical and timely emergency response teams to save lives during terrorist attacks, as is the case with Mali.

Another outcome of the assessment of the ECOWAS Counter-Terrorism Strategy is the revelation that the majority of ECOWAS' member states are failing to pprevent and combat violent religious radicalism/extremism within their national borders. Rampant unemployment, widespread poverty, rising inequality, and poor service delivery in West African countries are nurturing a breeding ground for extremism and fundamentalism. It is recommended that countries need to prioritize prudent macroeconomic management, broad-based economic empowerment, and job creation so as to avoid making communities vulnerable to terrorist recruitment. In addition, countries need to complement military counterterrorism approaches with nonmilitary approaches that include reconciliation, community dialogue, reintegration, and deradicalization.

Lastly, the assessment revealed that in seeking to promote regional and international cooperation on terrorism-related matters, member states are contributing to ECOWAS' joint forces, which are fighting terrorism within the subregion, while also cooperating differently within the framework of a regional approach toward countering terrorism. This is quite encouraging and should be built upon by the member states.

CONCLUSION

This chapter sought to assess the ECOWAS Counter-Terrorism Strategy with a view to appraise its effectiveness and track the emerging challenges and complexities that obstruct progress while also identifying possible areas that require interventions. It evaluated the extent to which the agreed interventions as outlined in the ECOWAS Counter-Terrorism Strategy have been implemented, and how these interventions have assisted to contain and eliminate terrorist threats within the subregion.

The assessment has revealed that the strategy is assisting in providing a framework to facilitate a more viable regional and collaborative approach to counterterrorism. Whilst ECOWAS has managed to establish the relevant institutions, as well as facilitate regional coordination and forge collaborations to effectively implement the ECOWAS Counter-Terrorism Strategy, challenges relating to capacity deficiencies, the persistence of socioeconomic environments that are conducive for religious fundamentalism and extremism;

and varying levels of political will and commitment are all undermining the efficacy and impact of the strategy.

REFERENCES

African Development Bank. 2018. West Africa Economic Outlook 2018. https://www.afdb.org/fileadmin/uploads/afdb/Documents/Publications/2018AEO/African_Economic_Outlook_2018_West-Africa.pdf. Accessed October 28, 2018.

Akanji, O. Olajide. 2019. "Sub-regional Security Challenge: ECOWAS and the War on Terrorism in West Africa." *Insight on Africa* 11(1): 94–112.

Argomaniz, Javier, Bures Oldrich, and Christian Kaunert (Eds.). (2105). *A Decade of EU Counter-terrorism and Intelligence: A Critical Assessment.* New York: Routledge.

Asongu, Simplice, and Jacinta Nwachukwu. 2018. "Fighting Terrorism: Empirics on Policy Harmonization." *German Economic Review* 19(3): 237–59.

Best, Steve, and Anthony J. Nocella. 2004. "Defining Terrorism." *Animal Liberation Philosophy and Policy Journal* 2(2): 1–18

Borelli, Marguerite. 2017. "ASEAN Counter-terrorism Weaknesses." *Counter Terrorist Trends and Analyses* 9(9): 14–20.

Botha, Anneli. 2007. Relationship Between Africa and International Terrorism: Causes and Linkages. Paper Presented at the Conference on Southern African and International Terrorism Dialogue. Brenthurst Foundation, Tswalu. South Africa. January 25–27, 2007.

Bures, Oldrich. 2006. "EU Counterterrorism Policy: A Paper Tiger?" *Terrorism and Political Violence* 18(1): 57–78.

Center for Democracy and Development. 2018. ECOWAS Counter-Terrorism Strategy Tracker. Fact Sheet, May, 2–11. https://www.africaportal.org/publications/ecowas-counter-terrorism-strategy-tracker/. Accessed September 19, 2018.

De Castro, Renato Cruz. 2004. "Addressing International Terrorism in Southeast Asia: A Matter of Strategic or Functional Approach?" *Contemporary Southeast Asia* 26(2): 193–217.

ECOWAS. 1999. Protocol Relating to the Mechanism for Conflict Prevention, Management, Resolution, Peacekeeping and Security. https://www.zif-berlin.org/fileadmin/uploads/analyse/dokumente/ECOWAS_Protocol_ConflictPrevention.pdf. Accessed September 12, 2018.

ECOWAS. 2008. ECOWAS Conflict Prevention Framework. REGULATION MSC/REG. 1/01/08. ECOWAS Commission, Abuja, Nigeria. January. http://documentation.ecowas.int/download/en/publications/Conflict%20Prevention%20frmework.pdf. Accessed September 12, 2018.

ECOWAS. 2010. Revised Treaty of the Economic Community of West African States (ECOWAS). ECOWAS Commission, Abuja, Nigeria.

ECOWAS. 2013. ECOWAS Political Declaration and Common Position Against Terrorism. http://www.edup.ecowas.int/wp-content/uploads/2016/11/Ecowas-CT-strategy_ENGLISH-Published.pdf. Accessed September 12, 2018.

Emmers, Ralf. 2009. "Comprehensive Security and Resilience in Southeast Asia: ASEAN's Approach to Terrorism." *Pacific Review 22*(2): 159–77.

Hassan, Muhsin. 2012. *Understanding Drivers of Violent Extremism: The Case of Al-Shabaab and Somali Youth.* Combating Terrorism Center. Department of Social Sciences, United States Military Academy; West Point. August 23.

Institute for Economics and Peace. 2018. Global Terrorism Index: Measuring and Understanding the Impact of Terrorism. New York, http://visionofhumanity.org/app /uploads/2018/12/Global-Terrorism-Index-2018-1.pdf. Accessed October 18, 2018.

Institute for Economics and Peace. 2014. Global Terrorism Index: Measuring and Understanding the Impact of Terrorism. New York, https://reliefweb.int/sites/ reliefweb.int/files/resources/Global%20Terrorism%20Index%20Report%202014 .pdf. Accessed: October 18, 2018.

Institute for Economics and Peace. 2016. *Global Index Terrorism: Measuring and Understanding the Impact of Terrorism.* New York. http://economicsandpeace .org/wp-content/uploads/2016/11/Global-Terrorism-Index-2016.2.pdf. Accessed: October 18, 2018.

Maiangwa, Benjamin. 2017. "Assessing the Responses of the Economic Community of West African States to the Recurring and Emerging Security Threats in West Africa." *Journal of Asian and African Studies* 52(1): 103–20.

Mannik, Erik. 2009. Terrorism: Its Past, Present and Future Prospects. http:// www.ksk.edu.ee/en/wp-content/uploads/2011/03/KVUOA_Toimetised_12-M%C3 %A4nnik.pdf. Accessed: September 30, 2018.

Pujol-Mazzini, Anna. 2018. "Islamist Terrorist Groups Are Turning Their Attention to West Africa." *Washington Post.* July 3. https://www.washingtonpost.com/news /worldviews/wp/2018/07/03/islamist-terrorist-groups-are-turning-their-attention -to-west-africa/?noredirect=on&utm_term=.965d06e41493. Accessed October 31, 2018.

Ray, Nivedita. 2016. "rowing Threat of Terrorism in Africa: The Case of Boko Haram." *Indian Council of World Affairs (ICWA) Issue Brief,* 20.

Salihu, Naila. 2015. "The Center Can Hold: Towards a Regional Approach to Combating West Africa's Terrorists." *Kofi Annan International Peacekeeping Training Centre. Policy Brief, 1 July 2015,* http://www.kaiptc.org/Publications /Policy-Briefs/Policy-Briefs/2015-KAIPTC-Policy-Brief---Naila-Salihu.aspx. Accessed 12 October 2018.

Tejpar, Johan, and Adriana Lins de Albuquerque. 2015. Challenges to Peace and Security in West Africa: The Role of ECOWAS. Studies in African Security, FOI Memo, 5382.

United Nations Economic Commission for Africa. 2018. *A Study on the Global Governance Architecture for Combating Illicit Financial Flows.* Addis Ababa, Ethiopia.

United Nations. 1994. Declaration on Measures to Eliminate International Terrorism Annex to UN General Assembly Resolution 49/60 Measure to Eliminate International Terrorism. 84th Plenary Meeting of the UN General Assembly. December 9, 1994. UN Doc. A/Res/60/49. New York. http://www.un.org/documents/ga/res/49/ a49r060.htm. Accessed September 30, 2018.

United Nations. 2017. UN Office for West Africa and the Sahel. January 2018
    Monthly Forecast Security Council Report. https://www.securitycouncilreport.org
    /monthly-forecast/2018-01/west_africa_and_the_sahel.php. Accessed September
    24, 2018.
US Department of State. 2018. Country Reports on Terrorism 2017. September
    19. https://www.state.gov/documents/organization/283100.pdf. Accessed: January
    4, 2018.
World Bank. 2019. Armed Forces Personnel, Total. http://data.worldbank.org/
    indicator/MS.MIL.TOTL.P1. Accessed January 5, 2019.

Chapter 8

The US Counterterrorism Regime in Africa

George Klay Kieh Jr.

The aftermath of the September 11, 2001 terrorist attacks on the American homeland by Al-Qaeda witnessed the meteoric rise of the African continent on the United States' national security agenda. As Kieh and Kalu (2012: 3) observed, "On September 11, 2001, the foundation of the United States was jolted as a result of the terrorist attacks launched against the homeland by Al Qaeda . . . The attacks were both brazen and horrific. The terrorists used planes belonging to various American airlines to launch the attacks on the towers of the World Trade Center and the Pentagon."

Significantly, Africa's rise on the American national security agenda was propelled by several interlocking factors. The framing one was the "Global War on Terror," which was launched by the George W. Bush administration in the aftermath of 9/11 (Kieh 2014a). The United States realized that its "Global War on Terror" required the participation and support of various countries around the world, including those in Africa. Hence, Africa became what Minx and Prince (2012:19) referred to "another front in the U.S.' Global War on Terror (GWOT)."

Another factor is that several African states have large Muslim populations. Although the Bush administration and subsequent ones declared that Muslims are not the target of the "Global War on Terror," praxis has demonstrated that American policy-makers are concerned about Muslims because of what they termed "Jihadist-based terrorism"—terrorism that has been, and continues to be, undertaken by Islamic-based groups such as Al-Qaeda (Saine 2012). In 2001, when GWOT was launched by the Bush administration, for example, Mauritania's population was 99.9 percent Muslim; Morocco was 99 percent; Algeria was at 98 percent; Egypt stood at 94 percent; Senegal stood at 94

187

percent; and Gambia, Mali and Niger stood at 90 percent each (Pew Research Center 2009).

In addition, the United States is desirous of preventing "so-called failed states or fragile states [in Africa] from providing sanctuary to terrorist groups" (Kwesi-Aning and Atuobi 2009:1). That is, the thinking of American policy-makers is that African states that were and are experiencing state fragility and state failure and the associated weak capacity to exercise full, effective, and efficient control over their respective territories provide propitious environments for terrorist groups to exploit.

Further, American policy-makers were, and remain, concerned that terrorist organizations could adversely affect US economic interests by jeopardizing access to the African continent's vast oil, gas, and mineral resources. These natural resources are critical to supplying the American industrial and manufacturing complexes, and the resulting continued socioeconomic development of the United States (Adibe 2014). For example, the Gulf of Guinea region, which has large deposits of oil and gas, has become a major area of focus in GWOT and the broader American foreign and security policy toward Africa. In sum, the United States is interested in safeguarding the Gulf of Guinea region, as well as individual African states that are pivotal to supplying the United States with oil and minerals.

Against this background, this chapter has several interrelated objectives. A key one is to examine U.S.-Africa relations. The rationale is to interrogate the ways in which American foreign policy toward Africa has contributed to sowing the seeds of undemocratic governance and socioeconomic malaise, which in turn has contributed to the engagement in terrorism by various African-based groups such as Al-Shabaab and Boko Haram, as well as external groups such as Al-Qaeda and the Islamic State of Iraq and Syria (ISIS), which have affiliate organizations in various parts of the African continent. Another is to probe US counterterrorism policies, especially to locate Africa within these crucibles. As well, the chapter will map out the major US counterterrorism strategies in Africa. This will be followed by an assessment of the progress and challenges these strategies have experienced. Finally, based on the evaluation of US counterterrorism strategies in Africa, the chapter will proffer some suggestions for rethinking these counterterrorism strategies.

U.S.-AFRICA RELATIONS: A BACKGROUND

The examination of U.S.-Africa relations is critical to understanding the roots of "terrorism from below"—the engagement in acts of terrorism by various non-state actors such as Al-Shabaab and Boko Haram (Jalata 2016). Relations between the United States and Africa were framed by the imperatives of the

"Cold War" between the American-led bloc and the Soviet-led one (Adibe 2014; Kalu 2014).This was because the "third wave of independence" (the largest), which began sweeping across the African continent in 1960 commenced about fifteen years after the beginning of the "Cold War." Hence, both power blocs sought to woo African states into their respective camps using various inducements, such as foreign aid. The raison d'être was for African states to serve the national interests of the leaders and constituent member states of the two major power blocs. In the case of the United States, as Kalu (2014: 62) argues, "Historically, [it] has always measured its relations with Africa on the extent to which such a relationship advances America's economic and geostrategic interest." In other words, neither the United States nor any global power has an interest in promoting human security in Africa. Instead, it has, and continues to be about using African states as handmaids to serve the national interests of the United States and other global powers.

In this vein, the United States has pursued two contradictory pathways in its relations with African states: On the one hand, in its policy rhetoric, the United States has professed to be the champion of democracy, including the promotion and protection of human rights. However, on the other hand, in its policy praxis, during the "Cold War" (1945–1990), the United States established and maintained "asymmetrical, neocolonial and paternalistic relationship with some of the most repressive regimes—Mobutu (Zaire, now the Democratic Republic of Congo), Barre (Somalia), Arap Moi (Kenya), Doe (Liberia), and Mubarak (Egypt)" (Kieh 2014a: 191). As the foot soldiers for the promotion of American national interests, these autocratic regimes were supported with foreign aid, including weapons, to ensure their maintenance of power. However, US support for these regimes was provided amid the vitriolic violations of human rights (Freedom House 2022) and human needs deficit and the associated mass and abject poverty, social malaise, and other vagaries of material deprivation (United Nations Development Program 2022). One of the resulting effects was the development of mass resentment for these regimes and the United States. For example, the US support for the autocratic regime of Mohammed Said Barre in Somalia contributed to the ultimate collapse of the regime and the eruption of a civil war in 1988 (Elmi and Barise 2006; Kieh 2002). In addition, the failure of the Barre regime to provide the requisite leadership in promoting human security, and the aftermath of the civil war led to the establishment of insurgent groups, including Al Shabab, that used terrorism both in a targeted and random manner. Further, some Somali developed an anti-American orientation, against the backdrop of the role of the United States in providing the oxygen that kept authoritarianism well and alive in their country.

Interestingly, with the end of the "Cold War" and the resulting collapse of the Soviet Union in 1990, the United States was forced to rethink its anti-democracy and antidevelopment policy towards Africa (Kieh 2014a). The result of the policy review was what I referred to elsewhere as "cynical disengagement" (Kieh 2014a: 191). That is, after supporting authoritarian regimes in Africa during the "Cold War," and the resulting crises and conflicts in several of the client states such as Somalia, Liberia, and the Zaire (now the Democratic Republic of Congo), the United States retreated from Africa. Subsequently, amid the chaos and violence in client states like Liberia, Somalia, and the Democratic Republic of the Congo, the United States for-mulated and implemented a so-called new policy toward Africa anchored on a framework that Chase et al. (1999:1) called "pivotal states"—states that are critical to the promotion of the economic and strategic interests of the United States. Consequently, the emergent "pivotal states" in Africa included Egypt, Ethiopia, Kenya, and Nigeria. Then, after 9/11, the list of "pivotal states" in Africa was expanded to include countries like Djibouti. For example, about a year after 9/11, the United States "established in Djibouti for the Combined Joint Task Force-Horn of Africa" (Kieh 2014b:171). Similarly, the United States reached "base access agreements with several African states, including Gabon, Kenya, Mali, Morocco, Tunisia, Namibia, São Tomé and Principe, Senegal, Uganda and Zambia" (Kieh 2014b: 171; Volman 2009:3). Specifically, these base access agreements give the U.S. "access to local bases and other facilities to be used by American forces as transit bases or as for-ward operating bases for combat, surveillance, and other military operations" (Kieh 2014b: 171; Volman 2009: 3).In addition, in 2007, the U.S. established AFRICOM as a major featured of its post-"Cold War" and post-9/11 policy toward Africa. In this way, the United States will have the military tool to protect its economic and strategic interests in Africa, including unfettered access to oil.

Overall, despite the end of the "Cold War," the pivot of US policy toward Africa has remained unchanged: The promotion of US economic and strategic interests in various African states, including using authoritarian regimes as the handmaids. Thus, while the United States has continued to trumpet its pro-democracy and pro-development rhetoric, the bottom line is that American interests supersede the promotion of democracy and socio-economic development in Africa. In other words, human security in Africa remains subordinated to the imperatives of American economic and strategic interests in Africa. Thus, the George H. W. Bush, Clinton, George W. Bush, Obama, the Trump, and Biden administrations have supported, and continue to support ,various authoritarian regimes in Africa, including in Djibouti, Egypt, and Gabon (Freedom House 2022).

AMERICAN COUNTERTERRORISM POLICY

The US counterterrorism policy is a derivative of the annual national security strategy that is formulated by the incumbent administration. In this vein, the initial counterterrorism policy was formulated by the George W. Bush administration in 2002, in the aftermath of 9/11 (White House 2002). President Bush outlined the major contours of the policy in a joint address delivered to the US Congress on September 20, 2011, framed by what the Council on Foreign Relations (2005: 2) referred to as a "global open-ended war on terror." In his address, President Bush asserted: "Our war on terror begins with al Qaeda, but it does not end there. It will not end until every terrorist group of global reach has been found, stopped and defeated" (Bush 2001: 1). In addition, about three days later, President Bush issued Executive Order 13224, which gave the US government authority to "designate and block the assets of foreign individuals and entities that commit, or pose a significant risk of committing acts of terrorism" The subsequent US National Security Strategy for 2002 provided the framework for American counterterrorism policy toward Africa:

> Together with our European allies, we help strengthen Africa's fragile states help build indigenous capability to secure porous borders and help build up law enforcement and intelligence infrastructure to deny haven for terrorists. . . . Africa's great size and diversity requires a security strategy that focuses on bilateral engagement and builds coalition of the willing. (White House 2002:9–10)

Here are two major derivatives from the U.S.' counter-terrorism policy towards Africa. A key one is that the United States will foster cooperation and collaboration as the mainstays to "strengthen alliances to defeat global terrorism and work to prevent attacks against [the United States] and [its] friends' (The White House 2002:1). The other is the pursuance of unilateral, bilateral, and multinational efforts that are designed to prevent terrorist organizations from threatening and using weapons of mass destruction against the United States and its allies.

Since the emergence of the post-9/11 era, the US counterterrorism policy toward Africa has served as the road map for each administration—George W. Bush, Obama, and Trump. Interestingly, while the Biden administration that came to power in 2021 has maintained the fundaments of the US counter terrorism policy toward Africa, it has enunciated an approach that locates the former in the broader crucible of US foreign policy. This "new approach" is outlined in the US National Security Strategy for 2022. Three major issues can be discerned from the emergent counterterrorism policy toward Africa and the other regions of the world:

1. Counterterrorism will be linked with other US national security issues.
2. Counterterrorism should be aligned with the dynamism of terrorist threats (Shiel et al. 2021).
3. The United States will expand its counterterrorism tool box by making investments "in a broader set of tools to tackle emerging threats" (Shiel et al. 2021:1)

AMERICAN COUNTERTERRORISM STRATEGIES IN AFRICA: NATURE AND SCOPE

Background

The United States has formulated and implemented a plethora of counterterrorism strategies, including initiatives and programs, in Africa. Given the multiplicity of these programs, this section of the chapter will focus on some of the major ones. This will be done by deciphering the major contours of each strategy, and the geographical expanse within the context of the African continent. The common thread that weaves together these counterterrorism strategies is their "preponderant reliance on the use of military means" (Kieh and Kalu 2012:6; Kieh 2012:123). This reflects two major framers of the US counterterrorism strategies in Africa. A key one is that terrorism is a target that can be engaged. The other is that the use of military means is the most effective way to defeat terrorism.

Pan-Sahel Initiative

The Pan-Sahel Initiative was the inaugural counterterrorism program established by the United States in Africa. Commencing operations in 2002, the Pan-Sahel Initiative comprised four African Sahelian states as the participants under American suzerainty: Chad, Mali, Mauritania, and Niger. Initially, the rationale was that the hotbed of Al Qaeda-led terrorist activities was the African Sahel region.

The overarching purpose of the Pan-Sahel region was to build the military-security capacities of the participating Sahelian states, so they in turn could assist the United States in prosecuting the African dimension of its "Global War on Terrorism." For example, special counterterrorism units were created within the military establishments of the participating African states and trained by American military personnel. In addition, the militaries of the participating African states received military-security equipment from the United States to buttress their capacities to engage in counterterrorism operations, including intelligence gathering, surveillance, and military offensives.

As Ellis (2004: 459) notes, "PSI consist[ed] of training military units from the four partner countries, mostly by soldiers from U.S. Special Forces from EUCOM. Also, involved in some aspects of the scheme [were] U.S. Marines, with some logistical work being sub-contracted to the private security company Pacific Architects and Engineers (PAE)."

The East African Counter-terrorism Initiative

The East African Counter-terrorism Initiative was established in 2003, with Djibouti, Eritrea, Ethiopia, Kenya, Tanzania, and Uganda as the participating countries. The focus was on the East African region. The initiative had several major goals:

1. The United States would provide training in counterterrorism operations to military units from the participating African countries.
2. The United States would provide training in border security for the coast guard and related military-security units from the participating states.
3. The United States would help with aviation security for the participating countries.
4. The United States would provide training for the police forces of the participating countries.
5. The United States will build the capacity of the participating states to enable them to counter the financing of terrorism.
6. The United States would build the capacity of the participating states to plan and undertake educational and outreach programs that are designed to counter terrorism.

About six years later, the United States developed and implemented an expansive initiative dubbed the Partnership for Regional East Africa Counterterrorism (PREACT). The participating countries are Burundi, Comoros, Djibouti, Ethiopia, Seychelles, Kenya, Mozambique, Rwanda, Seychelles, South Sudan, Sudan, Tanzania, and Uganda. Interestingly, the initiative includes Mozambique, which is in the Southern African region.

The initiative has several interlocking strategic objectives:

1. Reducing the operational capacity of terrorist networks;
2. Developing a rule of law framework for countering terrorism in partner nations;
3. Enhancing border security;
4. Countering the financing of terrorism; and
5. Reducing the appeal of radicalization and recruitment to violent extremism (U.S. Department of State 2022).

The Trans-Saharan Counter-terrorism Partnership (TSCTP)

The Trans-Saharan Counter-terrorism Partnership was established by the United States in 2005 as the successor to the Pan-Sahel Initiative. Initially, the participating African states are Algeria, Chad, Mali, Mauritania, Morocco, Niger, Nigeria, Senegal, and Tunisia. Subsequently, Burkina Faso and Libya were added. In terms of its scope, the TSCTP mainly covered the central, northern, and western regions of the African continent. In terms of the regional distribution of the member states, there is one participating state from Central Africa, four from North Africa, and six from West Africa.

The TSCTP has four major pillars that constitute the overarching strategic objectives:

1. The United States through its Special Operations Command provides training to military units from the participating states in the techniques of counterterrorism military operations.
2. The United States provides military equipment to the participating African states to enhance their counterterrorism capabilities.
3. The United States provides logistics to the participating states to support their counterterrorism operations.
4. The United States provides training to military and security units of the participating states in border protection as a bulwark against terrorist incursions, especially against the backdrop of the porosity of borders in Africa.

In 2021, the US Congress passed the Trans-Saharan Terrorism Partnership Program Act. The law was passed in recognition of what Schmidt and Minter (2021: 1) referred to as an acknowledgment of "the failure of U.S. counter-terrorism policies in North and West Africa." The thrust of the revised program is to "balance security activities with diplomatic and development efforts to address the political, socioeconomic, governance, and development challenges . . . that contribute to terrorism and violent extremism" (Schmidt and Minter 2021:1).

The African Coastal and Border Security Program (ACBSP)

The African Coastal and Border Security Program, which was established in 2003, has its roots in the US-established Coastal Security Program (CSP) of the 1980s. The CSP was designed to help build the capacity of coastal African states to effectively monitor and control their territorial waters in the efforts to prevent illegal fishing and mining activities. The ACBSP is a multipurpose initiative, and the participating countries include Angola, Chad, Djibouti, Eritrea, Ethiopia, Gabon, Kenya, Nigeria, São Tomé and Principe, and Uganda (Duncker 2007). The initiative's geographic scope spans the central, eastern, southern, and western regions of Africa.

Organizationally, the initiative has major counterterrorism elements. One is the training of the participating countries' coast guards in border security, including monitoring, detecting, and preventing incursions by terrorist organizations. Another is the provision of monitoring and communication equipment by the United States to the participating states to help enhance their intelligence collection capabilities, among others.

The U.S. Africa Command (AFRICOM)

The U.S. Africa Command (AFRICOM) was established in 2007 (Kwesi-Aning 2012). According to the George W. Bush administration, the rationale for establishing the military command was in recognition of "the growing strategic importance of Africa" (United States Africa Command 2022: 1). Operationally, the "U.S. Africa Command assumed responsibility for U.S. military activities in areas that had been part of three geographical commands previously and now included all of Africa except Egypt" (United States Africa Command 2022: 1).

The guiding framework for AFRICOM's role in counterterrorism is based on the building of the military-security capacities of selected African states to enable them to help protect the United States from terrorist attacks both on its homeland and its interests abroad. In his testimony before the Armed Services Committee of the US House of Representatives on March 17, 2022, General Stephen Townsend, the Commander of AFRICOM, articulated the framework thus:

> Deadly terrorism has metastasized to Africa . . . with al-Shabaab, al-Qaeda's fastest growing and most kinetically active affiliate, in East Africa, and ISIS and Al Qaeda groups in West Africa and elsewhere among the world's fastest growing, wealthiest and deadliest terrorist groups. They remain grave and growing threats that aspire to kill Americans there and, in our homeland. (Townsend 2022: 4)

Accordingly, AFRICOM's counterterrorism functions in Africa are anchored on three major pillars. A key one is the provision of military training in counterterrorism to units from participating countries. Another is the provision of military equipment to the counterterrorism units in the militaries of the participating countries. As well, AFRICOM establishes special military task forces for the purpose of undertaking counterterrorism operations on the African continent. Two major cases are the Combined Joint Task Force Horn of Africa, and the Joint Task Force AZ TEK SILENCE.

The Gulf of Guinea Maritime Security Initiative

The Gulf of Guinea Maritime Security Initiative comprises seventeen African countries, stretching from the western to the southern sections of Africa. The Gulf of Guinea region is important to the United States because it has vast reserves of oil. For example, the region accounts for about 60 percent of Africa's oil production (Morcos 2021).

Given the importance of oil to the continued industrial development of the United States, American policy-makers are concerned that the region would be vulnerable to terrorist incursions, including attacks and other acts of sabotage that could jeopardize both the flow of oil and the reserves. Thus, the overarching purpose of the initiative is to "secure the region from terrorist attacks" (Kieh 2014: 196). In order to achieve this goal, the United States provides training, equipment, and weapons to military and security units from the participating states to build their capacity to monitor, detect, prevent, and suppress terrorist incursions in the region.

The Drone Program

During the Obama administration, the United States decided that the use of unmanned drones was an effective counterterrorism strategy. Specifically, the drones are used for intelligence gathering and for launching strikes against various targets. This was because it does not involve the use of military personnel, who are vulnerable to attacks, and the resulting injuries and death in traditional counterterrorism military operations. In other words, if drones are attacked, including being shot down, it would have no implications for the safety of military personnel.

Accordingly, in the case of Africa, beginning in 2013, the United States began to negotiate bilateral agreements with various states for the purpose of these African countries serving as bases for the American drone program. The initial agreement was with Niger, which provided the United States with a bridgehead for collecting intelligence on the affiliates of Al-Qaeda in northern Mali and the broader Sahara region (Al Jazeera 2013:1; Kieh 2014a: 195). Subsequently, the United States signed drone basing agreements with other African countries, including Burkina Faso, Ethiopia, Mali, Morocco, Algeria, Somalia, and Sudan (Kieh 2014; a Queally 2012; Richman 2013; Schmidt 2013).

ASSESSING US COUNTERTERRORISM STRATEGIES IN AFRICA: PROGRESS AND CHALLENGES

Background

What progress has been made, and the shortcomings with the implementation of US counterterrorism strategies in Africa? In other words, has the pursuance of US counterterrorism strategies in Africa led to the possibility of containing and eventually eliminating the use of terror by non-state actors such as Al Shabaab, Boko Haram, and the surrogates of Al-Qaeda and ISIS? This *puzzle will frame this section of the chapter.*

Progress

The implementation of US counterterrorism strategies in Africa has yielded two major benefits. A key one is that under each of the strategies and the associated programs the military and security units from the participating African states have received training in counterterrorism. The training covered areas such as intelligence gathering and surveillance of non-state actors that use terrorism. In addition, special operations forces from the participating countries have developed their capacities to undertake counterterrorism military operations either offensively or defensively. Another benefit is that the participating African states in the various US-created and -managed counterterrorism strategies have received much needed equipment for undertaking a variety of counterterrorism activities, including intelligence collection and monitoring. Further, the United States has provided vehicles to help address the critical transportation needs of the military and security units from the participating African countries that are involved in counterterrorism operations.

Another counterterrorism area in which progress has been made is the capturing of some of the leaders and members of terrorist organizations. This success has contributed to adversely affecting the command and control functions of these groups. However, this success has been undermined by the fact that terrorist organizations operating on the African continent have demonstrated the capacity to replace their leaders who have either been captured or killed in counterterrorism military operations.

Challenges

On the other hand, US counter-terrorism strategies in Africa have some major shortcomings that have undermined them. First, the United States has turned the African continent into a "battlefield" on which the participating African states are required to fight terrorist organizations on behalf of the United

States. One of the resulting consequences for both the participating African states as well as the nonparticipating countries has been the harm visited on the well-being of the citizens of these African states, including injuries and deaths, incurred from terrorist attacks and counter-terrorism operations that are undertaken by the United States and the participating African states. In sum, the physical well-being of the citizens of the various African states, especially those that are the epicenters of US-led counterterrorism operations on the African continent, is being sacrificed to protect the citizens of the United States residing on the homeland and abroad, as well as American economic and strategic interests.

Second, the various initiatives reflect American unilateralism rather than the building of professed partnerships with African states on counterterrorism. For example, the interests, nature, objectives, and scope of the various initiatives were singularly determined by the United States. Consequently, the interests of the participating African states were not considered nor reflected in the various counterterrorism initiatives. Hence, the military and security forces of the participating African states are analogous to hired gendarmeries in the service of American national security interests.

Third, the way in which the United States has framed terrorism is problematic for two major reasons. One is that the United States declared "war" on a method. That is, terrorism is an instrument rather than an identifiable adversary. In addition, states, including the United States and the participating African states in the various counterterrorism initiatives have used, and continue to use terrorism against various individuals and groups. For example, the United States used various terroristic methods, including waterboarding and sleep deprivation, in its treatment of detainees at the Abu Ghraib Prison in Iraq (Gordon 2006). Similarly, virtually all the participating states in the various US-led counterterrorism initiatives have used and continue to use terror as an instrument for oppressing their own citizens, who are advocating for human security (Freedom House 2022).

Fourth, all of the US counterterrorism strategies are military-security centric. That is, these counterterrorism strategies rely exclusively on the military means as the foundationfor addressing terrorism "from below" (Jalata 2016: 29). In addition, the United States pays lip service to the inclusion of nonmilitary means in practice to its various counterterrorism strategies in Africa. Such an approach fails to take cognizance of the cultural, economic, political, and social factors, such as authoritarianism and socioeconomic malaise, including mass abject poverty and class inequities and inequalities, as well as primitive and predatory accumulation that provide the root causes of non-state actors engaging in terroristic acts. In addition, the preponderant reliance on the use of military means has undermined the purposes of the counterterrorism strategies by, among others, contributing to the recruitment efforts of terrorist organizations. As Nyang'oro and Walther (2013:105) argue, "The security focus of the U.S. counter-terrorism programs may have inadvertently increased the exact religious radicalization of local groups and collaboration with terrorist organizations that the U.S. designed [counter-terrorism initiatives] to eradicate and prevent."

Fifth, the U.S. has enlisted authoritarian and semi-authoritarian regimes in Africa as the motor forces for implementing its counter-terrorism strategies in the region. This has undermined the credibility of the strategies, because these semi-authoritarian and authoritarian regimes lack the moral authority and legitimacy that are required to mobilize their respective citizenries. In other words, these semi-authoritarian and authoritarian regimes are major contributors to the root causes of terrorism on the African continent. This is because they have suppressed the political human rights of their citizens and deprived them of the right to live prosperous and fulfilled lives (Freedom House 2022; United Nations Development Program 2022). In addition, the illegitimacy of these regimes has served as an important recruitment tool for the various groups that use terrorism, as well as the vehicle for winning empathy and support for the terrorist groups from the citizens of the participating African states.

Sixth, the participating African states have politicized the American counterterrorism initiatives as tools for suppressing the political human rights of individuals and organizations that are critical of the regimes in power for undemocratic governments and the crises of human development. For example, in Ethiopia, as Workneh (2019: 5) asserts, "The [government] has . . . repurpose[ed] counter-terrorism apparatuses—intelligence and surveillance systems, military equipment, and technical know-how—financed and set up by its Western allies to quell critical expression, organization and assembly domestically." Similarly, in Kenya, in 2015, for example, the government used the the prevention of terrorism to justify to "freez[ing] the bank accounts of two civil society organizations in Mombasa County [and] accusing them of financing terrorism" (Akwei 2019:1).

Seventh, Kenyan and Ugandan security forces have been notorious for committing vitriolic human rights abuses by, among others, subjecting terrorist suspects to myriad acts of inhumane and degrading treatment, including torture and murder (Open Society Foundations 2013). In addition, in Kenya, some members of Muslim communities have experienced sundry human rights abuses from the security forces based on their religion, and their often-baseless connections to Al Shabab (Open Society Foundations 2013). In the case of Nigeria, the Joint Task Force, the military-security linchpin of the counterterrorism operations, has committed various human rights abuses, including subjecting suspected supporters and fighters of Boko Haram to torture. As Sampson (2015: 25) observes, "whereas the terrorist activities violate rights of victims, JTF's actions have also resulted in significant human rights abuses against innocent civilians."

TOWARD THE RETHINKING OF US COUNTERTERRORISM STRATEGIES IN AFRICA

Clearly, on balance, US counterterrorism strategies in Africa have not achieved the desired results of ending terrorism, especially the threat it poses to American national security and the associated economic and strategic interests. Against this background, American counterterrorism strategies on the African continent need to be rethought. A key factor is the imperative of democratizing US foreign policy toward Africa. The rationale is that there is a glaring contradiction between US support for democratization and democracy in Africa and its consistent and persistent support for authoritarian and semi-authoritarian regimes in Africa. This approach has contributed to the discontent among the citizens of African states, who view the United States as an enabler of authoritarian governance and human insecurity (Kieh 2009; Kieh 2014a). In sum, the United States needs to match its pro-democracy and pro-development rhetoric in Africa with policy praxis.

Another major issue is the importance of ending the reliance of the various counterterrorism strategies on the military and security forces. Alternatively, the foundational pillars of the counterterrorism strategies should be a mixture of military and nonmilitary means. For example, American assistance to African states to address the scourge of mass abject poverty, unemployment, and access to clean drinking water and sanitation, among others, will help address the human insecurity issues that terrorist groups use for recruitment and the mobilization of support among the citizenries of various African countries. US assistance to African states needs to be de-securitized.

Further, the counterterrorism regimes of African states need to be depoliticized, and respectful of fundamental political human rights such as the freedoms of assembly, of the press, and of speech, as well as the due process of law. This will require, among other things, holding military and security units that are involved in counterterrorism operations accountable if they are accused of human rights violations. Makinda (2010:20) puts the case this way:

> Safeguarding the security of African states and peoples require policies that undercut the base of terrorism and, at the same time enhance norms, rules and institutions. In other words, the so-called war on terror should not been seen simply as a technical, management or military issue, but initiatives that minimize the conditions that give rise to terrorism while maximizing those that strengthen norms, rules and institutions.

As well, the unjust world capitalist system needs to be restructured, because it contributes to the conditions that engender terrorism in Africa. For example, the "system of unequal exchange" forces African states to pay more for manufactured goods that are produced by the United States and other core states, while receiving less for their primary products such as agricultural goods, minerals, and oil (Aghiri and Pearce 1972; Onimode 1988).This adversely affects the foreign exchange earnings of African states and their terms of trade (Aghiri and Pearce 1972; Onimode 1988). In turn, these twin problems militate against the capacity of African states to invest in the improvement of human material well-being. Alternatively, there is the urgency of establishing a new global economic order that is based on, among other things, partnership, equity and fairness among the countries of the "global south," including African states, and the "global north," including the United States. One of the resulting frontier issues should be the establishment of a system of fair pricing for primary products from Africa and the other countries of the "global south" and the manufactured goods that are produced by the United States and the other countries in the "global north." This will help to address Africa's terms of trade and foreign exchange earnings problems. In turn, this will give African states the capacity to invest in the material well-being of their citizens, including job creation, the redistribution of wealth and income as the axle for addressing mass abject poverty, and the establishment of first-rate educational and health systems. In addition, African states should have access to technology, so that they can industrialize, thereby being positioned to add value to their primary products by turning them into semi-manufactured and manufactured products.

CONCLUSION

Since the 9/11 terrorist attacks on its homeland by Al-Qaeda, the United States has enlisted various African states as "infantry forces" in its "Global War on Terror" (GWOT) that was launched by the George W. Bush administration and continued by subsequent American administrations. At the vortex of the prosecution of the US GWOT in Africa is a plethora of counterterrorism initiatives involving several African states in the various regions of the continent. After more than two decades, the American-established counterterrorism initiatives in Africa have had minimum successes. This include building the capacity of the participating African states in the areas of training, intelligence gathering, and surveillance and the provision of equipment. In addition, several leaders and members of the various groups that are committing terrorist acts such as Al Shabab, Boko Haram, Al-Qaeda, and ISIS have been arrested, and in some instances killed.

On the other hand, the American-created counterterrorism initiatives are fraught with several major problems, including military centricity, the primacy of American national security interests at the expense of the security of the participating states, especially their citizens, and the politicization and human rights violations by the security and military units that are involved in counterterrorism operations. For example, American-supplied weapons and equipment have been used to persecute the critics of the regimes of the participating states. Similarly, those who are suspected of either supporting or fighting for terrorist organizations are subjected to sundry human rights violations, including the denial of due process and inhumane and degrading treatment such as torture.

Against this backdrop, it is suggested that the U.S.' counter-terrorism initiatives in Africa need to be rethought and restructured, if they are to have the desired impact of mitigating the commission of terrorist acts by non-state actors. Among the suggestions are the exigency of addressing the contradiction between the U.S.' pro-democracy and pro-development rhetoric and its support for authoritarian and semi-authoritarian regimes in Africa, shifting from the preponderant reliance on military means to a mixture of military and non-military means, including the investment in human security, democratizing the domestic counter-terrorism regimes of the participating African states, and restructuring the world capitalist system on the basis of equity, equality and fairness.

Finally, the Biden administration's professed commitment to addressing of the root causes of terrorism in Africa must be matched by concrete actions. In other words, while the pronouncements and their subsequent inclusion in policy documents are encouraging signs, they must be translated into concrete actions on the African continent. If this is done, then US counterterrorism initiatives in Africa will begin to have the desired effects of undercutting the use of undemocratic governance and the crises of human material well-being as veneers by terrorist groups to recruit, especially alienated youth, who are the poster children for socioeconomic malaise, and mobilize support among the populace of the various African states.

REFERENCES

Al Jazeera. 2013. "Niger Agrees to U.S. Drone on Territory." January 30. 1.

Adibe, Clement. 2012. "From Benign Neglect to Strategic Engagement: The Shifting Dynamics of America's Policy Towards Africa." In *West Africa and the U.S. War on Terror.* Edited by George Klay Kieh Jr. and Kelechi A. Kalu. London: Routledge, 27–61.

Aghiri, Emmanuel, and Brian Pearce. 1972. *Unequal Exchange: A Study of the Imperialism of Modern Trade*. New York: Monthly Review Press.

Akwei, Adotei. 2019. The Impact of U.S. Counter-terrorism Efforts on Human Rights. Statement Delivered at the Hearing of the National Security Subcommittee of the Committee on Oversight and Reform of the House of Representatives. Washington D.C. December 17,

Bush, George W. 2001. Joint Address to the United States Congress on the 9/11 Terrorist Attack Against the United States. September 20.

Chase, Robert et al. 1999. "Introduction." In *Pivotal States: A New Framework for U.S. Policy in the Developing World*. Edited by Emily Hill et al. New York: W.W. Norton, 1–14.

Council on Foreign Relations. 2005. *How 9/11 Reshaped Foreign Policy*. New York: Council on Foreign Relations.

Duncker, John. 2007. "Globalization and Its Impact on the 'War on Terror.'" In *Africa and the War on Terrorism*. Edited by John Davis. Aldershot, UK: Ashgate Publishing, 63–79.

Elmi, Afyare Abdi, and Abdullahi Barise. 2006. "The Somali Conflict: Root Causes, Obstacles and Peacebuilding Strategies." *African Security Review* 15(1): 32–54.

Ellis, Stephen. 2004. "Briefing: The Pan-Sahel Initiative." *African Affairs* 103(412): 459–64.

Executive Order 13224. 2001.

Freedom House. 2022. Freedom in the World: Historical and Comparative Data, 1972–2021. Washington D.C.: Freedom House.

Gordon, Avery F. "Abu Ghraib: Imprisonment and the War on Terror." *Race and Class* 48(1): 42–59.

Jalata, Asafa. 2016. *Phases of Terrorism in the Age of Globalization*. Berlin: Springer.

Kalu, Kelechi A. 2014. "U.S.-Africa Security Relations in the Twenty-First Century: Trends and Implications. In *U.S.-Africa-Security Relations*. Edited by Kelechi A. Kalu and George Klay Kieh Jr. London: Routledge, 62–82.

Kieh, George Klay Jr.. 2002. "The Somali Civil War." In *Zones of Conflict in Africa: Theories and Cases*. Westport, CT: Praeger, 123–38.

Kieh, George Klay. 2009. "The Bush Administration's Stabilization Policy and the Second Liberian Civil War." In Assessing *the Bush Administration's Policy Toward Africa*. In Abdul Karim Bangura et al. Bloomington, Indiana: iUniverse Press, 211–27.

Kieh, George Klay. 2012. "Good Governance, West African regional Security and the U.S. War on Terror." In *West Africa and the U.S. War on Terror*. Edited by George Klay Kieh Jr. and Kelechi A. Kalu. London: Routledge, 122–143.

Kieh, George Klay. 2014a. "Rethinking U.S.-Africa Security Relations." In *U.S.-Africa-Security Relations*. Edited by Kelechi A. Kalu and George Klay Kieh, Jr. London: Routledge, 191–216.

Kieh, George Klay. 2014b. "The Obama Administration's Policy Toward Africa." In *Obama and the World: New Directions in U.S. Foreign Policy*. Edited by Indejeet Parmar et al. London: Routledge, 165–84.

Kieh, George Klay Jr., and Kelechi A. Kalu. 2012 "Introduction: The Travails of the U.S. War on Terrorism." In *West Africa and the U.S. War on Terror*. Edited by George Klay Kieh Jr. and Kelechi A. Kalu. London: Routledge, 3–18.

Kwesi-Aning, Emmanuel, and Samuel Atuobi. 2009. *Security Threats, Trafficking and Terrorism in the Sahel.* Mimeo.

Kwesi-Aning, Emmanuel. 2012. "The U.S. African Command (AFRICOM): Issues and Perspectives." In *U.S.-Africa-Security Relations.* Edited by Kelechi A. Kalu and George Klay Kieh Jr. London: Routledge, 147–168.

Makinda, Samuel. 2010. "Terrorism, Counter-terrorism and Norms in Africa." *African Security Review* 15(3): 19–31.

Minx, Dean, and Vinton Prince. 2012. "Sub-Saharan Africa: Another Front in the U.S. Global War on Terror." In *West Africa and the U.S. War on Terror*. Edited by George Klay Kieh Jr. and Kelechi A. Kalu. London: Routledge, 19–34.

Morcos, Pierre. 2011. A Transatlantic Approach to Address Growing Maritime Insecurity in Gulf of Guinea. Center for Strategic and International Studies. February 1.

Nyang'oro, Julius, and Andrea Walthier. 2012. "The U.S. Trans-Saharan Counter-terrorism Partnership: An Evaluation. In *West Africa and the U.S. War on Terror*. Edited by George Klay Kieh Jr. and Kelechi A. Kalu. London: Routledge, 87–106.

Onimode, Bade. 1988. *A Political Economy of the African Crisis*. London: Zed Books.

Open Society Foundations. 2013. Counter-terrorism and Human Rights Abuses in Kenya and Uganda: The World Cup Bombing and Beyond. New York: Open Society Foundations.

Pew Research Center. 2009. Mapping the Global Muslim Population. Washington D.C.: Pew Forum for Religion and Public Life.

Queally, Jon. 2012. "A Retort to U.S. Military Expansion in Africa: Dismantle Africa." *Common Dreams*. December 24.

Richman, Sheldon. 2013. "The Ominous U.S. Presence in Northeast Africa." Empires' Futures of Freedom Foundations. January 31.

Sampson. Terwase. 2015. "Between Boko Haram and the Joint Task Force: Assessing the Dilemma of Counter-terrorism and Human Rights in Northern Nigeria*."* *Journal; of African Law* 59(1): 25–63.

Schmidt, Eric. 2013. "U.S. Weighs Base for Spy Drones in North Africa." *New York Times*. January 29.

Schmidt, Elizabeth, and William Minter. 2021. "Can We Demilitarize U.S. Policy in Africa?" *Foreign Policy in Focus*. July 28.

Shiel, Annie et al. 2021. Insight into Biden's Counter-terrorism Thinking Suggests More of the Same," *Just Society*. October 18.

Townsend, Stephen (General). 2022. Statement: Investing in America's Security in Africa: A Continent of Growing Strategic Importance. Testimony Before the Armed Services Committee of the U.S. House of Representatives. March 17.

United Nations Development Program. 2022. *Human Development Report, 2021*. New York: United Nations Development Program.

U.S. African Command (AFRICOM). 2022. History of U.S. Africa Command. www .africom.mil. Accessed March 2, 2022.

U.S. Department of State. 2022. Programs and Initiatives, 2022. www.state.gov/ bureau-of counterterrorism programs and initiatives. Accessed March 1, 2022.

Volman, Daniel. 2009. "China, India, Russia and the United States: The Scramble for African oil and the Militarization of the Continent." *Current African Issues* 43. Uppsala, Sweden: Nordic Institute for African Studies,

White House. 2002. *The National Security Strategy of the United States*. Washington, DC: The White House.

White House. 2022. *The National Security Strategy of the United States.* Washington, DC: The White House.

Workneh, Tewodros.2019. "Counter-terrorism in Ethiopia: Manufacturing Insecurity, Monopolizing Speech." *Internet Policy Review* 8(1): 1–22.

PART IV

LESSONS AND INSIGHT

Chapter 9

Toward Addressing the Scourge of Insurgency and Terrorism in Africa

George Klay Kieh Jr. and Kelechi A. Kalu

Where they are lodged, insurgencies and terrorism continue to have adverse effects on many African countries. One of the major negative consequences of insurgencies and terrorism is their contributions to state fragility and the resulting ramifications for stability. For example, the Fragile State Index for 2022, which is published by the Fund for Peace, shows that Somalia (score of 110/120), Mali (with a score of 98.6), and Nigeria (with a score of 97.2/120) are top-tier fragile states (Fund for Peace 2022).

Another adverse effect is the loss of human lives. In January–March 2022, for example, there were 379 terrorist attacks in Africa; and these were carried out by various non-state actors, including Al-Shabab, Boko Haram, Al-Qaeda, and ISIS (African Center for the Study and Research on Terrorism 2022). The attacks resulted in about 2,824 deaths (African Center for the Study and Research on Terrorism 2022). Cooke et al. (2016:11) provide a summation of the overall impact of insurgencies and terrorism on human security thus:

> Since the early 2000s, violent extremist organizations have expanded their ambitions, capacities and geographical reach into the Sahel and West Africa, with devastating impact on human security and economic development. Attacks by AQIM and Boko Haram have killed tens of thousands of people and displaced millions more within and across national borders.

What lessons have been learned from the seemingly unending cycle of insurgencies and state and non-state-led terrorism? What are some of the ways the African continent can address the root causes of insurgency and terrorism?

These two questions will frame this chapter. To address these issues, the chapter is divided into two major parts. In the first part, lessons about insurgencies, terrorism, and counterterrorism are drawn from the constituent chapters of the book. Second, some insights are proffered for addressing the scourge of insurgency and terrorism.

THE LESSONS

The book's constituent chapters provide several lessons about the root causes, nature, and dynamics of insurgency and terrorism, as well as the travails of counterterrorism in Africa. These lessons apply to African states that are experiencing insurgencies and terrorism and those that have not. For the latter, with few exceptions, the factors that lead to insurgency and terrorism are athwart to inclusive politics, committed, effective, and competent governance. Hence, if they are not addressed, then insurgencies and terrorism could ensue. For example, according to Freedom House (2022), in 2021, for Africa, there were eight democratic countries; twenty-two hybrid countries (semi-authoritarian); and twenty-four authoritarian countries. In sum, there were forty-six nondemocratic states in Africa in 2021. Similarly, in the area of human development, in 2019, ten African countries—Niger, Central African Republic, Chad, Burundi, South Sudan, Mali, Burkina Faso, Sierra Leone, Mozambique, and Eritrea—had the lowest human development index in the world (United Nations Development Program 2020).

Against this backdrop, the major lessons learned can be summarized thus:

1. That as colonial states in Africa governed with force and violence, and to the extent that the postindependence states are still unreformed, force and violence remain the preferred strategies for responding to political agitations for inclusion.
2. That the issues that drove the agitations for independence—political and economic development to end external exploitations of Africa's resources and governance based on the rule of law—remain unresolved and are manifest in expressed grievances by ethnic, religious, and economic minorities;
3. To the extent that governments, in collusion with external natural resource mining and drilling firms, ignore these domestic grievances and agitations, anti-government forces will continue to fester across Africa;
4. Without resolving the internal issues of economic development and political inclusion, no amount of external support will pacify the

lived experiences of the masses that help in recruiting the youth into anti-government forces for terrorism and insurgency-related activities.

5. Unreformed states and governance create opportunities for persistent agitations for political inclusion; for example, in the case of Somalia and Nigeria.
6. Without knowledge and attention to local political contexts and grievances, external interventions and regime change efforts merely exacerbate and deepen existing anti-government forces' agitations for power and political inclusion.
7. The strategy of power-sharing can help to address community grievances and the effective involvement of the people in the economic development of their communities to ensure government legitimacy and support that are necessary for denying anti-government forces the opportunity to use community grievances as recruitment tools.
8. That the nature of the inherited colonial state in Africa needs to be reformed to ensure its relevance for mitigating terrorism by promoting political and economic stability and sustainable peace.
9. While anti-government forces have both internal and external dimensions, resolving insurgent and terrorist-related issues can only be effectively carried out domestically between African governments and their people.

In addition, there are two major supplementary lessons. A key one is that diminished state capacity leads to challenges by aggrieved groups in society. The other is that the existence of under-governed and ungoverned territories in African states is a breeding ground for terrorists/jihadists. Hence, coordinated policies and regional commitments are necessary for combating transnational networks of anti-government forces like Al-Qaeda. And if external partners coordinate their counterterrorism strategies and tactics and work with African governments to institutionalize good governance, peacebuilding, and government engagement with the citizens, this can help end anti-government activities and significantly reduce the menace of global jihadists and insurgent terrorism. In the end, the issue of insurgency and terrorism across African countries is rooted in the unresolved questions of legitimacy and authority, and in whose interest existing leaders govern their various countries.

BEYOND INSURGENCY AND TERRORISM
IN AFRICA? SOME INSIGHTS

Background

The root causes of insurgency and terrorism are lodged in the postcolonial state in Africa. In other words, the postcolonial state in Africa is plagued by contradictions. These contradictions are inherent in the nature, character, mission, political economy, and public policies of the postcolonial state. Hence, insurgency and terrorism both from "above" (the state) and "below" (non-state actors) (Martin 2003) will continue with their deleterious effects. And the various military-centric counterinsurgency and counterterrorism initiatives that are specifically targeted against non-state actors will have the desired impact in the bowels of the non-reconstituted postcolonial state in Africa.

Against this backdrop, this section of the chapter is intended to proffer some suggestions for addressing the root causes of insurgency and terrorism in Africa. Specifically, the suggestions revolve around issues such as the pedigree of the postcolonial state, undemocratic governance, ethno-communal conflicts, and human insecurity. While the suggestions do not constitute an exhaustive list of the root causes of civil conflicts and wars on the African continent, they, as we have discussed, were prominent causal factors in the various civil wars that plagued the region, including the cases in this volume.

The Drivers: Citizens and Leaders

Citizens and leaders must be the key drivers of societal transformation in Africa. In terms of the citizens, they must develop certain major characteristics. A key one is a civic nationalism that appreciates and adapts to ethnic, religious, and regional differences across communities. This entails a commitment to the country above all other loyalties, especially ethnic, regional, and religious. Citizens must support, grant legitimacy, and recognize the authority of leaders who exemplify civic nationalism. In this vein, the nationalist orientation would enable citizens to transcend the boundaries of social identities and build a partnership that is based on service to their countries. Another major characteristic is civic education (Mirra et al. 2013). Nationalistic citizens would need to learn and acquire civil knowledge that will enable them to participate in the affairs of their respective polities in an informed manner. As well, citizens must be consistently engaged in the affairs of their respective countries. This will help to ensure that leaders supported to govern well are held accountable.

In the case of the leaders at both the national and local levels, they must have two major orientations: service and transformation. In the case of the former, servant leadership, as Greenleaf (1970: 1) asserts would require that the leaders be "servant(s) first . . . care is taken by the servant-leader(s) to make sure that other people's highest priority are being served." Similarly, in the latter case, transformational leadership requires "leaders who seek new ideas and perspectives to create a new path of growth and prosperity. . . . [T]hey mobilize [citizens] to make a fundamental change in [society]" (Korejan and Shahbazi (2016: 454).

State Reconstitution

As we have argued elsewhere, the democratic reconstitution of the postcolonial state in Africa is indispensable to the minimization and avoidance of civil conflicts in Africa (Kalu and Kieh 2021). This is because the state sets the parameters within which societal activities spanning the broad spectrum of spheres—from cultural to social—take place. In this vein, the postcolonial state in Africa (with few exceptions) has performed the aforementioned role in two major contradictory ways. On the one hand, it has created propitious conditions for the ruling elites and their relations to enjoy the full battery of the material comfort of life. But, on the other hand, it had visited abject poverty, social malaise, and deprivation on the majority of Africans. As Ihonvbere (1995: 148–49) argues,

> The post-colonial state [is] a continuation of the colonial state with very minimal changes, mostly in terms of personnel rather than structures, functions and relations to civil society. Thus, it remained an interventionist, exploitative, and repressive as its predecessor. It is therefore inappropriate to expect good governance, transparency, social harmony, respect for human rights, adherence to the rule of law, and political stability in social formations presided over by weak and non-hegemonic elites.

The poor performance of African states led Samatar and Samatar (2002:5) to observe that the state in Africa is the "wrong type." Thus, Africa needs a new state type. In this vein, several major issues are germane to the state reconstitution project. A key one is the centrality of a vision. This is because as Mutua (2002:11) observes, "The state itself is . . . a receptacle or empty vessel." Using Mutua's metaphors, the state is receptive to the dominant vision that is plucked into it or deposited in it. And the emergent vision shapes and guides the nature, character, mission, and political economy of the state.

Against this backdrop, the new state in Africa must have certain major attributes. A major one is the imperative of the autonomy of the state

(Edigheji 2005; Mkandawire 2001). This means the states in Africa must be independent of the control of all social forces, including classes, and external actors so that they can make policies in the interest of the broader citizenry. Another dimension is embeddedness (Edigheji 2005; Evans 1995). This requires the "maintenance of strategic relations with the wider society" (Seddon and Belton-Jones 1995). In addition, the state must be protective (Ansell 2019; Mbaku 2018). At the core is the protection of citizens from what Galtung (1969: 173–80) calls "structural violence," physical violence, and exploitation by both internal and external forces. Similarly, the state must be productive (Mbaku 1999; Mkandawire 2001). This includes the formulation and implementation of policies that would, among others, help generate employment, promote viable and rewarding economic activities, and ensure agricultural productivity and the resulting impact on food security. Further, the state must empower citizens so that they can play pivotal roles in the formulation and implementation of public policies. As Eyaben (2011: 2) asserts, "Empowerment happens when [citizens] imagine their world differently, and to realize that vision by changing the relations of power that have kept them in poverty, restricted their voice(s), and deprived them of their autonomy."

Governance

The issue of governance is discussed at two major levels: the genre, and the organizational policy. In the case of the genre or type of governance, democratic governance is proffered (Bevir 2006; Haque 2016). The rationale is that democratic governance transcends the technicist-centric "good governance" model that is championed by the developed liberal democracies and their Bretton Woods institutions—the International Monetary Fund and the World Bank. That is, democratic governance is about the empowerment of citizens. As Bevir (2006: 426) argues, "citizens play an active role in making and implementing public policy," within the framework of the rule of law. This means that asking citizens to adapt to civic nationalism also requires political inclusion, and inviting citizens to be part of the solutions to economic and political challenges facing their states.

At the organizational cum policy level, there are several major dimensions, and these include respect for political rights and civil liberties, accountability, transparency, the rule of law, "checks and balances," peaceful co-existence and tolerance, and inclusion and equity in power relations. In terms of political rights and civil liberties, all citizens, irrespective of their social identities, must have the freedom to participate in the political process through running for office (if eligible), voting, and peacefully protesting repugnant government policies and actions. Similarly, among others, all citizens must enjoy the freedoms of assembly, association, religion, thought, movement, and the press.

The essence of accountability without exceptions is the extent to which public officials and citizens are held responsible for their actions within the established rule of laws. In the case of public officials, this can be done in three major ways: vertical accountability, horizontal accountability, and diagonal accountability. Horizontal accountability entails public officials and public institutions holding one another accountable (Luhrmann et al. 2020). Vertical accountability revolves around citizens holding public officials accountable through various means, including elections (Luhrmann et al. 2020). Similarly, diagonal accountability focuses on nongovernmental actors such as civil society organizations and the media holding government officials responsible for their actions (Luhrmann et al. 2020).

Transparency is another major area, especially against the backdrop of the perennial lack of openness in the operations of the governments of states in Africa. Citizens' knowledge about the operations of their governments is important for several reasons (Hollyer et al. 2011). A key one is that it positions citizens to exercise "vertical accountability" over the government more effectively. Another reason is that transparency serves as a deterrent against engagement in corrupt activities by public officials, who are fearful that their actions will become public knowledge in a matter of time, and will moderate their rent-seeking behaviors. Further, openness helps build the trust of citizens in their governments.

And, the "rule of law," ensures that everyone, irrespective of their socioeconomic status or role in society, is answerable to the law and legal process for their official behavior (Waldron 2021). In other words, the "rule of law" ensures that all citizens, including the head of state and head of government, as well as top government officials, are not above the law. The effective enforcement of this foundational plank of democratic governance is important for several major reasons. For example, the "rule of law" militates against the "culture of impunity," which is a major cornerstone of authoritarian and hybrid states in Africa. This is done by ensuring, among others, that no one is given preferential treatment in the application and enforcement of the laws, irrespective of political and socioeconomic status and connections in society. Also, a rule of the law-based public policy increases the citizens' confidence and trust in the legal system as a fair and impartial arbiter of disputes. As well, the "rule of law" minimizes the resort to extra-legal means in the settlement of disputes, especially the use of violence. And as discussed previously, the rule of law enables citizens to have faith in the legal system as a platform to address their grievances fairly and in conformity with a verifiable law. Consistently abiding by the rule of law will significantly provide citizens government access that can embolden citizens to eschew tendencies that attract them to anti-government forces, insurgency, and terrorism because of exclusionary political strategies that lack accountability.

A system of "checks and balances" is also indispensable to ensuring democratic governance (Holcombe 2018). Essentially, this would require the distribution of authority among the three major branches of government— legislative, executive, and judicial—in ways that enable each of them to have both sufficient and necessary authority to checkmate the excesses of the other branches. The effective and efficient operation of a system of checks and balances makes it difficult for a public official or a branch of government to subordinate other branches and usurp their authority. In sum, the system of "checks and balances" curtails authoritarian tendencies, especially in a democratic system of governance.

Another important element is the imperative of peaceful coexistence and tolerance. Since the overwhelming majority of African states are, inter alia, multiethnic and multireligious, it will be critical for these divergent groups to coexist peacefully. Among others, this will require respect for one another and a commitment to resolve differences peacefully. In addition, effective, enabling, and empowering states in Africa are those that create and enable access to their citizens without privileging any group in the allocation of resources, like jobs in the public sector and project locations for socioeconomic development. In essence, as Mengisteab (2007: 111) cautions, an "ethnic state" is an anathema to democratic governance. Equally, tolerance of divergent views and ways of life is a major pillar of democratic governance. This means that at the broader societal levels, enshrined civic education is necessary for citizens to learn and practice tolerance of divergent cultures, religions, social, and political views. Cumulatively, peaceful coexistence and tolerance are indispensable to the maintenance of peace and stability.

As well, power relations must be restructured at various levels, both within the broader society and the government. In terms of the larger society, for example, restructuring the framework that provides access to power, without gender discrimination, is necessary to ensure that women are active and effective contributors to economic growth and maintenance of peace and security in Africa. The historical privileging of men has not led African states and peoples out of the malaise of economic dependency on commodity exports, foreign aid, and incessant debt crises. To be sure, privileging men over women has not resulted in a feeling of sustainable peace and security in many postcolonial states across the continent. Although, there has been an appreciable level of improvement in the quest to dismantle the vestiges of patriarchy, for example, in Rwanda and Ghana, much work needs to be done in many other states. Essentially, equity in power relations between men and women must be anchored on the foundational principle that patriarchy is an unjust and undemocratic system of subjugation that is an anathema to democratic governance. Alternatively, women and men must have equal opportunities, and be equally rewarded for doing the same work; and this must start with enforceable legislation for the education of boys and girls. In addition, women should have an equal role in policy-making and implementation in all spheres of society. At the governmental level, constitutional design and the resulting constitutionalism must ensure that no official of government, branch, or agency has the preponderance of power that would lead to suzerainty. Indeed, cultural, religious, and political exclusion of women in schools, public, and private economic opportunities have partly led to the increasing presence of women in the rank and files of young women who are forced into prostitution, marriages, and as suicide bombers by jihadists like Boko Haram and, other criminal and terrorist groups.

NATIONHOOD

Undoubtedly, nation-building has been an elusive quest in Africa (Udogu 1999). This is because the state and its custodians, by and large, have privileged one ethnic group over the others in, inter alia, the allocation of resources. In addition, some dominant ethnic groups tend to demonstrate hubris toward the other ethnic groups by, among others, disparaging their humanity and their cultures. And these attitudes have and continue to contribute to conflicts, including civil wars, as has been the case in Nigeria, Rwanda, South Sudan, and Ethiopia.

Hence, since various multiethnic states in Africa have failed to anchor their nation-building projects on inclusive politics and policies, peaceful coexistence, and democratic pluralism, citizens have tended to shift their loyalties to various ethnic groups (Osaghae 2005). This is because they believe that their ethnic groups accord them greater citizen rights and privileges than the state. Thus, poor and ineffective nation-building strategies result in the problem of competing loyalties to the state and ethnic groups. Importantly, the absence of nationhood as embodied in the nation-state has engendered citizens' treatment of the state as an irritant that is irrelevant to their lives.

Given the importance of civic nationalism to the establishment and maintenance of long-term peace and stability, multiethnic African states need to rethink their nation-building projects, starting with reforms and restructuring of the state as a framework for collective efforts in political and economic governance. The emergent post-rethinking nation-building projects should include several major elements. As has been discussed, a key one is a shared vision that represents the interest of all the groups, while making the interests of the state (the collective) paramount. Another is the centrality of inclusion.

All the ethno-communal groups should be treated equally by the state and its custodians. In addition, the members of these groups should have equal rights and privileges of citizenship in all spheres. As well, an enabling environment of mutual respect for differences in society is critical. Linked to this is mutual respect for each group's culture. An effective state provides the physical security for all its citizens and groups to contribute their best in securing sustainable security, peace, and economic wealth and influence of the state.

Human Material Well-being

Background

The human material well-being deficit has been a major contributing factor to insurgencies and terrorism from "below" in Africa. At the core is the Janus-faced nature of the African state: On the one hand, the state in Africa provides propitious conditions for the members of the various local ruling classes and their relations to live fulfilled lives (Kieh 2017). However, on the other hand, the state visits mass deprivation, including abject poverty and social malaise, on the vast majority of Africans (Kieh 2017). The major resultant effect is that the majority of the citizens become alienated from the state and disaffected with the custodians of state power at various historical junctures. Ultimately, this contributes to the erosion of the legitimacy of the state and the authority of its governments. Insurgent groups then use the disaffection and alienation of citizens from the state and its regimes as the motor force (either real or pretentious) for undertaking armed violence against incumbent regimes.

The material well-being of citizens as a core element of human security must be at the apex of the agenda for managing and resolving civil conflicts, including civil wars. Similarly, in those African states in which civil wars have ended, the post-conflict peacebuilding agenda must give priority to the advancement of human material well-being as the foundation for building durable peace (Kalu and Kieh 2021). In this sense, political stability, economic well-being, and durable peace will result in effective counterinsurgency policies to end the delegitimization efforts of anti-government forces across Africa. While liberal democracy is important, for example, it should not be delinked from human material well-being. This is because freedom transcends the political realm and includes the economic, social, and other spheres (Marshall 1950; Sen 1999).

Poverty

Economic deprivation, political exclusion, and the constant survival mode that is the condition of many Africans, especially young people, leave them vulnerable to recruitment into conflict projects that often incubate intrastate violence and wars. Therefore, the prevalence of poverty in Africa is one of the major paradoxes of a region that is well endowed with natural resources, including agricultural ones, minerals of varying types, and oil. In 2020, for example, about 40 percent of the population in Africa subsisted at or below US $1.90 a day (Donnonfeld 2020). In the region's two largest economies, Nigeria and South Africa, the poverty rate was 46 percent and 26 percent of the population respectively (Hendrik 2021).

For Africans to exit the "poverty trap" requires the implementation of major economic and political inclusion strategies that enhance the authority of state agents and promote civic nationalism of the citizenry. Several major strategies are noteworthy in both the short and long term. In the short term, given the severity of poverty on the African continent, governments should consider conditional cash transfers; for example, parents ensuring that their children are enrolled and stay in school. As Millan et al. (2019:119) posit, "[Conditional cash transfers are] short-term poverty reduction [strategies] via cash transfers, and long-term enhanced poverty reduction through investment in human capital." Without effective government intervention, especially in the under-governed and ungoverned spaces, anti-government forces, insurgents, and terrorists will continue to provide positive and negative incentives to citizens without viable life and security-preserving alternatives.

In the long term, at the core is the consideration of a new development paradigm that is "people-centered and community-oriented" (Torjman 1998: 1). Based on this framework, specific policies can be formulated and implemented. For example, a policy that transparently enforces political inclusion, equitable distribution of wealth and income, and fair access to justice to win the hearts and minds of the citizens and communities will advance the cause for national peace and security. This is quite important because, as will be discussed later, small groups own disproportionate shares of the wealth and income, which is a source of visible feelings of deprivation and unfairness amongst the citizens. Another policy option is public investment in quality education, from the elementary to the tertiary level. The thrust should be on the development of the knowledge base and skills sets of students in various subject areas. Then, at the tertiary level, the focus should be on preparing students to specialize in various fields spanning the broad gamut of disciplines—from the arts and humanities to the natural sciences. The rationale is that poverty and the broader crises of development that plague the African continent require the expertise of trained personnel from multiple disciplines. In addition, vocational education should also be prioritized. This will enable students who are desirous of learning trades such as carpentry and plumbing, to do so. The acquired vocational skills will position the students to seek employment, establish small businesses, and become employers of labor.

Job creation should also be pursued as a major plank in the efforts to address the scourge of poverty. In terms of the role of the state, it should formulate and implement various policies that will create favorable conditions for the creation of jobs, for example, the use of policy incentives to encourage local entrepreneurship. This can be done by, among others, providing low-interest loans, a duty-free privilege for some time, a tax holiday for a while, and preferential treatment over foreign businesses in the awarding of public contracts and training.

Also, the development of the physical infrastructure such as roads, bridges, communications, water, the electrical grid, and storage facilities will contribute to socioeconomic development in two major ways. First, it will help facilitate commerce between and among the various parts of a country, make goods accessible, reduce the difficulties of doing business, and enable entrepreneurs to generate revenues and employment opportunities. Secondly, infrastructural policies, competently implemented, to provide amenities like electricity and pipe-borne water, will help trigger entrepreneurship, create employment opportunities, and improve the quality of life for all citizens in the country.

With enhanced educational learning in the arts, humanities, science, and technology in a framework of a stable political system, African states should invest in the development of a technological base for smart industrialization that preserves the built communities for future generations. This will enable businesses to manufacture value-added products that can be competitive and generate employment opportunities for the well-being of the citizens while ensuring a greater amount of revenue for business than the perennial reliance on the export of primary products such as coffee, cocoa, oil, and minerals athwart sustainable value-added productive economic activities.

Further, strategic industrial and trade policies should be developed by the state that will entail the identification of industries and products that are critical to economic security. In turn, the state can use its various levers, for example, duty-free and tax breaks, to support these industries and products, while simultaneously supporting all nonstrategic businesses and products.

Quality health care is also an important area that is indispensable to addressing poverty. The state should invest in the development of a first-rate public health care system as a "public good" that is available to all citizens, irrespective of their class or positions. In other words, quality health care should be a universal right for all citizens. Quality health care starts with establishing and maintaining quality medical schools and training centers to produce qualified medical personnel, like doctors, nurses, pharmacists, and hospital administrators to staff state-of-the-art medical facilities—hospitals and health centers, supplies, equipment, and other medical logistics. And, such medical services and facilities must be accessible to people, irrespective of their locations—rural and urban—and at an affordable cost.

Lastly, to end the plague of corruption—the basis for primitive accumulation of capital by most public officials who deploy the agency of their respective offices for rent-seeking—sustained efforts should be made to address corruption at the core of the system that created and maintained African states and its impacts on the fabric of governance in various countries. In their peculation, these state managers employ various means such as the stealing of public funds, bribery, extortion, fraudulent contracts, and procurement schemes to amass personal wealth. In turn, these illicit acts deprive the citizenry of the financial resources that should be invested in addressing their material deprivation. A major anti-corruption mechanism is the establishment of an anti-corruption body—fully independent of the executive and the legislative branches of government—that is clothed with investigative and prosecutorial authority outside of the sphere of the Ministry of Justice. Such an approach would help to give the anti-corruption body the independence that is imperative for the effective dispensation of its functions and responsibilities.

Wealth and Income

The distribution of wealth and income in Africa is skewed in favor of the members of the ruling class. In terms of wealth, Nigeria and South Africa, the African Continent's two largest economies provide good examples of the gross disparities in the distribution of wealth and income (Squazzin 2021). In Nigeria, in 2017, "five of Nigeria's wealthiest people, including Africa's richest man, Aliko Dangote, [had] a combined wealth of $29.9 billion—more than the country's entire 2017 budget" (Oxfam International 2021). As for South Africa, in 2020, "the richest 10% of the population own[ed] more than 85% of household wealth" (Squazzin 2020: 1).

In terms of the distribution of income in Africa, in 2019, the top 10 percent cornered about 50 percent (Robilliard 2020) of the total income, leaving the bottom 90 percent with the remaining 50 percent. The distribution of income is inequitable, and thisis a major reason for the prevalence of poverty on the African continent that is often used as an excuse by ethnic entrepreneurs and terrorists to violently challenge government authorities and legitimacy.

Contrary to the claim by some, the skewed distribution of wealth and income in Africa is not the result of differences in work ethics and skills. Instead, inequities in wealth and income are by-products of structural factors such as disparities in access to political and socioeconomic power between the ruling class and the masses that are embedded in Africa's political economy. Accordingly, the solution to inequities in wealth and income lies in "altering the social, political and economic structures that create and maintain income [and wealth] inequality" (Carter 2020) through the use of exclusive access based on class, role, and position.

Employment

According to the World Bank, in 2019, the unemployment rate in Africa stood at about 6.6 percent. In a continent where census figures lack legitimacy, especially in the larger states, where educational facilities are mostly underperforming, and with the population explosion in a context without adequate education and employment opportunities, we think the figures from international institutions, like the World Bank, grossly underreport the depth of the region's unemployment problem. Thus, the data on unemployment in Africa that is provided by the various international organizations, especially the International Labor Organization (ILO), fails to adequately and fully capture the severity of the unemployment crisis in Africa. Even anecdotal evidence suggests that a large swath of the eligible labor force in Africa is unemployed or underemployed. To be sure, youth unemployment is underestimated at about 10.7 percent (International Labor Organization 2020). In terms of the African continent's two largest economies—Nigeria and South Africa—he data does not capture the severity of the unemployment crisis. For example, in the case of Nigeria, in 2020, the unemployment rate was about 33.3 percent (Oluwole 2021). For South Africa, the unemployment rate stood at about 34.4 percent (Oluwole 2021). In terms of youth unemployment, the rate was about 53.4 percent in Nigeria, and about 64.4 percent in South Africa (Trending Economics 2021).

What are some of the solutions to the unemployment crisis in Africa? One major solution is strategic public investment in capacity building for teachers across the educational system; as a condition for effective teaching. A stable educational system without incessant strikes and the need for teachers to supplement their incomes in other economic activities are necessary for imparting useful knowledge and the requisite skill sets in various fields that will help graduates to become marketable and potentially spark their entrepreneurial spirits and aspirations. This should include vocational education that will enable people to develop various technical skills. In this vein, the state should provide an enabling environment for job creation and the associated "adequate wages," and good working conditions that are likely to generate more employment opportunities.

Food security

Food insecurity in Africa is one of the major challenges confronting the continent. For example, in 2020, an estimated 100 million people faced what the African Center for Strategic Studies (2021: 4) referred to as "catastrophic levels of food insecurity." Among the African states that face the highest increases in food insecurity were the Democratic Republic of Congo, Mali, Chad, Ethiopia, Sudan, Cameroon, and Zimbabwe (African Center for Strategic Studies 2021); and, except for Zimbabwe, these countries are also suffering from intrastate wars. Importantly, food insecurity is linked to various diseases that are consequences of hunger and malnutrition, including high blood pressure, heart disease, and diabetes.

Food insecurity in Africa is a multidimensional phenomenon that includes violent conflicts, inadequate food production, availability and access challenges, and climate change. In the case of violent conflicts, existing cultivated farms, farmlands, and food supplies are destroyed; and in time, it becomes difficult to continue agricultural activities, which consequently results in food insecurity. Investment in an agricultural food chain is another major solution that will encourage sustainable food production, food safety, and reduction in food insecurity. As Pawlak and Kalodziejczak (2020: 2) observe, "The agricultural sector plays a strategic role in improving the availability of food and achieving food security." Thus, increased food production and effective and efficient distribution will help address the availability problem. In addition, efforts should be made to ensure that food products are reasonably priced, by considering the objective economic conditions in the various African states' economic policies and implementations. Further, internal and continental efforts should be made to address the root causes of climate change and its resulting adverse effects on agricultural productivity. This requires governments across the African continent to work together to reduce the emission of harmful gases into the atmosphere that continues to negatively impact food production, availability of clean drinking water, and the health of the citizens. For example, climate change has, among others, contributed to drought in various African states, especially those in the continent's Sahel region.

Housing

Poor economic growth and income inequality are evident in the housing crisis and its adverse effects, like homelessness and slums housing, e.g., in Nairobi, Lagos, and Accra. The shortage of affordable housing on the African Continent is quite pervasive. For example, in Kenya, there is a gap of about two million homes. Similarly, in Egypt, the shortage of affordable housing has, for example, resulted in about 12 million people "liv[ing] in informal buildings (Oxford Business Group 2021). As has been raised, one of the adverse consequences of the housing crisis in Africa is the emergence of slum communities, especially in major cities like Lagos, Nigeria; Nairobi, Kenya; and Johannesburg, South Africa. In this vein, in 2020, about 59 percent of the people residing in urban centers live in slums (Habitat for Humanity 2021).

Addressing the daunting challenges of the housing crisis in Africa will require a multidimensional and integrated approach that seeks to weave together the major factors. As the Africa Report (2021: 1) argues, "[Housing development must be linked to a broader system of financial inclusion, a strong regulatory and institutional framework to govern service delivery and construction, resilient economic demand for service, long-term low-cost capital, and technology and innovation." Addressing housing shortage as an aspect of peace and security requires enforceable land tenure reform laws, planned communities, and focused efforts in creating employment opportunities at all levels that enable citizens to earn an income they can survive and thrive on. The derivatives have to include the construction of affordable housing, providing credit to purchase homes, addressing the lacuna of slum communities, and providing quality housing for economically poor segments of the urban populations.

Water and sanitation

The twin problems of access to clean drinking water and acceptable sanitation are quite pervasive on the African continent. For example, about 400 million people in sub-Saharan Africa do not have access to basic drinking water (Holtz and Golubski 2021:1). The problem is made worse in several cases by the privatization of water. This means that drinking water that communities are used to fetching from streams is now commoditized and sold at prices that are sometimes unaffordable to the poor. Policies that commoditized a basic gift of nature, like water is antithetical to Goal 6 of the United Nations Sustainable Development Goals (Holtz and Golubski 2021), especially in situations where many families do not have an income earner. An overarching solution is for African states to make investments in the provision of safe drinking water so that it can be available to citizens, irrespective of socioeconomic status and location. In short, as a "fundamental human right recognized by the United Nations," safe drinking water should be a "public good" that is available and accessible to all the residents of a country (Holtz and Golubski 2021).

Similarly, acceptable sanitation is a major challenge in Africa. For example, in 2020, only about 12 percent of the population in sub-Saharan Africa had access to basic sanitation facilities (One World in Data 2021). The problem is exacerbated by the fact that about 18 percent of the population engaged in open defecation (One World in Data 2021), with consequences for the health and well-being of the citizens in that community. The remedies must link sanitation with access to clean drinking water and hygiene, both of which assume formal and informal educational opportunities for members of the community on the necessity of good sanitation practices for their health.

That is, the major requirement for an effective sanitation system is the avail-ability of water and the practicing of good hygiene by the residents of specific communities and urban centers across states in the continent of Africa. City, municipal, and urban public services that construct public lavatory facilities to militate against open defecation, and a functioning garbage collection and disposal system will significantly contribute to sustainable solutions to the current challenges with water and sanitation infrastructures in many countries in the continent.

CONCLUSION

This book has attempted to address two major questions: What are the major causes of insurgencies and terrorism in Africa? What steps need to be taken to address the root causes that contribute to these acts of conflict? First, insur-gencies and terrorism "from below" are caused by several factors. Among them are undemocratic governance, socioeconomic malaise, inequalities in income and wealth, and the instrumentalization of ethnicity and other pri-mordial affinities. In terms of undemocratic governance, since the postcolo-nial era, African states (with few exceptions) have retained the authoritarian governance system that was bequeathed to them by the colonial powers. This has been reflected in, among others, vitriolic human rights abuses, economic and political exclusions, and the holding of fraudulent elections. As for human material well-being, the postcolonial state in Africa and its various regimes have performed two contradictory functions: On the one hand, the custodians of state power have created propitious conditions for the members of the ruling classes and their relations to enjoy the material comfort of life; and on the other hand, the ruling elites visit abject poverty and deprivation on the majority of the citizens. Similarly, the custodians of state power have instrumentalized ethnic and other primordial identities as the core of their "divide and rule" strategy. That is, state managers in various African states have privileged one ethnic group over the others, and allotted to the privi-leged primordial group's disproportionate amount of the national resources. This visible practice of political and economic exclusions is directly tied to several instances of insurgencies and terrorism across the continent of Africa.

Against the backdrop of the major causes of insurgencies and terrorism, the remedial measures must be tailored to the specific circumstances of the various countries, as well as taking cognizance of shared factors among African states. The overarching shared causal factor that is the root cause of insurgencies and terrorism (both from "above" and "below") in Africa is the pedigree of the postcolonial state. Thus, the democratic reconstitution of the postcolonial state in Africa should be the centerpiece of the efforts to address insurgencies and terrorism. Undoubtedly, a democratic state that is anchored on human security will provide the best framework for addressing the maladies of authoritarianism, the human material well-being deficit, and ethnic privileging and exclusion.

Finally, the transformation of African states will require the commitment and involvement of two major sets of actors: citizens and leaders. In the case of the former, citizens need to be informed about the affairs of their countries and governments and to provide oversight. This will help check the regime in power. Leaders at various levels constitute the other major set of actors. Essentially, leaders must subordinate their interests to the general welfare of the state. For example, public funds must be used for the general good of the citizenry, and not serve as a source for the private accumulation of wealth by state managers. Further, leaders must be visionary and transformative in their orientation. This would mean, inter alia, the development of the requisite political will to jettison customs, traditions, rules, processes, and policies that do not serve the general good. And the imperative of demonstrating the willingness to formulate and implement policies that will ensure that Africans enjoy what Marshall (1950:3) called "social citizenship."

REFERENCES

African Center for Strategic Studies. 2021. Food Insecurity Crisis Mounting in Africa. February 16.

African Center for the Study and Research on Terrorism. 2022. The Quarterly Africa Terrorism Bulletin Period of 1st January-31st March 2022. June 28.

Africa Report. 2021. Africa Housing Revolution Needs More Than Bricks and Mortars. February 19.

Ansell, Christopher. 2019. *The Protective State.* Cambridge: Cambridge University Press.

Bevir, Mark. 2006. "Democratic Governance: Systems and Radical Perspectives." *Public Administration Review* 66(3): 426–36.

Carter, Valerie. 2020. "Income Inequality." *Encyclopedia Britannica*. www.britannica .com. Accessed July 26, 2021.

Cooke, Jennifer et al. 2016. *Militancy and the Arc of Instability: Violent Extremism in the Sahel*. Washington DC: Center for Strategic and International Studies.

Donnefeld, Zachary. 2020. "What Is the Future of Poverty in Africa?" *ISS Today* March 2, 1–2.

Edigheji, Omano. 2005. *A Democratic Developmental State in Africa? A Concept Paper*. Johannesburg: Center for Policy Studies.

Evans, Peter. 1995. *Embedded Autonomy: States and Industrial Transformation*. Princeton, NJ: Princeton University Press.

Eyaben, Rosalind. 2011. *Supporting Pathways of Women's Empowerment: A Brief Guide for International Development Organizations.* Pathway Policy Paper. Brighton: Pathways of Women's Empowerment, RPC.

Freedom House. 2022. Freedom in the World, 2021. Washington, DC: Freedom House.

Fund for Peace. 2022. Fragile States Index, 2022. Washington, DC: Fund for Peace.

Galtung, John. 1969. "Violence, Peace and Peace Research." *Journal of Peace Research* 6(3): 167–91.

Greenleaf, Robert. 1970. *The Servant as a Leader.* South Orange, NJ: Robert K. Greenleaf Publishing Center.

Habitat for Humanity. 2021. "What is Affordable Housing? Affordable Housing in Developing Countries. www.habitat.org. Accessed March 2, 2021.

Haque, M. Shamsul. 2016. "Understanding Democratic Governance: Practical Trends and Theoretical Puzzles." *Asian Journal of Political Science* 24(3): 340–47.

Hendrik, Jurie. 2021. "African Countries Continue to Have the Highest Poverty Rates in the World." *Development Aid* February 25: 1.

Holcombe, Randall G. 2018. "Checks and Balances: Enforcing Constitutional Constraints." *Economics* 6(57):1–12.

Hollyer, James R. et al. 2011. "Democracy and Transparency." *Journal of Politics* 73(4): 1191–1205.

Hotlz, Leo, and Christina Golubski. 2021. "Addressing Africa's Extreme Water Insecurity. Brookings Institution's Africa in Focus Series. July 23.

Ihonvbere, Julius. 1995. "Beyond Governance: The State and Democratization in Sub-Saharan Africa." *Journal of Asian and African Studies* 50(1): 141–58.

International Labor Organization. 2020. Global Employment Trends for Youth: Africa. Geneva, Switzerland: ILO

Kalu, Kelechi A., and George Klay Kieh Jr. 2021. "Conclusion: Building Durable Peace in Africa's Post-Conflict States: Lessons and Insights." In *Peacebuilding in Africa.* Edited by Kelechi A. Kalu and George Klay Kieh Jr. Lanham, MD: Lexington Books, 237–56.

Kieh, George Klay. 2017. "The Janus-Faced Liberian State," *Liberian Studies Journal* 42(1 & 2): 36–72.

Korejan, M. Moradian, and H. Shahbazi. 2016. "An Analysis of the Transformational Leadership Theory." *Journal of Fundamental and Applied Science* 8(3): 452–61.

Luhrmann, Anna et al. 2020. "Constraining Governments: New Indices of Vertical, Horizontal, and Diagonal Accountability." *American Political Science Review* 114(3): 811–820.

Marshall, T. H. 1950. *Citizenship and Social Class, and Other Essays.* Cambridge: Cambridge University Press.

Martin, Gus. 2003. *Understanding Terrorism: Challenges, Prospects, and Issues.* 1st ed. Thousand Oaks, CA: Sage.

Mbaku, John Mukum. 2018. "Making the State Relevant in African Societies." In *Preparing Africa for the Twenty-First Century.* Edited by John Mukum Mbaku. Aldershot, UK: Ashgate, 299–334.

Mengisteab, Kidane. 2007. "State-Building in Ethiopia." In *Beyond State Failure and Collapse: Making the State Relevant in Africa.* Edited by George Klay Kieh Jr. Lanham, MD: Lexington Books, 99–114.

Millan, Teresa Molina et al. 2019. "Long-Term Impacts of Conditional Cash Transfers: Review of Evidence." *The World Bank Research Observer* 34(1): 229–59.

Mirra, Nicole et al. 2013. "Educating for a Critical Democracy. *Democracy and Education* 23(1): 1–10.

Mkandawire, Thandika. 2001. "Thinking About Developmental States in Africa." *Cambridge Journal of Economics* 25(3): 289–313.

Mutua, Makau. 2002. *Human Rights: A Political and Cultural Critique*. Philadelphia: University of Pennsylvania Press.

Oluwole, Victor. 221. "South Africa, Namibia, Nigeria Have the Highest Unemployment Rates in the World." *Business Insider/Africa*. August 25,1.

Osaghae, Eghosa. 2005. "State, Constitutionalism and the Management of Ethnicity in Africa." *African and Asian Studies* 4(1 & 2): 83–105.

Our World in Data. 2021 Sanitation. June.

OXFAM International. 2021. Nigeria: Extreme Inequality in Numbers. www.oxfam .org. Accessed March 15, 2021.

Oxford Business Group. 2021. Africa Looks to Solve Housing Shortage Amid Growing Population. www.oxford.businessgroup.com. Accessed March 2, 2021.

Pawlak, Karolina, and Malgazata Kolodziejczak. 2020. "The Role of Agriculture in Ensuring Food Security in Developing Countries: Considerations in the Context of the Problem of Sustainable Food Production." *Sustainability* 12: 1–20.

Robilliard, Anne-Sophie. 2020. What's About Income Inequality in Africa? World Inequality Lab, Issue Brief 2020-03.

Samatar, Abdi, and Ahmed Samatar. 2002. "Introduction." In *The African State: Reconsiderations*. Portsmouth, NH: Heinemann, 1–16.

Sen, Amartya.1999. *Development as Freedom*. New York: Alfred Knopf.

Seddon, David, and Tim Belton-Jones. 1995. "The Political Determinants of Economic Flexibility with Special Reference to the East Asian NICS." In *The Flexible Economy: Causes and Consequences of the Adaptability of National Economics*. Edited by Tony Killick. London & New York: Routledge, 325–64.

Squazzin, Anthony. 2021. "South Africa Wealth Gap Unchanged Since Apartheid, Group Says." *Bloomberg Equality*. August 5: 1.

Trending Economics. 2021. "Youth Unemployment Rates in Nigeria and South Africa." Data Set. www.trendingeconomics.com. Accessed April 2, 2021.

Torjman, S. 1998. *Community-Based Poverty Reduction*. Ottawa, Canada: The Caledon Institute of Social Policy.

United Nations Development Program. 2020. *Human Development Report. 2019*. New York: United Nations Development Program.

Udogu, E. Ike. 1999."The Issue of Ethnicity and Democratization in Africa: Toward the Millennium." *Journal of Black Studies* 29(6): 790–808.

Waldron, Jeremy. 2021. "The Role of Law and the Role of the Courts." *Global Constitutionalism* 10(1): 91–105.

World Bank. 2020. Data Bank. Washington D.C.: World Bank.

Index

About the Editors and Contributors

George Klay Kieh Jr. is currently the Dean of the Barbara Jordan-Mickey Leland School of Public Affairs and Professor of Political Science at Texas Southern University and Professor in the Graduate Program in International Relations at the African Methodist Episcopal University (AMEU), Liberia. Prior to that, he served as the Interim Chair of the Department of Criminology and Dean of the College of Arts and Sciences at the University of West Georgia, Dean of International Affairs at Grand Valley State University, and Chair of the Department of Political Science at Morehouse College. . His research interests include peace and conflict studies and security studies.

Kelechi Kalu is a Professor of Political Science at the University of California, Riverside. As the Founding Vice Provost of International Affairs at UC Riverside (2015–2020), he was responsible for setting the vision for UCR's internationalization efforts. He previously served as Associate Provost for Global Strategies and International Affairs and Professor of African American and African Studies at The Ohio State University (2012 – 2015). Before his Associate Provost role, he served as the Director of the Center for African Studies at The Ohio State University. He was a Korea Foundation Visiting Scholar at the Graduate School of International Studies & The Institute for Development and Human Security at Ewha Womans University, South Korea (2011–2012), and as Faculty affiliate at the Mershon Center for International Security Studies at The Ohio State University. His research and teaching interests are in international politics, African political economy, and US-Africa relations.

Angela Ajodo-Adehanjoko is Associate Professor of Political Science at the Federal University of Lafia, Nasarawa State, Federal Republic of Nigeria. Her research interests include conflict and gender studies.

Sylvester Akhaine-Odion is Professor of Political Science at Lagos State University and chair of the board of trustees of the Center for Constitutionalism and Demilitarization, Federal Republic of Nigeria, and editor of *Constitution: Journal of Constitutional Development*. His research interests include comparative politics, political economy, human rights diplomacy, and global governance.

Al Chukwuma Okoli is Senior Lecturer in Political Science at the Federal University of Lafia, Nasarawa State, Federal Republic of Nigeria. His research interests include liberal political ecology, security studies, gender, and development

Clayton Hazvinei Vhumbunu is currently Senior Lecturer, Department of Political Studies and Governance, University of Free State, South Africa. Prior to that, he served as a Research Fellow in International Relations in the School of Social Sciences and Lecturer in the School of Management at the University of KwaZulu-Natal (UKZN) in Durban, South Africa. He has also worked in the Ministry of Regional Integration and International Cooperation in Zimbabwe and has been an Associate Researcher at the Southern African Research and Documentation Center (SARDC), a regional think tank based in Harare, Zimbabwe. His research interests are in the areas of international relations, regional integration, conflict management, public policy and governance, and China-Africa relations.

Mohammed Ingiriis is Research Fellow at the African Leadership Center, King's College, London, and the associate editor of the *Journal of Somali Studies*. His research interests include the Somali state, society, and politics.

www.ingramcontent.com/pod-product-compliance
Lightning Source LLC
Chambersburg PA
CBHW031126270326
41929CB00011B/1515